NORWEGI
WO

A TRADITION OF BUILDING

NORWEGIAN WOOD

A TRADITION OF BUILDING

JERRI HOLAN

FOREWORD BY CHRISTIAN NORBERG-SCHULZ

Rizzoli
NEW YORK

Front jacket: Detail of Finnes loft, *ca. 1250, Voss, Sogn.*

Back jacket: A loft *and its companion* bur, *1786, Kviteseid, Telemark.*

Frontispieces: page 1—Elevation drawing of a Saint Andrew's cross from Gol Church, ca. 1170, Gol, Hallingdal; page 2—Eidsborg Church, ca. 1200, Eidsborg, Telemark.

Note to illustrations: All buildings have been photographed in their original locations unless otherwise noted.

First published in the United States of America in 1990 by
RIZZOLI INTERNATIONAL PUBLICATIONS, INC.
300 Park Avenue South
New York, New York 10010

Library of Congress Cataloging-in-Publication Data

Holan, Jerri.
    Norwegian wood.

    Bibliography.
    1. Building, Wooden—
Norway.   2. Architecture—
Norway.   I. Title.
NA1261.H65   1990   721′.0448′09485   88–4692
ISBN 0–8478–0954–4
ISBN 0–8478–0955–2 (pbk.)

Design by Abigail Sturges

Set in type by Rainsford Type, Danbury, Connecticut
Printed and bound by Tien Wah Press, Singapore

Contents

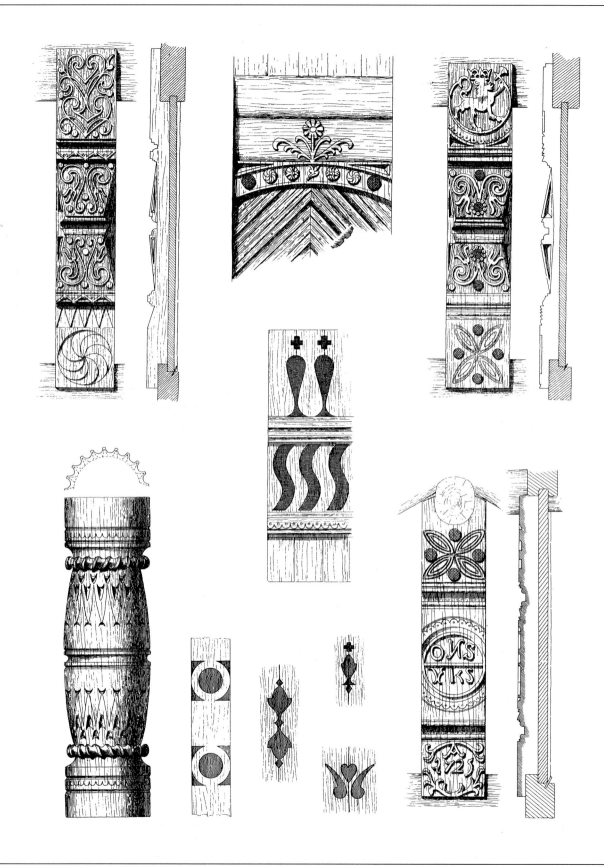

Foreword

Jerri Holan's title is well chosen. As an architect and a carpenter, she visited Norway to experience a culture where wood is not just one material among others, but a kind of basic environmental fact. Norway belongs to a Nordic "wood culture," in contrast to the "stone cultures" of Mediterranean countries. In the North we have since time immemorial grown up surrounded by wooden walls, we have as children played on wooden floors, and we have known the exciting mystery of the forest.

Drawings of details from Stærnes loft, ca. 1725, Rollag, Numedal.

The Finnish architect Reima Pietilä asserts that the dream of Nordic man is a "cave of wood." Indeed, we need "caves" for protection against a harsh climate, and these must be of the warm material wood in order to offer comfort during the long winters, and even colorful to make us remember the green trees and the flowers of summer. Conversely, in the hot southern countries, walls and floors of hard stone offer a cool retreat.

These facts may seem banal, but they determine architecture and tune the psyche of man. The term "wood culture" therefore means something more than the mere presence of wooden houses and artifacts. It implies that the inhabitants of the North have a deep emotional relationship to the material wood. It gives them a sense of belonging and security, and satisfies a need for "home." This presupposes a poetic understanding of the environment. In the past, Nordic people identified with their given world, and their understanding found its expression in the Norwegian fairy tales and the magnificent Finnish epos, *Kalevala*. In these literary works the forces of nature are kept and conveyed, in order to help the individual experience the meaning of the environment, or its "beauty," to use the terminology of Jerri Holan.

But meaning and beauty were not only "told" by means of poetic language—they were also made visible in buildings and objects. In Heidegger's words: "The buildings bring the inhabited landscape close to man, and at the same time place neighborly dwelling under the expanse of the sky." Thus, by means of architecture the earth becomes the native ground where life takes place. In the "rose-painted" Norwegian *stue* (dwelling house) the summer survived through the winter, and snow and cold became part of a total world of outside and inside, memory and expectation. We could also say that the building establishes and expresses a friendship between man and his environment.

This friendship determined structures that were in tune with nature and place, in contrast to the ruthless exploitation of the natural resources of modern times. What was produced, thus, became profoundly meaningful; it was the fruit of the land and expressed man's toil. As the "treasury" of the farm, the articulate and ornate façade of the Norwegian *loft* (storehouse) particularly well illustrates this deeper meaning of "Norwegian wood."

But how does the "expanse of the sky," that is, the larger dimension that makes the neighborhood part of a "world," enter the picture? The sky itself tells us how. The Nordic sky is very different from the southern one. Whereas the sky of the Mediterranean countries is a high dome that is filled with the light of the burning sun, the Nordic sky is "low" and mostly gray, and since the sun never rises toward the zenith, it casts long shadows. Only in winter, does the sky sometimes appear as a dark, embracing cupola, pierced by innumerable stars, giving the environment a cosmic dimension. The "dark light" of the stave church interior fixes and expresses this environmental quality. In this building, the posts or staves rise like the trees of the forest toward the dark ceiling, and humans coming from the enclosing horizontality of the *stue* are transported into a superior world. Like the churches on the European continent, the stave church leads the worshipper toward the altar along a path accompanied by light, but in Norway light has become a pattern of starlike points.

The *stue*, the *loft*, and the stave church represent not only symbolic forms, but also concrete structures realized through *making*. They belong at once to the eye, the hand, and the mind, and thus to life. Two technical methods were used by the Norwegian builders: *log* and *stave* construction. In the *stue* the horizontal logs create an earthly cave of wood; in the church the vertical staves make ascension to heaven manifest; and in the *loft* the two are combined to express how the earth bears fruit when it receives the blessings of the sky.

The wooden buildings of Norway constitute a microcosmos. They show how life took place *here*, and because of the free status of the Norwegian farmer throughout history, they have reached an exceptionally high level of expression. A tradition of this kind preserves its basic characteristics during the course of time. The *stue* and the *loft* are in fact *types* that were repeated for centuries. Nevertheless, they were subject to significant variations according to time and place. As expressions of constancy and change, they make us remember Louis Kahn's words: "What will be has always been."

CHRISTIAN NORBERG-SCHULZ

Preface and Acknowledgments

The original intent of the following pages was simply to present traditional Norwegian buildings, a small but rich manifestation of wooden architecture in a particular place. But after long discussions with a variety of individuals, I decided that a very important aspect of my subject was the art of craftsmanship, or how craftsmanship leads to beauty, as exemplified by the Norwegian buildings.

Today, beauty is the expression of the individual personality; in earlier times, it was the expression of humanity. Yet, one intuitively feels that beauty is neither old nor new, it is timeless. It is a quality that people recognize in traditional buildings of the past but rarely in contemporary architecture.

My studies have led me to conclude that an operational idea of beauty exists and, prior to modern times, was always used. This idea of beauty stands in contrast to today's building culture, or construction industry, because it hinges upon concepts implicit in the practice of craftsmanship, or explicit in the way of making things. It is my contention that beauty is derived from a craftsman's approach to making things, from the construction process itself. The beautiful ornamental quality that characterizes Norway's traditional buildings reveals the importance of this process when building was still considered a craft and an art.

Today's architects and builders seem to have forgotten that the marriage of fine materials and good techniques offer the most inspiration for the building arts. Obviously, the past provides many contrasts to present-day practices and its builders naturally had a limited choice of materials. But the lessons provided by a vernacular building culture are, nonetheless, valid. They reflect the craft of building when tradition, rather than new invention, stimulated builders: the beauty of this was that the tradition revealed certain existential meaning. This kind of meaning, along with the joy and purpose of craftsmen, is lacking in today's architecture. Consequently, we admire traditional buildings not because of their past, but because they have an enduring present.

In order to familiarize myself with the essence of the traditional architecture I describe as "Norwegian wood," I conducted discussions with people in many realms of life. The information I gleaned from architects, stave-church specialists, farmers, and craftsmen, reinforced my original feelings about the nature of Norway's building culture and the nature of creating beautiful buildings: the message of Norway's vernacular reiterates how the use of beauty gave the Norwegians a coherent and integrated environment; and these conversations confirmed that the idea of beauty is not absent in our building culture today, only its application is missing.

In speaking with Sverre Fehn, a renowned Scandinavian architect, for example, I confirmed that the simple measure of a footstep or an intuition about certain dimensions are precise guides used in any relevant building process. Walking with Herr Glad, the current occupant of Kruke Farm, I discovered that three of his father's entire farms were devastated by fire, and that each time the farm was rebuilt on its original site, its character could be faithfully reproduced because its buildings and construction methods were traditional. The master builder for each reconstruction had only to assure that correct procedures were followed in order to create the appropriate structures, as everyone knew the building "types." As a result, the quality of the farm was only the result of inherited traditions. A knifemaker, Aasmun Voldbakken, explained why people perceive stave churches as being alive, animistic. A stave church had a living identity, independent of its creator, derived from its own particular functions, and because the builders emphasized this unique identity in all its parts, a beautiful church appears animate. Håkon Christie, a leading stave-church historian, spoke to me about the essence of these churches: they are there, *now*; they are the result of the right thing in the right place. The current master woodworker at the Viking Ship Museum in Oslo, Erik Fridstrøm, gave me a clue to the Oseberg Viking Ship's holistic finesse—the wood-carver and the shipbuilder were the same man so that the details of his ship were intimately matched to the skeleton of what such a ship needed to be.

Sod roof of a ridge-pole dwelling house, early 1800s, from Numedal, now at the Kongsberg Folk Museum.

But it was when Frue Tveita allowed me to sleep in the traditional bed in her old *loft* or when Herr Lundevall drove me to see his favorite *loft* (though his own are spectacular) that I finally began to feel the nature of this wooden architecture. Or perhaps it was when Arne Berg, a noted farm historian, pinpointed the distinct character of Norway's buildings as compared to Sweden's or Finland's that I understood its quality: the buildings stood testimony to a strong, unique tradition of wood building in a certain landscape. The exact moment of understanding is difficult to recall, and it is not important. But just as Gunnar Granberg, a Norwegian architect, said, the craftsmen's knowledge was a given: rather than thinking about it, they simply built the buildings.

It is impossible to acknowledge all the inspiration I have received during the undertaking of this project. Yet, some individuals must be mentioned to whom I owe a specific word of thanks. I would like to thank Christopher Alexander for teaching me the spirit of a building language, and Ingrid King for the encouragement she always gives me when I try to speak such a language. In particular I would like to express my gratitude to Christian Norberg-Schulz for his help, for his infinite knowledge, and for the poetic understanding he has given me, which guides my thoughts. In addition, I would like to acknowledge Håkon Christie for his contextual advice and interpretations regarding stave churches.

I would also like to thank the American-Scandinavian Foundation, the Fulbright Grant Program, the Norway America Association, and the Oslo Arkitekturhøgskolen for allowing me the opportunity to pursue my interests.

Most especially, I must express appreciation to my personal friends and professional associates who gave so much of their time and effort to this endeavor: Gunnar Granberg, Lars Elton, Harald Skram, Rod Maack, Bill Mastin, Bob Lee, Michael Conford, Elvin Fritz, and Stephanie Salomon. I am also deeply indebted to the special people who brought life to this project and gave meaning to my time in Scandinavia: Siri Tveita, for all the help with translations and for teaching me not to ski; Børre Sveen, for conducting me to remote churches and showing me Viking ways along Christian paths; Susan Dahl, for guiding me through Sweden and Finland with boundless patience for my attempts at photographing in the never-ending rain; and all the people I met in the Norwegian countryside who always managed, somehow, to repair my old moped, and who provided me with too many cookies and too much coffee and offered warm beds and help during my travels. And, finally, thanks to my mother and brother who took care of me, abroad and at home, during the various stages of this book.

J.H.

1. INTRODUCTION

The beauty that we see in a vernacular landscape is the image of our common humanity: hard work, stubborn hope, and mutual forbearance. Landscapes which make these qualities manifest can be called beautiful. Their beauty is not simply an aspect but their very essence and it derives from the human presence.
—John B. Jackson

Fig. 1.1. Gol Church, ca. 1170, from Gol, Hallingdal, now at the Norwegian Folk Museum, Oslo.

T he traditional architecture of Norway is the product of a folk culture; it evolved to meet the needs of a distinct way of life, and lies harmoniously integrated into a distinct terrain. Traditional cultures—like Norway's—appear holistic because they seldom distinguished between visions of life, work, art, and religion. Consequently, their buildings naturally reinforced the unchanging and timeless essence of a particular place. In Norway, this essence was retained until relatively recently; it was only in the middle of the last century that traditional buildings finally gave way to modern ones and lost their unique sense of the art of building.

Fig. 1.2. Havsten loft, *ca. 1600, Gransherad, Telemark.*

Folk architecture is that of the majority of people, often predominantly rural, and constitutes the bulk of our environment—the anonymous buildings. In contrast, monumental, or "high," architecture is produced for the ruling class, the elite, the church, or the city dwellers, and it is usually derived from broader, international trends. Norway, historically, had very small distinctions between its social strata, even in terms of egalitarian Scandinavia, and had no urban tradition to speak of until the nineteenth century. What it did have, from the Middle Ages until the Industrial Revolution, was a strong rural class that was close to its ruling members. The ruling class, in fact, arose from its rural society; Norway's medieval kings were farmers as well. Thus Norwegian art and architecture were influenced predominantly by local sources. In spite of, or perhaps because of, its rural traditions, Norway's highest achievements in both art and building were executed in the same medium: wood. Its architecture was the art of building. Consequently, the differences between "high" art and "common" art are negligible in this country as are distinctions between folk and monumental architecture: the traditional buildings of Norway are, simultaneously both.

Norway's traditional architecture had an unusually long and continuous history, which began prior to the Middle Ages. The buildings that evolved in this country are inspiring because they were an intimate marriage between native materials and refined techniques, occurring within a distinct landscape. The builders were always guided by the physical presence of wood and the omnipresence of nature—their buildings were hidden in the remote pine valleys of a relatively isolated and rugged land.

In this forested part of the northern world, the tree gave Nordic man his structures. Norway was a vast coniferous forest belt, and the development of its wooden buildings should be viewed in this qualitative context. In contrast to southern Europe, where forests do not dominate the landscape and stone building, historically, was more common, northern Europe's landscape was covered with forests and a strong wood-building culture evolved from the fifth century onward. Of course, wood building occurred in the south and stone building developed in the north but, in general, wooden buildings persevered as archetypal images through the ages in northern Europe. As a result, distinctions can be made between the various "wood cultures" that evolved.

The wooden vernacular of Europe can be tied, in a broad historical context, to the kinds of forests found in its different regions. In landscapes where open, deciduous forests existed, such as Germany, Switzerland, France, and England, the skeletal system of transparent post-and-beam construction developed. In areas where seemingly boundless coniferous forests grew, such as Russia, Central Europe, and Finland, solid, closed log buildings were the dominant type of construction.[1] In Scandinavia, the wood culture was a practical mixture of both bay and monolithic systems.

Eventually, these two archetypal construction methods interacted and produced many beautiful building variations all over the European continent throughout the ages. In Scandinavia, the mix occurred early, sometime during the Viking era (ca. A.D. 800–1000). It produced an exceptionally rich variety of wooden vernacular in Norway, which eventually surpassed other similar building cultures in quality and construction methods.

The Viking era was probably the most significant period of Scandinavia's early history. It was an age of expansion that affected all areas of Scandinavian life, socially, economically, and architecturally. When the Vikings first stormed the northern European landscape, they cultivated large areas of Nordic forest and built thousands of farms and villages. The first townships emerged as marketplaces, and abroad, the Vikings created an extensive network of colonies and trade routes. The ships kept the Scandinavians in contact with other cultural centers and hence made available technology that had evolved elsewhere in Europe.[2] As a result, the Vikings later incorporated much of this experience into their native culture and their traditional wood buildings. The technology was especially significant in Norway where wood construction persisted longer than in most countries.

Every country has a particular set of traditional buildings that accords with its way of life. The most revealing aspect of any kind of vernacular building is how these building types were adapted to enhance life in different places because, ultimately, the "kernel" of a building's message is a way of life. Traditional buildings in most parts of the world usually reflect the intimate knowledge of a climate, a building material, and an activity typical of its culture and this is evident in Norway's architecture.

The Norwegians consistently constructed well-crafted wooden buildings for almost 800 years, and it is not surprising that they developed certain buildings and ways of making them that suited their particular activities. The use of similar buildings for such a long period of time was dictated by Norway's environment and agricultural way of life, and the beauty of this tradition is particularly strong. The life and soul of a place depend greatly on the events that take place within it, and Norway's buildings could not have survived for so long had not their world and events remained coherent. Many of these buildings are separated in time and location, yet they always constituted a familiar family of events. They represented shared experiences and knowledge of a particular landscape. The buildings were a cultural heritage that held common meaning, and they contained an idea of beauty that assured unity in their building culture.

Norway's traditional architecture is represented by only two groups of wooden buildings: farms and stave churches. As Christian Norberg-Schulz describes the buildings, "The old, Norwegian architecture is a good example of identity and harmony between buildings. In principle, the private farm's image includes the composition of many types of houses and one single, public building: the stave church. Roof over roof, the stave church rises toward the sky and gathers the farms around itself to a family of houses."[3] Yet, the architecture found in this country is surprisingly rich

and also quite varied given the country's apparently simple, agrarian life-style. Even within the broad spectrum of wooden architecture, including the beautiful traditions of Swiss chalets, German hall houses, and Russian log churches, both groups of Norwegian buildings claim a high degree of originality.

Scandinavia, historically, was more agrarian than the rest of northern Europe, and as was the case in its neighboring countries, farming was the primary source of livelihood for Norwegians. Their daily life was carried out on farmsteads that were isolated, individual groups of log buildings. Beginning some time toward the end of the Viking period, about A.D. 1000, and continuing through the first half of the eighteenth century, the Norwegians skillfully built farms to suit their particular needs. The pride of each farm was the *loft*, a two-story structure that functioned as a storage building on all traditional Norwegian farms. During the seventeenth and eighteenth centuries, the finest woodworking skills were lavished on this building form, which thus represented the highest achievement of Norwegian wood-building techniques. Its companion was the traditional dwelling, or *stue*, which reflected the *loft's* character in its refined log construction.

In a thinly populated country such as Norway, few public buildings graced the landscape during medieval times. The rare exception was the stave church. These churches, built between 1050 and 1350, usually stood alone against a group of farms and represented a sacred aspect of medieval life. Inspired creations of the Norwegians' world, they were the culmination of a highly refined structural system. The stave churches of Norway are examples of some of the finest wooden buildings in Europe and are, at the same time, some of the oldest. Because they embody some of the most advanced framing techniques preserved in wooden architecture from the Middle Ages, it is not surprising that this degree of sophistication is evident in

Fig. 1.3. Traditional dwelling house (stue), early eighteenth century, from the Hans Nissen Farm, Trondheim, now at the Trøndelag Folk Museum, Trondheim.

a religious structure: their existence today is testimony to the masterly skills that only a church could gather in the sparse farming communities. Although their exact origins have yet to be determined, they represent an important step in the development of wooden architecture, as they confirm the high state of technology achieved by wooden construction methods during the Middle Ages. What is surprising is that these buildings have survived for so long, even more so when one realizes that most medieval buildings remaining today were built of stone.

The development of architectural and artistic forms in Norway was always tied directly to the craft of wood carving. While most early cultures used wood for some of their buildings and crafts, in Norway, no other material was used for the majority of buildings until the nineteenth century, and wood was even used for the most sacred and important structures—the stave churches. Similar to masons and sculptors in other medieval cultures, in Norway, builders were both local workers and specialists on the farms and churches. Construction methods developed for church buildings were later incorporated into farm structures, and pagan and Christian wood carvings were used on both farms and churches. The give-and-take of sacred and profane, the blending of both mundane and specialized skills, characterizes Norwegian wooden buildings.

Architecturally, the wooden stave churches and farms represent the sacred and the secular, the public and the private, the medieval and the Renaissance in Norway. The stave churches and *loft* are, in fact, cultural images: they are symbols that represent the Norwegians' world, that manifest truth, and that constitute culture. An image is something people are familiar with—in terms of buildings, a type that fulfills certain ideals, or functions, well. The form of a building first reflects its function and second, reflects the traditions and customs by which we perceive a particular world; it is the latter that gives us understanding. As Christian Norberg-Schulz defines it, "The word *understanding* here does not mean scientific knowledge; rather, it is a concept that denotes the experience of meanings. The understanding of a culture is not a subjective product, but an interpretation of a world."[4]

What finally generates the customs and traditions of a building culture, what gives it character, is the vision of life that people share. In Norway, prior to the nineteenth century, farming communities were the repositories for the deeply rooted customs embedded in their myths and legends. Historically, most parts of the country had little contact with one another or with foreign countries so that the farming culture retained a mystical and magical conception of life. This romantic conception existed independently of official religion and was reflected in rich oral traditions that included a wealth of poetry.[5] These customs and traditions provided a strong source of structure for Norwegian life in its vast wilderness and also affected the character of buildings through an abundant development of handiwork and crafts. Perhaps because their mountainous landscape was more demanding than those of neighboring countries, the Norwegians created fairy tales and buildings that were defiantly cheerful in the face of the rough, Nordic climate—a solution that reflected the way that Norwegians lived close to nature without subordinating it.

The wood culture that sprang up in Norway during the Middle Ages was not wealthy given the limited resources of a harsh landscape, in contrast to Sweden, whose gentle valleys had always supported a large number of well-to-do farmers. Until the seventeenth century, the restricted economy curtailed Norway's opportunities for importing building materials other than wood, and in the construction of stave churches and farms, the margin for error and waste was small. Wood was plentiful, although the labor required to prepare it, transport it, and shape it was not. Difficult conditions forced the culture to amass a large body of knowledge regarding their native material. This store of cultural "wealth," along with the country's immaterial beliefs, inspired the creative powers of builders for many generations.

Architecture is the result of many forces: materials, climate, labor, and economics are pragmatic factors, but cultural traditions, social patterns, and political values are what ultimately give any art its local expression. Not surprisingly, the latter were more important for shaping the character of Norway's buildings. The unique expression of Norway's architecture leads one to believe that building methods were treated differently in this part of the world. Norway's history reveals cultural and natural forces that led to the development of its woodworking techniques, and it also reveals the prototypes that led to its traditional buildings. Log and frame-type constructions were known in various parts of northern Europe as were most of the Norwegian building types used. Yet, the value of craftsmanship in Norway's architecture distinguished it from other, similar wood cultures such as Sweden's or Finland's.

Tradition is the essence of any vernacular. In Norway, tradition hinges upon a high degree of craftsmanship. During the Viking period, wood carving was greatly esteemed in the courts and was one of the country's most distinguished arts. In the Old Norse sagas, wood carving and carpentry were described as highly reputed crafts, only entrusted to men of rank, and Viking shipbuilders were extremely well regarded. The sagas told of Norway's history from the ninth and tenth centuries and of the kings who settled the country. Originally related verbally, they were written down formally by Icelandic skaldic poets in the thirteenth and fourteenth centuries; and although they are often imprecise in fact, the sagas were the only source of history in the Middle Ages. Given the strong oral tradition in Norway, the tales persisted through the ages and descriptions of craftsmanship obviously inspired succeeding generations of builders in the land.

The sagas confirm that few countries had such a long tradition of highly regarded woodworking skills. From the master builders before them, the Norwegians inherited a keen sense of form and proportion based on the natural properties of wood. The builders of the Viking ships (ca. 900), the stave churches (ca. 1200), and the farms (ca. 1700) lived on the same land, used the same materials, and built the same types of buildings for centuries. Not surprisingly, a sensitive handling of wood is apparent in Norway's buildings. The inherent bond between technique and artistic sensibility in a traditional building craft can be seen in the seemingly decorative details so characteristic of these buildings. This ornamentation was an act of love toward construction itself, without which the buildings would be incomplete.

Wood, of course, lends itself to carved decoration and is easily molded but it also has certain inherent structural characteristics. As a construction material, wood has qualities that stone and brick do not possess. Wood has great strength and elasticity in comparison with its weight and has an ability to absorb the stress and strain involved in covering a wide area far exceeding the capacity of a horizontal stone member. The principal unit of wood building is the tree trunk, which can be used more or less in its natural shape either as a vertical or a horizontal supporting and load-bearing member. It can also be split into planks and used to fill in open spaces between the supports.[6] With an understanding of these structural properties, the Norwegian builders developed refined building methods that were in accord with their native material. Ultimately, what the Norwegian builders inherited from generation to generation was the patience of craftsmen who, rhythmically and repeti-

Fig. 1.4. Norwegian loft *and its matching, one-story storehouse (*bur*), ca. 1730, from Rauland, Telemark, now at the Skien Folk Museum. A typical* loft *from Telemark was always distinguished by particularly fine craftsmanship and wood carving.*

tiously, in harmony with natural forces, chiseled wooden buildings to satisfy a way of life.

In order to understand Norway's wood-building culture, one must understand the traditional processes a craftsman followed in constructing a building, from its site, to its structure, to its details. One looks at the land first, then at the buildings on the land, then at how they are made; and in so doing, one begins to understand that while the scale of building changes from site to detail—that is, from large to small—the creative impulse behind a traditional building process remains the same: a beautiful building represents a consistency of thought between site, building, and detail.

A traditional building culture such as Norway's is usually distinguished by buildings whose forms are dictated by the demands of the environment. A specific type of construction is always associated with these forms, and it is used by most members of a given society. This traditional construction process, when executed with the knowledge and precision of a craftsman, turns building into the *art* of building. In this sense, a craftsman's way of making buildings replicates a way of thinking. Norway's vernacular reflects a certain order precisely because such craftsmanship dominated the building culture. Consequently, its buildings illustrate the act of "making" in its deepest sense—that is, the revealing and enhancing of structure or reality. As opposed to mere building, "making" is an act of emphasizing the given structure in any situation, whether a site, a building, or a detail.

At the level of a site, the process can be seen as enhancing the given structure of the land so that it illuminates a particular environmental quality. It begins with the topography of Norway's rugged landscape and the types of settlements it demands. When a builder chose a site on which to dwell in this country, he did so to

make a place in his world, and his buildings generally responded to the specific qualities of a certain region. As a result, the geographical regions of Norway are the existential, or structural, source of differences within this building culture, and these variations provide the basis for a holistic approach to its architecture.

Craftsmen had to modify traditional buildings so that they could live better in their particular countryside. According to Christian Norberg-Schulz, the way a culture interacts with its environment, its general landscape as well as its particular elements—such as the mountains and fjords, sun, and snow in Norway—is "dwelling," and this is apparent in how a culture "makes" its buildings. To construct a dwelling is not an act of building shelter but an act of acknowledging the environment's qualities, bringing them close to one's self, so that the builder becomes part of his unique universe. When one "belongs" to a landscape in this manner, human existence is meaningful and—as had been earlier posited by Heidegger—one dwells poetically.[7]

In this manner, traditional buildings have meaning as they reveal what is significant for a specific culture. Certain archetypal buildings were adopted in traditional cultures for general purposes. Over time, these types were modified for specific activities and uses within the culture and, as expressed by architect and theorist Christopher Alexander, a "building pattern" arose. These archetypal buildings, such as *loft* and churches in Norway, provided a functional base from which to initiate the building process, while the final patterns reflected the unique character of the culture's "building language." In Alexander's words, the relationship between buildings, how they support certain activities, and how they are built, together form a building language. In Norway, the strength of such a language can be seen in its perseverance for 800 years.

Fig. 1.5. Swedish loft, *early nineteenth century, from the Delsbo Farmstead, Hälsingland, now at the Skansen Folk Museum, Stockholm. Compared to Norwegian* loft, *the Swedish structures generally have a more restrained character.*

Christopher Alexander notes, "A building pattern and event together is given by culture and the repetition of both gives an underlying structure to the world."[8] From his viewpoint, activities such as cooking, and events such as marriages differ from culture to culture, and these are anchored in a specific landscape and associated with a certain structure. These "patterns" are always related to the activities that occur within the structures and vice versa. Building patterns do not create the activities nor do the activities create the spaces. Yet, when the two are congruent, when they support and enhance one another, a harmonious, stable configuration that resolves the forces of their interaction is achieved. When a certain type of gallery porch worked well in a Norwegian dwelling, its pattern was repeated throughout a region although it was made a little differently for each individual family.

In this way, building patterns define a culture's typical activities; *loft*, for example, represent the Norwegians' need to store food for their long winters. Patterns reflect a common understanding of attitudes, how life makes sense in a particular place. According to Alexander, a list of any culture's building patterns reveals a way of life, and such patterns are alive to the extent that they enhance life's situations.[9]

Yet, the study of a culture's settlements and buildings does not provide an interpretation of a world or explain why it emerges in a particular manner. At this level, there is little to distinguish Norway's building patterns from Sweden's. One needs to look beyond practical considerations and delve into the craftsman's way of thinking, his building language: why he thought a post worked better one way than another; how use and beauty were equated. This is not a subjective process. On the contrary, it is both objective and precise and manifests itself in the way a building is put together, how its details are "made" to enhance a structure.

In Norway, details give buildings their characteristic quality. By emphasizing certain details and their place within a building, a Norwegian craftsman illuminated a structure. Without consciously pursuing beauty, builders followed basic ground rules inherent in timber building, and over time their building language achieved a natural ornamental expression. An ornament's deepest function is to clarify and accentuate an existing situation or reality. Ornament, in this sense, produces a beauty that is always tied to time and place and is not superficial. In this way, tradition taught the Norwegian builders the basic forms and techniques so that they could pay attention to the important individual building situations. One could say that the builders were, in effect, making ornaments. Yet, the ability of a Norwegian builder to express a building's true character required more than skill; it required craftsmanship.

Technology is knowledge that can be passed on, standardized; it has little to do with quality. On the other hand, the craftsman's knowledge is developed as an individual attribute over the course of time. His technique can only be learned, not taught, and it has everything to do with judgement. A craftsman knows that every detail he constructs has a physical result; if a Norwegian builder was truly aware of all the forces affecting his building, if he had built many such buildings, his details both resolved a building situation and conveyed an ornamental quality. Therefore, he intuitively regards beauty at every point in his construction process. In this way, beauty is essentially a matter of experiences and values derived from a particular world. As Sōetsu Yanagi, a Japanese art historian, explains, "If there were no standards, judgments of beauty would lose their basis."[10]

The use of such standards by traditional Norwegian builders is obvious in the way they made their buildings—there was always a proper and an improper way of constructing a *loft* or a church. Almost naturally, from the construction procedures

Fig. 1.6. Rear view of Gol Church, ca. 1170, from Gol, Hallingdal, now at the Norwegian Folk Museum, Oslo.

themselves, the builders derived an ornamental quality for their structures; this was not an afterthought. Similarly, Louis Kahn describes "making" in terms of aesthetics: "Aesthetics are realized out of the singularity of a making in which someone, sensitive to how rules derived from the laws of nature might be employed, makes an aesthetic principle. Aesthetics come after one makes something, not before." [11] Norwegian craftsmen thus assured their buildings a timeless quality.

The stave churches and farm buildings of Norway are images of a particular world at a particular time, just as our buildings are today. Yet in contradistinction to our culture, the character of Norway's buildings is the consequence of a thoughtful building process. If the ornamental quality of a building culture is understood from a builder's point of view, it can never be confirmed when speaking about the intentions of craftsmen from the past. The quality comes from a certain thought process derived from living in a particular world. To understand a culture fully is almost to understand a way of thinking. One sees this in the literature of Norway, where the cold climate and overwhelming force of the landscape generated a special need for its people to interpret reality in a romantic manner. The folk legends and fairy tales of Norway perhaps best express the nature of the Norwegian mind. They are a key to understanding this culture's reality. Knut Hamsun echoes this:

> We can't conceive of a sun that would shine and burn mercilessly. Our fairy tales deal with the earth and what is beneath it; they are the product of the imagination of peasants in leather breeches, they come out of dark winter nights spent in log cabins with smoke vents in the roof. The truly rustic, earthbound poetry of the tales from Gudbrandsdal—these were our creation. Our fairy tales don't make us shudder; they are fanciful and amusing; they make us laugh. Hadn't we created something out of the mystery and the wild beauty of the sea? [12]

The wooden buildings in Norway are an expression created directly from the raw material of a land's soul. They crystallize the character of the landscape, the temperament of its people, and the essence of a building material. From the clear structure of their building patterns to their precise details, beyond the demands of functional requirements, the Norwegians revealed the art of building as it should be.

2. SITE

The locale has a great influence on the forms within which the imagination creates.
—Henrik Ibsen

Fig. 2.1. Loft from a cotter's farm, ca. 1775–1825, from Mjøen, Oppdal, now at the Norwegian Folk Museum, Oslo. Norway's traditional wooden buildings stood out reassuringly in the bleak winter landscape.

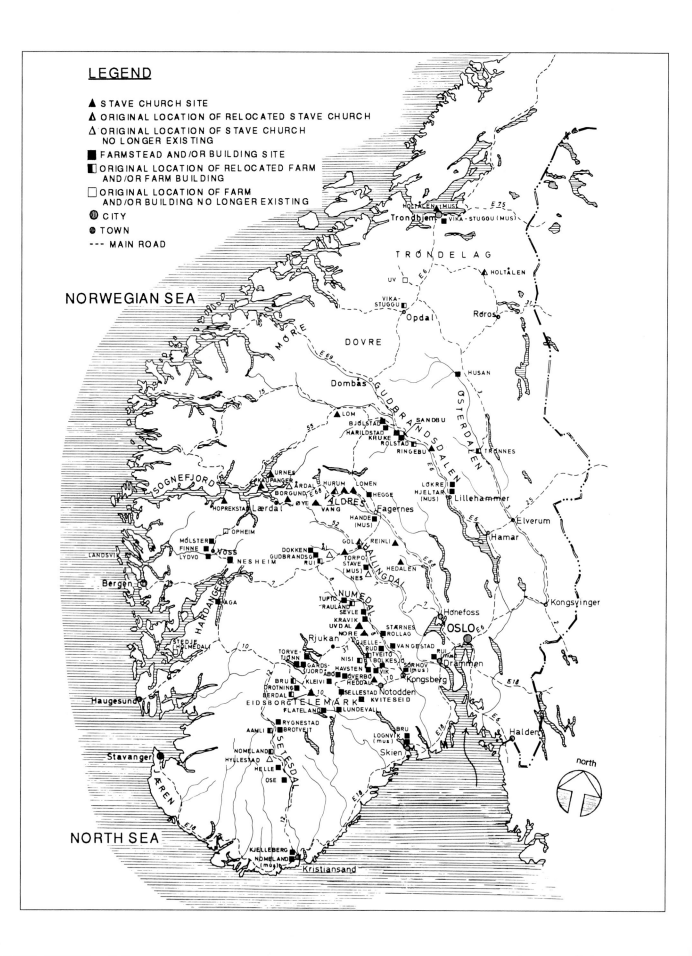

LEGEND

▲ STAVE CHURCH SITE
△ ORIGINAL LOCATION OF RELOCATED STAVE CHURCH
△ ORIGINAL LOCATION OF STAVE CHURCH
  NO LONGER EXISTING
■ FARMSTEAD AND/OR BUILDING SITE
◧ ORIGINAL LOCATION OF RELOCATED FARM
  AND/OR FARM BUILDING
□ ORIGINAL LOCATION OF FARM
  AND/OR BUILDING NO LONGER EXISTING
◉ CITY
◉ TOWN
--- MAIN ROAD

NORWEGIAN SEA

NORTH SEA

TRØNDELAG

DOVRE

MØRE

SOGNEFJORD

VALDRES

HALLINGDAL

NUMEDAL

HARDANGER

GUDBRANDSDALEN

ØSTERDALEN

SETESDAL

EIDSBORG TELEMARK

JÆREN

north

HOLTÅLEN (MUS)
Trondhjem
VIKA-STUGGU (MUS)
HOLTÅLEN
UV
VIKA-STUGGU
Opdal
Røros
Dombås
HUSAN
LOM
BJØLSTAD
SANDBU
HARILDSTAD
KRUKE
ROLSTAD
RINGEBU
TRØNNES
URNES
KAUPANGER
ÅRDAL
HURUM
LOMEN
LØKRE
HJELTAR (MUS)
Lillehammer
BORGUND
ØYE
VANG
HEGGE
Fagernes
HOPREKSTAD
Lærdal
HANDE (MUS)
Elverum
OPHEIM
Hamar
GOL
REINLI
MØLSTER
FINNE
LYDVO
DOKKEN
GUDBRANDSG.
RUI
TORPO STAVE (MUS)
NES
HEDALEN
Voss
NESHEIM
LANDSVIK
Bergen
AGA
TUPTO
RAULAND
SEVLE
KRAVIK
UVDAL
NORE
STÆRNES
ROLLAG
Hønefoss
Kongsvinger
STEDJE HOLMEDAL
Rjukan
GJELLE-RUD
VANGESTAD
RUI (mus)
OSLO
TORVE-TJØNN
NISI
TVEITO
BOLKESJO
SØRHOV (mus)
Drammen
GARDS-SJORD
HAVSTEN
ABO
VIK
OVERBØ
HEDDAL
Kongsberg
BRU
DROTNING
KLEIVI
BERDAL
SELLESTAD
Notodden
KVITESEID
Haugesund
FLATELAND
LUNDEVAL
RYGNESTAD
AAMLI
BROTVEIT
BRU
LOGNVIK (mus)
Halden
NOMELAND
HYLLESTAD
Skien
HELLE
OSE
Stavanger
KJELLEBERG
NOMELAND (mus)
Kristiansand

E75
E6
E6
E6
E6
E16
E18
E18
E18
55
52
50
7
7
10
12
9
2
25
31
69
75

A genuine response to physical surroundings is one of architecture's most important qualities. Solving the problem of how to dwell in a particular region—that is, how to place buildings in their terrain while preserving and enhancing that terrain's natural attributes—requires an understanding of the land. The result, in most traditional architecture, is a quality tied to a particular site, or more generally, to a specific landscape.

The way the sun shines, or does not shine, the seasons that bring snow, the mountains that generate wind or rain, are all significant in determining a settlement—it is not only human events that create its character. The way in which a builder responds to these qualities reflects his ability to dwell within a particular landscape. Christian Norberg-Schulz describes this similarly: "The man-made place visualizes, complements, and symbolizes man's understanding of his environment."[1]

The land provides the major source for a culture's identity and one's sense of living in a particular world. Buildings give a similar sense of identity to a culture, being rooted in and derived from the same landscape. Whereas a building site by itself does not determine form, the act of building can be seen as a reinforcement of the structure already determined by the site. Architecture's purpose is to make a site become a place. As Spiro Kostof explains, "Architecture, in the end, is nothing more and nothing less than the gift of making places for some human purpose."[2]

The breathtaking landscape of Norway is directly tied to its architectural manifestation. The country's jagged coast and deep fjords, where steep mountains abruptly meet the dark, open Norwegian Sea, contrast sharply with Finland's inviting countryside, with its rounded rocky forms, and with Sweden's gently sloping terrain. In this landscape, people had to come to terms with the overwhelming force of nature. "To settle in Norway means to find a place in 'wild,' untamed nature, between rocks and dark, gloomy conifers, probably next to a swift stream of water—in contrast to Denmark's rolling landscape."[3]

Nature has a totality, a place has a particular identity, and these can both be described in qualitative terms. Qualities such as light, warmth, wetness, dryness, and vegetation leave a strong feeling within us of a place. It is to the extent that a building culture responds to such qualities, that its structures appear natural in their settings, that they feel more or less whole. In traditional societies, settlement patterns preserve their environment, and this is the case in Norway.

The initial impact of Norwegian buildings lies in their relationship to the landscape: the buildings belong so completely to their sites that one almost cannot imagine the countryside without them; the unity of site, plan, and materials evokes harmony with the landscape. The buildings seem to illuminate their world of rugged nature and, somehow, reinforce it.

Norway is an abruptly mountainous country with an average altitude of about 1,600 meters (5,200 feet) above sea level. The profile diagram of Norway and Sweden (fig. 2.3) reveals their contrasting terrains. The dramatic range of large, dry valleys in the eastern districts contrasts with the huge mountains and deep fjords of the western, coastal regions. Unlike the country's cold interior, the western regions enjoy a mild, damp climate along the Atlantic coast. Even in the north, the numerous fjords are normally ice-free year-round. This seaboard provided the route from the south by which the country generally became known, the "North-way" or Norway, inhabited by "North-men," or Norsemen.

Communication between different regions of Norway had a great impact on its settlements. If an area had access to a well-traveled route, it was apt to incorporate foreign styles and customs; if not, its buildings and crafts retained a strong local character not tied to prevailing stylistic trends. In the Middle Ages and throughout the seventeenth and eighteenth centuries, the latter type of settlements dotted the vast rural landscape. The many and varied Norwegian valleys were often quite cut off from one another, and this prevented easy access and communication between native regions. In some places, as in the southern Agder Valley, people remained isolated as late as the early twentieth century. This resulted in a wide variety of building traditions and crafts in which local influences were stronger than national trends.

Historically, transportation in Norway was by water and in most places boats were the most essential means of communication. Given the geological structure of the landscape, coastal waters were the natural routes for social and commercial intercourse. Roads existed, though they were not much more than tracks, but they were generally less significant than rivers, lakes, and seas. Often a church or farm was oriented more to buildings on the other side of a fjord or valley than to its immediate landbound neighbors. This was due to natural obstacles or winter conditions, which allowed only boat travel on the many lakes and fjords. However, the steepness of Norway's terrain often meant that rivers were too swift to be navigable. Consequently, land routes by way of river valleys were used. In the winter, the routes were usually traversed with skis, though sledges were also common; and in the summer, it was relatively easy to travel inland by way of the high treeless plateaus called *vidder* in Norwegian.

Today, landbound relationships exist between settlements, the pursuit of small-scale fishing has been abandoned, grain fields are now pastures, land is worked with machines rather than hand tools, and the church is no longer a parish's focal point. Nowadays, with automobiles and railroads, and with the scale of modern buildings, the rugged terrain might not seem so impassable, but in the not-so-distant past, communication and transportation were not taken for granted. If one imagines the land populated at a time when even a horse was a luxury, the impact of such geography can hardly be overestimated.

The rugged landscape influenced the development of Norwegian building patterns, especially in the farm complexes. The multistructured and fragmented landscape led to a unique settlement pattern: isolated, single farmsteads. It made sense for the inhabitants of a country with scarce amounts of tillable soil to settle in small groups of buildings rather than towns, and naturally, the churches followed the farms into the remote countryside. Norway's rural tradition remained strong well into the nineteenth century, and farmers, consequently, always remained close to nature.

Norway's topology also results in severe climatic conditions, which had important consequences for its traditional building patterns. The country's northern location leads to long winter and short summer seasons; in addition, its coastal position means its subarctic climate is conditioned by westerly winds, which bring warm currents of moisture and, when forced over the seaside mountains, produce

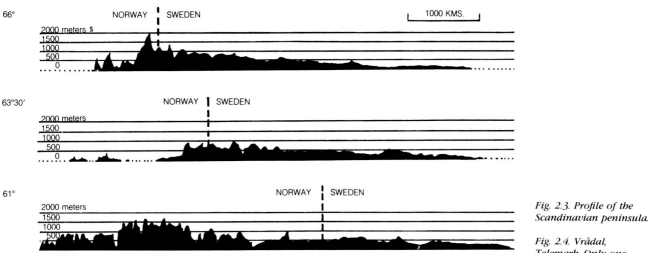

66°

NORWAY SWEDEN

1000 KMS.

2000 meters **s**
1500
1000
500
0

63°30'

NORWAY SWEDEN

2000 meters
1500
1000
500
0

61°

NORWAY SWEDEN

2000 meters
1500
1000
500

Fig. 2.3. Profile of the Scandinavian peninsula.

Fig. 2.4. Vrådal, Telemark. Only one farm is situated on the entire mountain.

Fig. 2.5. Roof of Lom Church, ca. 1150–1170, Lom, Gudbrandsdal. The only dragon head to survive the Middle Ages was discovered here and was replicated for use on this and other churches. Pagan imagery persisted even after the acceptance of Christianity in Norway, and appeared alongside the less familiar Christian icons in churches. The original dragon carving is now in the Maihaugen Folk Museum, Lillehammer.

copious amounts of rain and snow. The concern for conditions of sun, wind, rain, and snow found in most folk cultures cannot be overemphasized in Norway's vernacular architecture. The forces of winter—which in some places lasted up to nine months—offered no second chance if one did not pay attention to the elements. The settlement pattern of individual, single farms made an awareness of climate even more necessary. Self-sufficiency was demanded of all who would dwell here.

The balance between man and nature was almost a life-and-death struggle in some parts of Norway. In many places, life was a constant battle against semistarvation, cold, and disease, a fact that led builders to choose their sites carefully. One is repeatedly struck by the knowledge and discrimination of the builders in their selection of sites and materials suitable to the local microclimate and in their adaptation of traditional models to these conditions.[4]

Surviving the winter season was an important part of rural Norwegian life that also manifested itself culturally. Folk arts flourished in the daily round of farm life during the dark, northern winters. Consequently, this culture contained an abundance of storytellers, weavers, and wood-carvers, who always found a warm welcome and a place by the hearth on a long, cold winter evening. And during the endless summer nights, folktales were narrated of fairies at work, spinning gold from the mountains. As late as the twentieth century, Henrik Ibsen echoed the power of these stories:

> "It's so cool and beautiful up here. See there the mountain glowing red as gold. One might suppose it was the elfin folk displaying all their rich and secret hoard."
> "Do you then not believe such things exist?"
> "That these things still exist, I think I surely know as well as you. But that's precisely why you shouldn't talk about such matters as the sun goes down."[5]

Norway's rough landscape, coupled with the Norwegians' belief in folklore, led to a romantic interpretation of the forces of nature. A family had to be protected from the giants who inhabited the rocks or the trolls who lived underground; it could not upset the dark forces too much. This protection took the form of dragon heads on top of churches or of lions sitting on top of a *loft*'s doorposts—signals to the spirits who roamed about to stay away (figs. 2.5, 2.6). The land was alive and a distinct rapport existed between it and the culture.

At a more practical level, land was precious in Norway. The rough landscape led to a historically poor economy, and the potential productivity of a site was an important factor in determining its appropriateness for a farm or parish. Ownership limits often had to extend far into the sea or woods in order for the farmer to eke out a living in such sparse countryside. Sometimes a church was built by the only farmer in the region who had sufficient means. Additionally, a farm site had to provide for successive generations of the same family. As a result, land was highly regarded and well cared for. The Norwegians' most important resource was the land, which provided the abundant pine forests that they transformed into boats, dwellings, and churches.

To live in Norway, one must like the crunch of snow, the endless summer sun, the isolation of the mountains, the serenity of a fire, and the swift or slow movement of water. These qualities comprise both a definite type of nature and a specific reality, which the Norwegians acknowledged in their buildings, just as they celebrated them in life. The beauty of Norwegian buildings lies in the builders' collaboration with the particular manifestations of nature. Its omnipresent spirit is preserved in the wooden buildings that remain today. The manner in which these buildings have been set into the landscape reflects the extensive knowledge and love the people had of their surroundings: they struck a balance between the harsh forces of nature and the personal requirements of dwelling. This symbiotic relationship is described by Christian Norberg-Schulz:

> In our divided, microstructured landscape, it isn't natural to gather settlements in large units where we together can meet life. Instead, we dream back to each hill with each small lake or brook. Likewise, we own these surroundings together and they have given us a deep common identity. Better than other building works, the stave church expresses the variety and complexity in the Norwegian world and its dark light brings the winter sky's mystery in to the people. The stave church is the expression for the fairy tale in our surroundings but not for the strong climate and hard toil. The daily life comes forward better in the closed and solid *stue* where people sought light and rest. But also here the Norwegian takes the woods with himself. Flickering hearths over rose-painted walls conjure forth again the trolls and giants. Such lives the Norwegian and such he shows that he is friends with the Norwegian nature.[6]

Fig. 2.6. Guardian lions were carved on the entrance to the Åbø Farm storehouse (fourteenth century, Hjartdal, Telemark) to ward off wandering spirits.

*Fig. 2.7. A small farm
sits boldly atop a knoll,
Vinje, Telemark.*

Pl. 1. Mølster Farm, sixteenth century, Voss, Sogn.

2

3

4

5

Pl. 2. Sandbu Farm, ca. 1882, Heidal, Gudbrandsdal.

Pl. 3. Animal tun, or courtyard, of Sandbu Farm.

Pl. 4. Sandbu Farm. The landowners built their homes on the sunny side of the valley, leaving the shady side to the cotters.

Pl. 5. Family tun of the Søndre Harildstad Farm, late eighteenth century, Heidal , Gudbrandsdal.

Pl. 6. Havsten loft, ca. 1600, Gransberad, Telemark.

Pl. 7. Second loft on Rygnestad Farm, ca. 1600, Rygnestad, Setesdal.

Pl. 8. Kviteseid loft *(or* stabbur*) and its* companion bur, *a smaller, matching storehouse built for additional space, 1786, Kviteseid, Telemark.*

Pl. 9. Kleivi loft, *ca. 1783, Åmotsdal, Telemark.*

Pl. 10. Rear façade of the Finnes loft, ca. 1250, Voss, Sogn.

Pl. 11. Door from the Helle Haugo loft, seventeenth century, Helle, Setesdal.

Pl. 12. Aamli stue, *late seventeenth century, from Valle, Setesdal, now at the Norwegian Folk Museum, Oslo.*

Pl. 13. Guest room interior of Ramberg stua, *ca. 1790, Heddal, Telemark.*

Pl. 14. Rygnestad Farm,
1591, Rygnestad,
Setesdal.

Farms

First and foremost, we attach ourselves to the artistic qualities in the old farms, with the sunburnt brown and the weatherworn gray houses with roofs of natural materials—turf, stone, and shingles. We admire the fine changing dimensions and angles in the little askew houses which lean toward each other. The artists especially have taught us to see this, understandably it revolves around the casual quality of the houses. But we see also the intended values. Maybe the architect's view is more logical for in the architect's eyes, the sure and fine manner in which the houses are placed in the terrain gives the reason for appreciation. The houses perform together with the shape of the landscape in an harmonious manner, without competing with it. But simultaneously so that it is clear that this is man's work in nature.
—Peter Anker and István Rácz

T he old farms in Norway represent the daily relationship a Norwegian had with his world. Grouped together in discernible patterns, the buildings of a farm are connected directly to the earth, their horizontal walls delimiting the edges of fields. A Norwegian farm rooted firmly in the terrain reveals how people lived in this particular landscape in the past: humbly, yet proudly. This was the culture's response to its rugged landscape.

In contrast to the rural villages of Sweden, the Norwegian farm was a village in itself. For many centuries, the farm was the Norwegian's universe, substituting for the *civitas*, or civilization, of European towns and villages. In fact, the Norwegian word for the farm courtyard, *tun*, has the same root as the English "*town*."[7] Yet, in contrast to a town, a *tun* combined the communality of daily life with the personal freedom allowed by the private realm of dwelling.

Unlike most other European countries, Norway developed an urban environment quite late in its history. Instead of building villages, the Norwegians divided their landscape into rural districts, called *bygder*, (singular—*bygde*), early in the Middle Ages. These districts were composed of several scattered farms and were bordered by natural barriers such as fjords or mountains. When religion was introduced to the country later in the Middle Ages, the *bygde* defined a church's parish and could also be an administrative unit such as a township. This type of land division is still generally in existence today.

In the Middle Ages most farms were owned by kings, who themselves were farmers and warriors. In the agricultural Norwegian society, ownership of land was of central importance. In Norway the *bonde*, a farmer who ran his own establishment, and even more significant, the *odelsbonde*, a free or yeoman farmer living on inherited ancestral land, formed the aristocracy and the most important class in early Scandinavian history. Because of them, the complex family inheritance law regarding land·ownership, the *odelslov*, or allodium law, still exists in a diluted form today, handed down from the Middle Ages.

The *odel* estate was looked on as family land; it remained in individual, not family, ownership. The owner held it for his ancestors, not for his descendants, or

Fig. 2.8. Øygarden Farm, eighteenth century, from Vågå, Gudbrandsdal, now at the Maihaugen Folk Museum, Lillehammer. Eastern valleys were quite prosperous and their large farms contained many buildings, added on over the years, so that they stood out like small villages in the landscape.

kin at large. When an owner found it necessary to dispose of his estate, he was required to offer it to members of the family from which it was directly descended. Only if they would not, or could not, buy it was he permitted to sell to someone outside the family. If he neglected to offer it within the family and sold it to an outsider, compensation was due to his kinsmen; in some cases, the sale was not considered valid.[8]

By preventing the monopolization of fertile lands by wealthier yeomen, the *odelslov* preserved building traditions: a complex of buildings would remain in use for centuries, ideally in the same family. The *odelslov* illustrates the deep attachment Norwegians have always had for their land and their buildings. It instilled a sense of pride in a farmer that was reflected in his buildings and his care of them. It also underscores the important aspect of time in regard to chosen sites: when a farmer chose the location of his farm, he chose it with the knowledge that many future generations of his family would dwell there.

Though Norway experienced alternating periods of prosperity and decline, the tradition of Norwegian farmhouses spans many centuries. Indeed, the roots of most of the well-known farms can be traced back to the Middle Ages. In actuality, farm settlements began with the longhouse, common in Norway during the Stone Age. This was a large building, spatially undifferentiated, of vertical post-and-plank construction, housing both people and animals with few room divisions. The type was used widely throughout Europe, especially in Germany, where these buildings can still be found. From the time of the longhouse, farm building in Norway continued until the middle of the nineteenth century. Then, modern techniques and land relocations (redivisions of inherited land among families due to its scarcity) changed the practice and nature of farming.

From 1150 to 1300, with the rising influence of Christianity, many kings passed their strongholds on to the church as a sign of good faith. After the black death, an epidemic of the bubonic plague that killed 70 percent of the population in Norway by 1350, a period of decay began. Many farms stood empty and unattended. The decline was further aggravated by the period of Danish rule in Norway, which began in 1380 and lasted until 1814.

However, starting in about 1537 with the invention of the water-powered saw, the Norwegian economy rose. This early tool enabled the Norwegians to cut wood into planks and export it in large enough quantities that wood became a major national resource. Consequently, throughout the seventeenth and eighteenth centuries, the wealthier farmers rejuvenated many of their old farms or built new ones. This golden age was the most prolific and fruitful period for farm building, and it can be discerned in all regions of Norway.

Siting the Farm

In order to get a feeling for how these farms were originally staked out, one must imagine Norway's virgin territory in the thirteenth century and must then imagine a settler attempting to locate a place where he could earn a living. He had to imagine a site in all seasons and for all uses. He had to understand the lay of the land and how to live upon it. In addition, certain places associated with spirits, myths, and legends were off-limits to a farmer in this culture, so he had to know the traditions of those who dwelled before him and those who would survive him.

The land a farmer chose might have extended from the riverbed at the bottom of a valley to the top of a mountain. The infields and outfields were the most important areas of a farm, and their locations determined where the farm buildings would be placed. From these fields the family would gain its livelihood. The choice of a farm site was also significantly affected by the amount and angle of sunlight it received, its exposure to wind, the slope of the land, and its irrigation. In addition, for his home, a farmer had to consider access and distances to rivers, hunting potential, the availability of pastures, highlands, and timber forests, and perhaps the possibility of a view.

The influence of these concerns on a farm site can be seen in the valley of Gudbrandsdal in east-central Norway. The old farms of Heidal in Gudbrandsdal are situated high up on the hillside facing the sun. Gudbrandsdal was formerly one of the richest valleys in Norway. Four types of grain were grown along the gentle slope of its mountains. The slope was used to the farmers' advantage, as they walked uphill and cut the grain by hand. Furthermore, there were abundant opportunities for hunting and fishing, reinforcing the area's high standard of living. The region lies off the Old King's Road and thus experienced the processions of many royal factions, the highest houses being the first to spot the visitors. In the daily ritual of rural life, these traveling parties occasioned much excitement, so an advantageous location was desirable. But the farms were never placed at the top of the mountain—because of wind—nor at the bottom—because of the lack of sun and the good grazing pastures located there.

The region is covered in snow for seven to eight months of the year, so sun hours and angles are extremely critical. The mountains are, in fact, described in terms of the sunny side or dark side. The wealthier farmers lived on the sunny side while the poorer ones on the dark side might receive no sun on their farms through-

Fig. 2.9. The imposing Sandbu Farm (ca. 1882, Heidal, Gudbrandsdal) looks out over the huge valley like a fortress.

Fig. 2.10. A plan and rendering of the Sandbu Farm as it appeared ca. 1882. A typical double courtyard (tun) would have had a barn between courtyards; here, however, the cookhouse and summer cottage separate the two.

out the entire year. The Sandbu Farm of Heidal dates back to the Middle Ages and has remained a good example of the more luxurious farmsteads in the area; it faces the sun and overlooks the valley and the tenant farmers across the river (figs. 2.9, 2.10, 2.11; pls. 2, 3, 4).

After the grainfields and other infields and outfields were decided upon, a family in Gudbrandsdal chose the site for its farm buildings. The prosperous farms of Heidal were organized around two courtyards (the *tun*), one for the family and one for the animals. It is in the choice of building locations that the qualitative aspects of living in a particular place become evident. Buildings might be placed in a clearing around a special *tun* tree or on a ledge with a view. Big trees or immovable rocks would be avoided, and the direction of the valley in relation to the sun would set the farm's orientation. The main dwelling house could overlook the valley, toward or away from the endless summer sun, and was placed in the *tun* according to custom, while the cookhouse would be located not too far from it. The storage house was located for all to see, close to the barn and conveniently near the road leading to the fields. Thus, the setting for a family's daily routine would be integrated into the landscape.

One other important aspect of dwelling in a given terrain is apparent in Norway's

FAMILY COURTYARD

ANIMAL COURTYARD

0   20   40   80 FT.

Fig. 2.11. The family tun *of Sandbu Farm.*

farms: those requirements unrelated to farming that a farmstead had to fulfill in order for it to constitute a center of daily life. Christian Norberg-Schulz has theorized, "If the surroundings seem overwhelming or frightening, the settlement must receive the visitor as a safe and protective shelter."[9] Farms in Gudbrandsdal tend to be more fortresslike, or more ordered, than in other regions of Norway. In Gudbrandsdal, renowned for its dominant broad valleyscape and long winters, the feeling evoked by the region's buildings is one of strength and safety. The Sandbu Farm, located in this part of the country, seems to proclaim that *here* man has dwelled for many winters and shall continue to do so.

The Heidal farms are only one example of how finely tuned Norwegian farms were to their particular regions. In other parts of Norway, different qualitative demands evoked different responses from their farm settings. In all regions, farmers had to understand the landscape and make correct choices or they would suffer the consequences for generations, be it a cold wind or the wrong sun angle. They had to be familiar with their world in order to live there. But in order to "dwell" there, they had to preserve, or enhance, their earth, so that it would continue to take care of them.

Amos Rapoport expresses the idea similarly: "A consistent relationship to nature is inherent in the sharing of a world view and other images and value systems that make possible the process of vernacular building."[10] In confronting nature, Norwegians had to determine what made sense in a particular environment, and their interpretation extended beyond functional considerations. The culture as a whole developed an attitude toward life in the north that was as practical as it was exuberant. Their vision is reflected in the siting of farmsteads which simultaneously blend into their surroundings and stand out strongly against them.

The *Tun*

The center of every Norwegian farm was the *tun*, the outdoor "room" around which the most important farm buildings were arranged. The *tun* was a meeting place for life's most auspicious events: marriages, births, deaths, and special days were all celebrated here. A farm's best buildings were placed around this courtyard, according to function and need and to their relative significance in the daily framework of Norwegian life.

As in most folk cultures, the Norwegian farmer knew what types of buildings he was going to build. His choices lay in the selection of the site itself and the location of his buildings. After he had chosen the area for his farm buildings, a farmer had to decide what the relationships of the various buildings to one another would be and how they would be grouped around the *tun*.

With the introduction of log building into Norway in the early Middle Ages, the traditional longhouse lost its dominance, and smaller structures took its place. This marked a progressive step for farm life as important activities now took place in specialized buildings. Farms began to resemble small villages set into the landscape and centered around a "town square," which was the *tun*. *Tun* configurations are described relative to the groupings of their "inhouses" and "outhouses." The inhouses—such as the dwelling house and cookhouse—primarily served the family, while the outhouses served the utilitarian aspects of farm life, such as storage and animal shelter. The former group held the "life" of the farm, the latter, the "tools." In some regions, only five to ten houses were built around a *tun*, while other farms could have up to thirty-five different buildings. The number of buildings on a farm

Fig. 2.12. A celebration in the family tun *of a farm, 1925.*

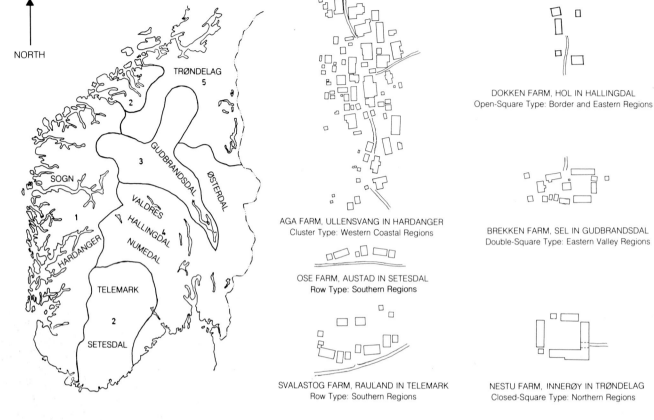

NORTH

TRØNDELAG 5

GUDBRANDSDAL

ØSTERDAL

SOGN

VALDRES

HALLINGDAL

3

NUMEDAL

HARDANGER

1

TELEMARK

2

SETESDAL

DOKKEN FARM, HOL IN HALLINGDAL
Open-Square Type: Border and Eastern Regions

AGA FARM, ULLENSVANG IN HARDANGER
Cluster Type: Western Coastal Regions

BREKKEN FARM, SEL IN GUDBRANDSDAL
Double-Square Type: Eastern Valley Regions

OSE FARM, AUSTAD IN SETESDAL
Row Type: Southern Regions

SVALASTOG FARM, RAULAND IN TELEMARK
Row Type: Southern Regions

NESTU FARM, INNERØY IN TRØNDELAG
Closed-Square Type: Northern Regions

Fig. 2.13. A regional map of farm types: 1. cluster tun; *2. row and irregular open-square* tun; *3. double* tun; *4. regular open-square* tun; *5. closed-square* tun.

Fig. 2.14. Schematic tun *types according to region.*

was determined both by the various functions needing to be housed and by the wealth and size of the family and the number of animals owned.

Naturally, the inhouses were given the most attention in a *tun* setting. A *tun* was thus partly determined by the landscape, partly by the function of its buildings, and partly by rural tradition. A farmer would determine what the land permitted, what he needed, and he would modify the region's ideal *tun* to fit the structure of his own farm.

According to Christian Norberg-Schulz, "Archetypal settlement configurations are found in all parts of the world. Towns and villages either belong to centralized, longitudinal, or cluster type organizations."[11] Such organizations are usually a result of specific topographies, and this is true in Norway. Norwegian farm patterns are categorized by the shape of their *tun*. In regions where the landscape had a clear structure such as a valley, the ideal *tun* had a definite geometric shape; in contrast, where land consisted of many different forms in the same region, such as fjords and mountains, *tun* were less geometric and more irregular. The row *tun*, double *tun*, and closed-square *tun* represent the former type, while the cluster *tun* and open-square *tun* represent the latter type (fig. 2.14). Whether a *tun* was open or closed was loosely a function of the distances between buildings. An open *tun* in the southern valleys might have 50 to 60 meters (180 feet) between its buildings; the half-closed *tun* in eastern valleys might have 30 to 40 meters (115 feet) between buildings; and the closed-square *tun* in the north might only have 15 to 20 meters (60 feet) between structures. Each region in Norway had a natural *tun* pattern that resolved dwelling requirements in a particular terrain and gave every farm its local character.

Western Regions. The coastal regions that lie west of the Oslo/Trondheim axis are almost one great plateau, scored deeply with fjords and narrow, glaciated valleys. This land was always fertile, but farming was often restricted to narrow strips along the shores and mountainsides and on the coastline's numerous islands. As a result, settlements were scattered but dense. From western areas it was possible to reach the central and eastern valleys through fjords and mountain passes or over the *vidder*. But communications between regions were often difficult, and many areas were quite isolated from the rest of the country. Consequently, these areas changed slowly, and conservative influences dominated their building traditions.

In this part of Norway the cluster type of *tun*, probably the oldest pattern of farm courtyards, can be found. Its character is organic and seems haphazard until one examines the unruly land forms of the area. Huge mountains and fjords characterize the region, making the preference for water transportation easy to understand. Even today, the main lines of communication are by sea. Farming was only one part of the local economy, which also included fishing and hunting. The population in this region, prior to the Middle Ages, was made up of a number of seaborne

Fig. 2.15. Mølster Farm, sixteenth century, Voss, Sogn. The two-family cluster farm lies in the right foreground, with the valley beyond it. The intimate, irregular grouping of the buildings lies in contrast to the vast valley beyond.

Fig. 2.16. Nesheim Farm, eighteenth century, Voss, Sogn. In this single-family tun, the irregularity of the cluster type is more apparent. The placement of the buildings at first seems quite random, but after closer examination one sees that the family cottage was situated on a rise for a view of the fjord and the barn built on a level area large enough for such a structure.

Fig. 2.17. Rygnestad Farm, 1591, Rygnestad, Setesdal. The row farm was the dominant type in Setesdal, forming streetlike façades along the narrow valleys.

Fig. 2.18. Gardsjord Farm, late seventeenth century, Rauland, Telemark. The uneven terrain of Telemark required the building of less regular row tun, with the loft and stue on opposite sides of the row.

warrior-chieftans who could not sustain themselves through farming or trading but enriched themselves through plundering and raiding during the Viking period.

The farms were sometimes cooperative in the sense that two or three families shared a *tun*, fields, and tasks. Whether this was due to marriages between families or to a lack of land has not been determined, although the latter seems most likely, as people were apparently forced to live quite close together. The Mølster and Nesheim farms, located in Voss, Sogn, are the best-preserved examples of the cluster type (figs. 2.15, 2.16; pl. 1).

Southern and Border Regions. In the small, isolated valley systems of southern Norway, transportation and communication were often difficult, and many remote areas retained unchanging building patterns well into the nineteenth century. The majority of farmers owned their own land, and there were few transient classes, such as tenants or farmworkers, in these less wealthy regions. As a result, society was deeply conservative.

The row farm was most prevalent in the border zones between the eastern and western sections of the country and in the southern regions, where narrow and tight valleys dominate the landscape. This *tun* form dates back to the Middle Ages and resembles a street; it simply repeats the mountain structure in its building configurations. In this pattern, the inhouses, used for household activities, were usually on the higher side of the row, facing the sun, with the outhouses that supported the farm situated on the lower side. Frequently, several buildings shared the same roof, enhancing the streetlike character of the *tun*. This type is particularly common in Setesdal in southern Norway (fig. 2.17).

In Telemark the row configurations can also be found, but in a less rigid form than in Setesdal because of Telemark's complex and broken-up terrain. In addition, open-square *tun*, where buildings stand separately and independently from one another, were sometimes formed, depending on local geography. The deviations from purer geometric *tun*, such as the row or square forms, are common in Telemark because of the region's highly varied terrain. Perhaps nowhere else in Norway is the land more inconsistent: it is a junction of all the different land configurations in the country, with valleys and *vidder* running both south and west to the coastal

Fig. 2.19. Kultan Farm, eighteenth century, Åmotsdal, Telemark. The renowned builder, J. A. Rønjom, built this farm for himself, placing it sensitively in the broken-up Telemark landscape. Each building was placed first in relation to the topology and then in relation to the other buildings, while striving to maintain the general square tun layout.

Fig. 2.20. The Groven Farm, eighteenth century, in Åmotsdal, Telemark, maintains a less regular row form along its rather uneven terrain.

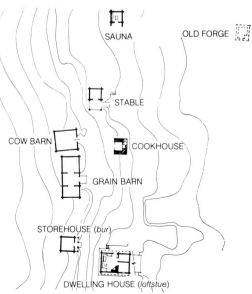

SAUNA

OLD FORGE

STABLE

COW BARN

COOKHOUSE

GRAIN BARN

STOREHOUSE (bur)

DWELLING HOUSE (loftstue)

Fig. 2.21. The Kollandsrud Farm, late eighteenth century, in Rødberg, Numedal, was moved from its original site nearby and restored with only five buildings rather than the eight usually associated with Numedal farms; the sauna house lies next to the fjord.

Fig. 2.22. Site plan of the Dokken Farm, late eighteenth century, Hol, Hallingdal. High up on a mountain overlooking the valley and Sudndalsfjord beyond, the farm represents the open, almost-square-tun form typical of border regions. The loftstue (a combined storage and dwelling house) is higher than the other buildings and dominates the courtyard.

communities. The description of the region as a miniature Norway is apt, and as a result, many ways of making a living thrived in this area, and farm courtyards of all types can be found here (figs. 2.18, 2.19, 2.20). Farther north, in Numedal and Hallingdal—regions that constitute border zones between the southern and eastern parts of Norway—a more orderly form of *tun* is found. This type usually features six to eight small buildings that define a somewhat symmetrical, open-square *tun*. Compared to Telemark, however, the simpler structure of these valley regions easily accommodated more regular configurations (figs. 2.21, 2.22).

Eastern Regions. The eastern border with Sweden is defined by the long mountain range called the Keel (or Kjølen). West of the southern part of this range lie two great valleys, Gudbrandsdal and Østerdal. Compared to the western and southern parts of Norway, transportation in this area was not difficult, and influences from Sweden and Finland can be detected in *tun* and building patterns.

The double *tun* arrangement, found commonly in the large valley of Gudbrandsdal in the east, consists of one closed-square *tun* intended for domestic use and one designed for the animals. Several buildings were placed next to each other to form one elevation of the square *tun*'s four facades, and there were usually no openings between buildings except for entrances. The two squares were divided by a large, symmetrical barn. This *tun* type, too, was a form known in the Middle Ages. The wealthier, land-owning farmers could afford this luxury, which was accommodated by the broad disposition of its wide valley. Typically, buildings were larger in this region than elsewhere in Norway. The symmetrical structure of the landscape allowed clear, well-ordered, geometric courtyards, usually square or rectangular, and these project a feeling of unity. With farming and hunting constituting the main sources of livelihood, the typical farmstead could easily contain thirty buildings. The many preserved courtyards of this type are some of the most architectonic in Norway. Their formal geometry stands out strongly against the broad valley (fig. 2.23, 2.24; pl. 5). Farther east, in the flatter, softer valleys of Østerdal, farming on a large scale was, as in Gudbrandsdal, easier to achieve than in other regions of Norway. This gave rise to big, square single-*tun* forms surrounded by large buildings—a pattern similar to that found in Gudbrandsdal. Mostly these were open-square *tun*, though sometimes they were closed. The topology of Østerdal recalls Sweden's, with its broad valleys and low mountains, and the traditional farms in this part of Norway resemble those in Sweden, where farm configurations of this type were common.

Northern Regions. Low passes lead north from Gudbrandsdal and Østerdal into a region of the country called Trøndelag, in medieval times, the northern limit of Norway proper. Today, the area is located in approximately the middle of the country around Trondheimsfjord. The interior here is colder and drier, with more of a continental climate than an Atlantic one. Trondheim was the nation's medieval capital, and rich and ample farming land has always existed in its broad valleys. Through Gudbrandsdal ran the Royal Highway, or High Road, from Oslo in the south to Trondheim in the north. It was the Old King's Road traversed by pilgrims on their way to the shrine of Saint Olav in Trondheim's Nidaros Cathedral. The valleys along this road were exposed to influences from abroad, especially from Sweden and Finland, and this was reflected in the traditional settlements. Trøndelag itself

Fig. 2.23. The double tun of Kruke Farm, ca. 1550–1686, in Heidal, Gudbrandsdal, is typical of this valley region; the traditional barn separates the family tun on the left from the animal tun on the right.

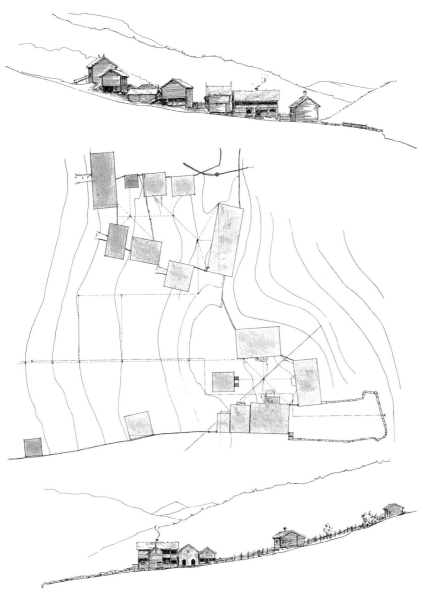

Fig. 2.24. Site and elevation plans of the Søndre Harildstad Farm as it appeared in the nineteenth century, Heidal, Gudbrandsdal. The double-tun farm lies directly north of the Kruke Farm, but unlike its neighbor, the two courtyards are not connected by a barn or farm house and remain independent of each other. The upper plan shows the animal tun, while the lower plan is the family tun. This land has been used as a farm site since the Middle Ages; these buildings, however, date from the end of the eighteenth century.

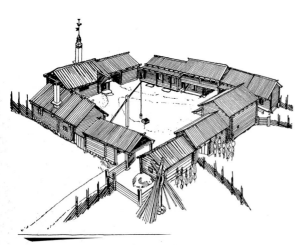

Fig. 2.25. The Mora Farm, sixteenth century, from Dalarna, Sweden, now at the Skansen Folk Museum, Stockholm. The principal buildings of the farm are built around the four sides of a square courtyard. The closed tun is similar to those of farms in eastern and northern valleys of Norway; these large courtyards seemed to enclose part of the huge, broad valleys and made the Nordic vastness more manageable.

Fig. 2.26. Four nineteenth-century closed-square courtyards in Østgardsgrend, Trøndelag. The tight cluster of tun illustrates the precise geometry such farms could achieve in the broad valleys of Trøndelag; their rigid configurations resemble those of Swedish farms.

had the resources to be self-sufficient but geographically was bound to be a junction.[12]

In Trøndelag, one finds another type of closed-square *tun*, which is usually defined by three or four long buildings. This configuration first appeared sometime during the nineteenth century and was the last of the five *tun* types to develop. It provided the basic model for Norwegian farms built during the nineteenth century. Prior to its appearance, regional farm patterns resembled Sweden's with open- and closed-square *tun* (figs. 2.25, 2.26).

The closed-square type of courtyard in these areas was certainly the most rigid of the various forms. Its enclosing walls were not composed of three or four buildings placed next to each other as was the case in Gudbrandsdal. Instead, each façade of the *tun* consisted of only one very large building. Perhaps the influence for this characteristic came from abroad: the pattern is reminiscent of courtyards in Sweden and Denmark where the terrain is flat and wide. It is also possible that the penchant for larger, longer buildings found in neighboring countries to the east influenced this later type of *tun*. Finland's well-known tradition of large symmetrical buildings probably spread through Sweden to northern Norway.

Trondheim has always been a natural place for foreign influences to infiltrate the country, and the region in which it was located was flat enough there to accommodate the unusual geometry of completely square courtyards. Apparently, there was no need to break down the farm into smaller buildings—a linear division of functions served just as well. And in such a clear, homogeneous terrain, it was possible to build a precisely structured *tun*.

Each *tun* form in Norway had its own order, which was derived from a larger

landscape; each *tun* used the earth itself as a measure of fitness. Heidegger's concept of dwelling best describes the order of Norwegian farms: "Mortals dwell in that they receive the sky as sky. They leave to the sun and the moon their journey, to the stars their courses, to the seasons their blessing and their inclemency; they do not turn night into day nor day into an harassed unrest."[13]

Farms in Norway were sensitively placed in their surroundings, and yet, they still appear as distinct entities. Part of the beauty of the farmstead groupings comes from the difficulty of siting buildings in the complex topology of Norway's landscape. The pattern of the land was so marked that it could not be ignored and had to be acknowledged. The farmers reiterated this pattern from region to region, from *tun* to *tun*. One can look at a *tun* and tell by its geometric pattern in precisely which part of the country it was built, even if it now resides in, or as, a museum, as many of them do today.

Traveling through the countryside, one finds that traditional farms are usually set in natural shelters—a knoll on a mountainside, for example, or the only level patch of land for miles around. In contrast, if the land was wide and open, a farm was laid out as a distinct and separate point in the homogeneous terrain. In fact, if one imagines such settings without the farms, one sees that the mountains or valleys are more complete *with* man's dwellings: the buildings emphasize the character of the land and their world becomes clearer.

The Norwegian farms were an expression of what rural life required in that harsh country, and the strength of the farmers' statements can still be felt today. The building groupings were not passive interpretations of geography, they were bold statements of what it meant to live in such a world.

Fig. 2.27. Nesset Farm, nineteenth century, from Meråker, Trøndelag, now at the Trøndelag Folk Museum, Trondheim. This farm is an example of the formal closed-square tun *with its large, linear buildings in the flat Trøndelag landscape.*

Churches

When Norway's valleys housed hundreds of stave churches, the land was really humanized, formed by the people. For the stave churches concretized, in a strange manner, the attitude towards life which is natural in the North's climate and landscape. Later periods tore down the stave and gave us roads and railroads instead. We have gotten the spoiled landscape in place of the humanized nature.
—Christian Norberg-Schulz

I n a country carved from glaciers, the wooden medieval churches of Norway appear as the natural outcroppings of a mysterious land. They seem to grow directly out of their austere northern geography, and one could not imagine them inhabiting any other landscape. Upon approaching a church site, one almost hears the spirits of ancient, untrammeled forces flowing by.

The site of a church is very different from that of a farm, both in a practical sense and in terms of what it symbolizes for a particular culture. A church represents an abstract and international ideal, not tied directly to any landscape; it is a public building made for worshipping and special events. A church signifies common agreement, a belief, a philosophy, and a shared image. It represents the spiritual aspect of life. The absolute east/west orientation of a church underscores the fact that man is bringing a unique type of building into the world—or onto the site—a symbolic structure that is imposed on, rather than inherently related to its local surroundings.

When Christianity was introduced to Norway in the eleventh century, via England, it had no church-building traditions to draw upon. Norwegians, steeped in pagan traditions, had to rely on their instinctive and extensive knowledge of the landscape in order to locate the proper sites for these structures. A Norwegian church during the Middle Ages had to obey Christian dogma, certainly, but it evolved as a unique structure paralleled neither by its Scandinavian neighbors nor in other lands.

Norway was a wild, lonely, and relatively unpopulated world in the Middle Ages. The short period during which the wooden stave churches were constructed—1030–1350—was dominated by two tendencies: a gradual consolidation of political unity and national independence; and a growing contact with the rest of Europe, especially after the acceptance of Christianity. At the beginning of the stave-church period, the country was marked by civil wars, in which various kings vied for supremacy, struggling to unify the country under one leader. Evil forces were still perceived as lurking in the dark conifer forests, which were brightened only by a few thinly scattered farms. Christianity promised to transform this chaos. It would gather all the farms under its protection and provide them with a universal image of one Almighty God. This concrete image would represent safety and a civilized humanity in a world filled with violent deeds and an overpowering nature. It would rise up out of the dark landscape and symbolize a new faith.

Fig. 2.28. Urnes Church, ca. 1030–1130, Lusterfjord (a branch of Sognefjord), Sogn. When Christianity reached Norway in the eleventh century, Norwegian farmers turned their formidable building skills to the construction of churches, often situating them close to bodies of water for easy access and high visibility. Two or three earlier churches were built on this site, but were destroyed by fire.

The site for a Norwegian church had to be commanding in order for the building to be influential. The structure itself had to work within the local environment—interpret it and portray it—in order to be understood by the local populace. Yet, it also had to maintain a universal image.

Today, the cultivated landscape makes the intentions of past church builders difficult to interpret, and many questions still remain about the origins of the stave churches. It is believed that during Norway's period of greatest prosperity in the thirteenth century, there were more than 1,000 stave churches; today only 22 remain to reveal how these buildings stood in the landscape. These remaining churches were probably the best-constructed examples of a particular group or were built in the most remote regions and therefore were the least disturbed through the ages.

The theory that churches were placed on old Viking ritual grounds, or *hov*, has been suggested but not proven except, perhaps, in two cases: in Uppsala (in southern Sweden) and in Mære (in northern Norway). The Norwegian location is particularly interesting as, historically, it was a known gathering place for pagan meetings. Excavations reveal that all the churches (both wood and stone) built on this old marsh since ancient times had problems with their foundations and would have been better located to the north or east of the original site.

A theory has also been proposed arguing that the *hov* was merely part of a pagan chieftain's farm, or a room also used for daily life on the farm. If one assumes that the church directly took over *hov* when it came into authority, it would have been difficult for members of the clergy to conduct regular services in such a private space without disrupting the farmer's routine. However, it is possible that this room-type *hov* provided some kind of physical model for the stave churches.

In spite of the uncertainty surrounding the initial structures, it is reasonable to assume that most churches were sited for other than practical reasons. In fact, church excavations of existing sites have shown that in some instances more than one church was erected on the same site over a period of many years—Kaupanger and Urnes are two such churches. Significance was obviously given to particular sites, but unfortunately, the only remaining clues as to why are scant literary descriptions.

The majority of church sites reveal that their locations are actually the result of many different factors. With the spread of Christianity in Norway, the richer farmers and kings took upon themselves the initial task of building the required churches. Consequently, a region could feasibly have more than one church, if more than one farmer or king chose to build such a structure. As the church and state authorities grew in stature during the Middle Ages, tithes, or special taxes, were introduced in order to raise or maintain churches. This led to an extensive program of church building in the twelfth century. Ideally, each district would have only one priest and one common church, preferably located near the priest's farm. This was not always possible, however, and much confusion arose in defining parishes. Regional economic factors then became decisive influences.

If the community had the resources to build a new church during the initial building phase—a *bygde* of wealthy farmers in a productive valley region, for example—an appropriate place was chosen for the one church. But if the community did not have sufficient means, one of the existing churches that had been built privately, perhaps by a rich patron king, was selected to serve as the main church. Consequently, any other unused church buildings were probably left alone or torn down for their materials. This might be conjecture, but it would explain why siting is not consistent and why it varies from parish to parish and from church to church. Some churches can be found in dominant locations, as at Urnes and Eidsborg, in

contrast to those at Heddal and Torpo; some are near farm settlements, while others are relatively isolated.

In the Valdres and Gudbrandsdal valleys, stave churches were usually located along fjords or rivers in various districts.[14] Water routes, the primary means of transportation in the Middle Ages, were also the means by which most wood was conveyed to a building site and were therefore a significant consideration in choosing where to construct a church. As a result, the majority of churches were built along water-accessible locations, such as the small church at Øye (pl. 20). Sogn contains the country's deepest fjord, Sognefjord, which stretches into an inland area, and many churches are still found in this district: Urnes Church is the most renowned and one of the oldest (fig. 2.28; pl. 15).

Because churches were situated in rural districts where the majority of people lived, the division of these areas into parishes was important. Initially, parishes were determined by topographical borders because they consisted of geographical areas defined by existing *bygder*. People sought the church most easily accessible to their farm's community, and thus, a stave church quite naturally became the focal point

Fig. 2.30. Lom Church, ca. 1150–1170, Lom, Gudbrandsdal. The Lom district lies between eastern and western Norway and boasts the highest mountain pass in northern Europe. The large church, with its tall spire, was visible from every point in the village.

of a particular region. It was not until the Reformation in 1536 that Norwegians imposed their own parish limits.

The churches in Gudbrandsdal and Valdres usually stood across a lake or fjord from a string of farms on the facing mountain where they were easily visible, as Lomen Church in Valdres still is today (fig. 2.29; pl. 19). Lom Church in Gudbrandsdal was placed on a peninsula at the junction of the region's two main rivers in front of its tall mountain; it could be seen from every point in the village (fig. 2.30). In contrast, Reinli Church was placed high up on the valley's mountainside overlooking the entire community (fig. 2.31). In Vang the church (ca. 1327), which has since been moved from Valdres, lay in the middle of the main group of farmsteads. Elsewhere in Valdres, as in Hedalen, which lies in the middle of a side valley with rich woods surrounding the community, the churches lay in remoter areas with less visual impact.

In spite of some confusion over borders and the limitations imposed by a region's natural characteristics, almost all the written descriptions of church sites from the early Middle Ages refer to a farm or farms in the same parish as the church. At that time, *bygder* were often known by the wealth or size of their royal farm estates.

The historian Arne Berg demonstrates the importance to church siting of the old, large farms in his description of Høre Church, known today as Hurum Church, in Valdres. The church lies centrally in Høresbygda, on a ridge that juts forward from the middle of a mountain's sunny side, a location that could be seen from most directions. Just above the church stood the houses of the five inhabitants of the Kvien Farm in a cluster. The farm buildings were so close that one of the church's stave masts could have reached from the old church and bell tower to their courtyards.[15]

The church was a public building that spiritually drew the private dwellings together, even if they only comprised a few scattered farms. It was a structure man could see rising above his horizon; it made him feel secure and consecrated his community as a settlement. The majority of stave-church sites known today reveal this basic kinship. Peter Anker, a noted Scandinavian art historian, describes the feeling engendered by such settings:

> On a lonely headland jutting into the Lusterfjord, a branch of Sognefjord, at a point where it has penetrated over a hundred miles into the west coast of Norway, stands the small wooden church of Urnes. It is one of the earliest datable churches in Norway. It is also one of the most isolated churches. Today, it must be one of the few places on the mainland which a visitor cannot reach by car or even on foot. [In 1980, a road was finally built.] In its very isolation it has a quality of exclusiveness. The visitor will be filled with anticipation as he sails up the fjord, surrounded by a range of high mountains rising steeply from both shores. From a far distance he catches sight of the green headland projecting from the massive cliffs, and soon he can make out the tarred, blackish-brown steeple of the church rising just over the tops of trees, silhouetted against the pale green hills and the grey rocks. Then, as he draws nearer to the little quay of Urnes hamlet, the steeple disappears from sight and the visitor has to walk a long way uphill from the sea until, passing the last orchards, he suddenly has the church in full view in front of him, situated in a wide open, slightly sloping meadow and surrounded by apparently limitless space and light. Around the churchyard is a low, irregular stone wall, and a few birch trees stand among the ancient tombstones at some distance from the building.
>
> When he turns his back to the church, the visitor has a magnificent view

Fig. 2.31. Reinli Church, ca. 1250–1300, Bagn, Valdres. The church overlooks two deep valleys; according to local legend, fairies moved the building to its present location while it was under construction at another site in the district.

of the landscape down to the sea and to the distant chains of snow-covered mountains on the other side of the fjord. In former times this sight would not have given rise to a feeling of solitude. The deep fjord was no obstacle but was indeed the very high road of the district, its only means of communication with the outer world, and the single route leading to the city of Bergen. No doubt there must have been very lively traffic of all kinds of vessels. Even today, the most populated parts of this region are along the fjord, and in the high Middle Ages, the districts of the inner Sognefjord were a fairly prosperous and important part of the kingdom, with numerous large farms and estates inhabited by powerful families.[16]

A short ferryboat ride away from Urnes, at Kaupanger Church, the setting is more integrated, with the church building placed on a prominent inlet overlooking a branch of northern Sognefjord (figs. 2.32, 2.33). At Borgund Church, also in Sogn, another effect is created as the church rises steeply next to an age-old salmon river nestled between two tall, rocky mountains: as one comes through the pass, by foot or by car, one is arrested by its sudden presence (pl. 22). And in remote Eidsborg, in Telemark, one senses why the simple nave-and-chancel church was situated across its small lake from the few farms (pl. 25). Its location was the perfect choice for this peaceful setting: the church could not have been placed anywhere else in that small parish without losing some of its presence, its protective relationship toward the farms.

The church was probably the most important building the majority of people in Norway would ever experience, and the choice of each site concretized a number

Fig. 2.32. Kaupanger Church, ca. 1190, Kaupanger, Sogn; painting by Knud Baade, ca. 1830. The church sits at the top of a small ridge, 200 meters (650 feet) from the beach. Kaupang means "market" in Norwegian; the church was located at the outskirts of this medieval market town. Today, it belongs to the manor seen to the left of the church.

of meanings, at both a local and universal level. In a rugged country of independent citizens, it was a rare public building that symbolized common agreement and acted as an important focus for an otherwise scattered community. The church represented a vision of local order at the same time that it hinted at a universal vision.

Special sites in the communities were selected to help the churches achieve their impact, and most were natural focal points for the surrounding region. In Norway, with its awe-inspiring and turbulent nature (compared to that of Sweden or Denmark), an influential site was especially necessary if the structure were not to be overwhelmed by its environs. The power of the Norwegian world was its nature, and the church sites took advantage of this in order to dominate their world. The prominent sites forced these buildings to rise and tower over their landscapes and gave them the power to stand up and to center the farms around them. Conversely, in emphasizing the structure of the landscape by compounding the effect of significant natural sites with symbolic religious structures, the Norwegian builders made the drama of their world even more visible, more apparent. They revealed how a church needed to stand in Norway's particular landscape.

If one begins looking at the way light entered these churches, or the way in which snow lay on their roofs, or storms battered their walls, or the way in which their foundations approached the problem of meeting the uneven ground, one begins to see how well the builders took care of their next task: the overall design of the churches was well suited to the exposed sites on which many of the churches were built. This brings us to a discussion of the buildings themselves.

Fig. 2.33. Kaupanger Church. This is the third structure built on the site; the Saga of King Sverre *tells of a fire in 1184 that burnt down one of the churches and excavations reveal that there was yet another church erected before the present one. The church, as it stands now, was restored in 1965 to its condition in 1600, when siding was added. The exterior gallery, added in the thirteenth century, is now gone.*

3. BUILDINGS

*Before a carpenter can make a chair, he must
have a pattern of a chair. The pattern is more
important than the actual chair because one
can destroy the chair, but not the pattern. It is
the mold from which all real things are cast.
And somewhere behind the walled façade of
reality, there is a timeless world in which these
molds are kept.*
—Christopher Alexander

*Fig. 3.1. Holtålen
Church, ca. 1050, from
Gauldalen, Trøndelag,
now at the Trøndelag
Folk Museum,
Trondheim, is one of the
earliest churches in
Norway. The
culmination of a highly
refined structural system,
the Norwegian stave
church is one of the
finest wooden building
types of Europe. The
presence of these
churches today, in some
cases eight centuries
after construction, is
testimony to the
masterly skills applied
to them.*

Vernacular building patterns throughout the world reinforce the time-less essence of their particular places. Such patterns give an underlying structure to the world. In the realm of Norwegian wooden architecture, the basic forms of the dwelling house (or *stue*), the storage house (or *loft*), and the stave church are repeated from one region to another.

Yet, the traditional structures found in Norway did not originate there; variations of stave churches and Norwegian farm buildings were common throughout Europe in the Middle Ages. As a result of Viking contact with other parts of the continent, new buildings and construction methods were probably introduced to the trading centers that sprang up along Norway's coast in the tenth century. These seasonal markets, which eventually grew into towns and larger cities such as Bergen, Trondheim, and Oslo, were probably the first places to use new building methods, which later spread throughout the countryside. In addition, the unsurpassed quality of Viking woodworking techniques, as evidenced by the ships themselves, had a strong impact on Norway's traditional buildings: the culture adapted and developed advanced construction methods at a very early date.

Consequently, the Norwegians easily transformed archetypal buildings, such as the *loft*, to their own specific needs. As Spiro Kostof expresses it, "A building type is an architectural form created for a specific purpose and only achieves its validity through repeated use."[1] A "pattern" emerges when a building type has been fully incorporated into a culture's building language, when its use becomes "traditional." Such building patterns express a specific way of life. In light of this, both the similarity of buildings separated by hundreds of years and miles, and the differences between buildings in apparently similar conditions, make sense.

The collective knowledge of a culture is embodied in its building patterns. These patterns comprise a language that defines the limited number of spatial arrangements that are suitable in a particular culture. Christopher Alexander describes a building language as a tapestry of life, which shows in the relationships among the patterns how the various parts of life fit together, and how they make sense, concretely, in space.[2]

Yet, within such a language, every building is made a little differently to reflect regional characteristics and its own unique forces. Given traditional building forms, a Norwegian farmer, for example, could pay attention to the problems demanded by his individual farmstead: where to place the door or gallery in relation to the *tun*, or in relation to this tree or that mountain. This authentic response to individual circumstances is typical in traditional architecture, and it is quite strong in Norway's. The further a building type had evolved in a region, the closer it came to an ideal pattern, and the closer it resolved common building situations. As time passed, a builder had to expend more effort if he was to make valid changes in such a pattern for his farmstead or church. Consequently, variations and innovations in Norway's buildings were a true response to circumstances and were not superfluous. To choose one pattern over another required an understanding of a pattern's function and

Fig. 3.2. Lillebuan Farm, nineteenth century, from Meldal, Trøndelag, now at the Trøndelag Folk Museum, Trondheim. Built by farmers, using the most basic of building methods—the horizontal laft technique—the solid, earth-hugging log structures of Norwegian farms served the everyday needs of farming communities.

Fig. 3.3. Torpo Church, ca. 1150–1175, Ål, Hallingdal. The high-reaching, vertical contruction of stave churches echoed the spiritual aspirations of Norwegians in the Middle Ages.

implied a certain sense of order—a feeling for what was appropriate and what would make the buildings better centers of activity in their different places. To perfect a building pattern, therefore, was not mere imitation; it was a conscious act of improving configurations that already worked well.

This process of adapting building types to enhance life in different environments is the most revealing aspect of any kind of vernacular architecture. Norway's traditional buildings, like those in most parts of the world, reflect an intimate knowledge of indigenous materials and activities as well as of a climate and locale.

Norwegian buildings are founded on a precise knowledge of the behavior, weathering, and natural forms of wood as well as the effects of time on it. The two building methods used in Norway—stave and log construction—have been adapted for many building types from culture to culture throughout the ages. Stave construction, the older of the two, involved the use of vertical planks to form the walls. Originally stuck in the ground with no supporting frame, the vertical timbers or planks were known as *palisades*. Later, they were raised and were placed on foundation beams with post frames. Log construction made use of timbers that were notched at the corners and horizontally stacked on top of one another. Although stave buildings required less wood than log structures, their thinner walls retained less heat.

The choice of structural system employed by a traditional culture depended on customs, available materials, and the level of local technology.[3] Similar to Norway, many other wood cultures commonly used a mixture of these two construction techniques and either method could have served both secular and sacred purposes. The log method, for example, reached a high point in church building in fifteenth-century Russia, and stave building was widely used for all types of dwellings throughout northern Europe in the Middle Ages.

In Norway, however, wood found its primary expression in stave-built churches and log-built farms. On the farms, the main construction of the dwelling house, the *stue* (plural—*stuer*), was composed of log walls, and the traditional storage building, the *loft* (plural—*loft*), was crafted from a combination of both log and stave work. For the churches, medieval builders used stave construction to create structures that remain, even today, unsurpassed in structural integrity and craftsmanship.

Norway's wise choice of structural systems is reflected in the refined forms of its log and stave building language. The expression of a building language becomes architecture only when it is executed with skillful understanding, and this is apparent in Norway's architecture. Climate, materials, and technology enable a society to build structures, but they remain only modifying factors behind the significant choice of forms—forms whose meanings are derived from a particular set of cultural values. If the world were determined only by calculation, buildings would lose all capacity for expression. In Norway's rugged countryside, builders chose stave construction to create churches that would rise above the tall pine trees and connect the buildings to an uneven ground. The choice of horizontal log walls for the farm buildings can be seen as a natural expression of daily life—hugging the earth, thick and protective in the northern landscape.

The fanciful farms and churches in Norway are expressive of more than just functional relationships: they manifest a vision of life. Vernacular architecture generally lacks theoretical or aesthetic pretensions, but this does not explain the dramatic, almost animistic, properties found in these buildings. The Nordic character is romantic and idealistic, molded by primordial natural forces which are still strongly perceived emotionally.[4] As a result, Norway's traditional architecture is predominantly local and romantic: each place has its own imagery, which alludes to a past

and which is not easily understood by other cultures. The Norwegians looked back to the Vikings and romanticized their symbols for cultural inspiration; they looked to nature and "humanized" its dark forces into gnomes, dwarves, and trolls. As Christian Norberg-Schulz explains, "The stave churches and *loft* in Norway appear subjective and complex, emphasized by wild silhouettes, with a variety of detailing and free ornament. They are intimate and idyllic; they have strong atmospheres and aim at expression."[5]

Although on the one hand, they appear to have evolved organically from the unrestrained landscape, traditional Norwegian buildings at the same time reveal quite refined structural systems. In fact, it was the skillful application of such systems that allowed builders to express their local character so vividly and to project an artistic sensibility. The romantic world of fantasy and nature in which the Norwegians lived marks these buildings, makes them somehow more complete. This character, finally, illuminates the builders' exuberant perception of reality.

If one, for instance, were to ask an old farmer how he perceives a stave church, he would relay the story about the giant trolls that live in the forests. According to the story, these evil trolls were the original inhabitants of the world and they threw huge rocks at the churches in order to destroy them, which is why churchyards have so many boulders. But the "nature spirits" of this wild, mysterious land lent invisible hands to help create strong buildings. That is why, the farmer believes, the churches are still preserved and so uniquely and beautifully formed.

With such tales, the Norwegians express their country's lively character. With similar romantic thoughts, they built their farms and churches. Their built expressions have, historically, withstood the test of time. Norway's choice of a building language was shared for more than eight centuries, and it can be seen as so many regional dialects, each talking about its own world. These buildings evoke a quality that is found in nature: they are full of similar elements yet no two are ever alike. In Norway that quality was created by physically repeating elements in a variety of combinations, so that each elemental pattern supported an activity, and the structure became the relationship between these patterns.[6] Throughout the country, the repeated patterns of wood reflected the consistent and cyclical events of this rural culture: here, in a *loft*, a farmer stored his goods every year and there, in his *stue*, the hearth burned continuously with warmth; across the fjord, in the stave church, the community gathered periodically to worship.

Fig. 3.4. Three-story loft, *ca. 1660, from the Brottveit Farm, Valle, Setesdal, and the one-story Aamli* årestue, *late seventeenth century, from Valle, Setesdal, both now at the Norwegian Folk Museum, Oslo. The two structures represent traditional* stue *and* loft *types.*

Farms

The special beauty of such buildings is not so much of the noble, the huge, or the lofty, as a beauty of the warm and familiar.
—Sōetsu Yanagi

The beauty of Norwegian farm buildings lies in their simple reflection of the forces and rural customs of each farm. Just as the *tun* configurations illuminated the Norwegian landscape, the individual buildings illuminated the structure of each courtyard and a family's way of life. The many and varied traditional buildings constructed during the fruitful period of the sixteenth and seventeenth centuries were built by men who made their living in the countryside and always had nature as a guiding force. Necessarily pragmatic, these farmers nevertheless retained many romantic notions of myths and legends, of the greatness of their Viking heritage. Their relative freedom and isolation allowed them to maintain such visions and to project their dreams and ideals onto their private wooden dwellings.

In addition to the influence of geographical factors, the variety of farms throughout Norway is the result of the fact that Norwegians always retained an exceptional degree of liberty, even during Denmark's long reign. Although Norwegian farmers were rarely wealthy, they were relatively independent. Conservative in nature, they were powerful and influential. In contrast to the situation on the continent at this time, property records reveal that the majority of peasants owned their own land by 1800—50 percent in Gudbrandsdal and up to 80 percent in Telemark, where land was less productive. By implication, one might assume that the social structure was egalitarian, but this was not the case. Different social strata were apparent and were reflected in the forms the buildings took. Naturally, the forms also reflected the variations in life-style that existed from place to place.

Norway's communal background reveals itself to be of importance when one realizes that the most significant building patterns arose from the common man, not from a remote ruling class or nobility. In the strictest sense, there were no formally monumental buildings to speak of in this culture. Authentic Norwegian architecture was not located in urban centers, rather, it was nestled on isolated farms in the deep, narrow valleys of mountainous regions. Even by the early 1800s there were no more than twenty cities in Norway, which held 9 percent of its population (compared to 25 percent in France or 30 percent in England). By 1850 the urban population had risen to only 12 percent. Obviously, then, local traditions affected Norway's architecture during its prolific building period, and these influences were also quite significant for its expression.

The buildings that developed on Norwegian farmsteads served similar purposes for more than 600 years. They reflected the demands of the landscape and they also portrayed the nature of an indigenous building material. The variety of strong buildings that emerged were constructed by men who lived and worked their entire lives with wood as a helping hand. Because most farmers were also skilled wood-

Fig. 3.5. Buildings from the Brottveit and Ose farms, ca. seventeenth century, from Valle and Ose, Setesdal, now at the Norwegian Folk Museum, Oslo. The original building patterns of farms were based on geographical factors, rural customs, and a family's way of life.

Fig. 3.6. Dwelling house from the Åspåsgarden Farm, ca. 1700, from Røros, Gudbrandsdal, now at the Trøndelag Folk Museum, Trondheim. The stue *incorporates both log and stave building methods—the fundamental techniques of Norwegian vernacular architecture.*

workers, the farm buildings naturally reflected the laws inherent in wood construction.

Log construction as a technique was widely known throughout northern Europe during the Middle Ages and was the primary method of building on Norway's farms. The development of the method and the high level of its articulation in Russia, Poland, Germany, Sweden, and in the traditional buildings of Finland illustrates its popularity. It seems natural to assume that the technique spread westward from eastern regions, where the earliest remains of log buildings are located. The extensive contact between the Vikings and eastern countries probably led to the technique's introduction in Norway, but because of scant evidence, this cannot be said with certainty.

Prior to Viking expansion, stave building is believed to have been the common means of construction, as evidenced by the many large hall-like buildings, or "longhouses," of the period. The technique of log building, or bonding logs, appears to have reached Scandinavia before the year A.D. 1000. The first instance of this building method in Norway was found on the Gokstad Viking ship in the form of a burial mound from the tenth century. The rough log building of the burial chamber contrasts with the refined strake construction of the ship, and this early evidence of log building might not be representative of the techniques actually used during that period. Log construction is difficult to document archaeologically because it leaves no traces in the earth the way vertical post members do; and, in general, the Scandinavian nations have fewer archaeological remains than most other countries. Therefore, while log building may have been a common construction method for secular buildings in Norway, it has left few remains prior to the thirteenth century.

As a building method, log construction is relatively simple: one log stacked horizontally over another provides a sturdy wall and a strong bond at the corners. The incorporation of the log method, or *laft* technique as it is known in Norwegian, which allowed for tighter and more solid buildings, brought about a radical change in building customs.

Gradually, the traditional elongated longhouses such as those found at the Viking strongholds in Trelleborg, Aggersborg, and Fyrkat in Denmark—built of staved walls—disappeared. In their place, shorter buildings were constructed. The length of a building was now determined by the natural dimensions of a felled log, and a

farmstead that had previously consisted of one or two large, hall-like buildings was now made up of groups of ten or twelve structures, each of which served a particular function. Animals and families no longer shared the same roof. What is more, the smaller, separate buildings reduced the risk of destruction by fire and the thicker, logged walls provided greater protection against the elements. In districts in which timber was scarce, such as in the western coastal regions, the vertical stave method persisted, particularly if the houses did not need much in the way of insulation. After the *laft* technique appeared, it became the primary construction method used on Norway's farm buildings. Stave construction was relegated to a secondary role, but it was still practiced along with log building, especially for secular purposes. Together, the two techniques provided the basic framework for Norwegian farmsteads for the next 600 years.

The common use of the *laft* technique in Norway began in the period following the Viking era, when many landholdings were passed from kings to the churches and farmers. The earliest extant farm buildings date from this time. After the Black Death, a new period of building began around 1535. At this time, the Reformation in Norway promoted contact with the European community, as did the rising Norwegian economy. Strengthened by the discovery and new use of natural resources, Norway's increased economic importance and wider international communication and trade produced a flowering of folk and building arts that culminated in the 1700s when log building reached its highest expression in Norway.

Between 1550 and 1650, an expansion of the agricultural industry occurred in Norway, encouraging the enlargement of old farms and the building of new ones. Because of the burgeoning industry, the farming class experienced an important change. The transition on farmsteads from tenancy to freeholdings started soon after 1660 when the Norwegian government began selling farms in order to gain capital to offset its past debts. In 1750 only 25 percent of Norway's farmers were freeholders; by 1800, the figure had grown to 75 percent. Through the course of the nineteenth century, tenancy almost completely disappeared. Conversely, a large and significant free class of cotters, or peasant workers, developed to serve the growing number of farms.

From this class came a proliferation of self-taught workers who specialized in the blossoming building crafts. These workers were influenced by a new group of

Fig. 3.7. The south gable wall of a traditional Finnish farmhouse, early nineteenth century, from Suojärvi, on the island of Seurasaari, South Karelia (formerly a Finnish territory, now part of the Soviet Union), now at the Helsinki Folk Museum. The traditional Karelian architecture is probably the purest source of log construction in Europe—emphasizing technique rather than ornamentation. The massive Karelian dwelling houses combined living and barn space under one roof; their influence is seen in the northern and eastern valleys of Norway where large farm structures were common.

craftsmen that had developed in the cities in response to the more precise demands of fine Renaissance and baroque furniture, which had formerly been imported from England and France. Because the rising number of cities during this period encouraged increased contact among urban and rural communities, international styles began to affect the larger houses being built on the more prosperous farms.

The influence of the urban artisans can be seen in the growth of regional building arts—such as baroque carving in Gudbrandsdal, and later in the eighteenth century, *rosemaling*, or rose-painting, in Telemark. By the end of the same century, these developments led to the formation of well-known building schools, such as the Klukstad School in Gudbrandsdal, and the growing fame of building specialists like Telemark's Jarand Aasmundson Rønjom. As a result, international styles developed even more quickly on Norwegian farmsteads. It is important to note that during this period of farm expansion, the majority of structures in most regions were erected by the farmers themselves with the help of their neighbors. Despite the growing number of large farmholds in parts of the country, few individual farmers had the means to employ specialists, and they continued to rely on their own skills to erect buildings. Nevertheless, they, too, were affected by the flourishing of local building crafts.

In 1814 Denmark ceded Norway to Sweden, and the following century was the beginning of Norway's modern history. By the time the industrial revolution began in the 1840s with the textile and paper industries, farming had become a business, and agricultural methods were modernized parallel with railroad and road developments. But the expanding economy could not keep up with the even faster-growing population. In the latter half of the century, waves of emigrants, primarily from the rural farming communities, left for America. By this time, a way of life had changed: farming on a family scale had declined, and traditional building methods had been taken over by mass-production processes. According to Gunnar Bugge and Christian Norberg-Schulz, "The articulate log and stave buildings gave way to monotonous buildings dressed in wainscot."[7]

It is not surprising that log building persisted much longer in Norway than in other wood cultures, remaining in common use until the late 1800s. The rural culture was tradition-bound, practical, and had faith in the tried ways of building in a harsh environment. Log building had been used for centuries and was a popular method executed with skill, with the result that the solid buildings withstood the severe climate for many years. Additionally, Norway always contained an abundant supply of good-quality wood. Even in the face of industrialization, the nature of the rural country made log construction eminently sensible.

In 1905 the union with Sweden was dissolved and Norway became an independent nation. Like most other countries at the turn of the nineteenth century, Norway experienced a romantic, nationalist movement characterized by a yearning for the greatness of its past. Building styles emerged that imitated details of stave churches while the period acknowledged the lost art of *laft* construction. As a result, outstanding buildings constructed by the old log method were moved from various farmsteads and gathered into open-air museums. The farmers who owned these remarkable buildings either could no longer afford their upkeep or needed room on their farms for modern structures. Because of the great number of well-crafted farm buildings that existed, it was necessary for the local communities to determine which buildings deserved to be maintained in the museums. The need to define building as an "art" form soon arose and, as a result, the museums came to be regarded as folk museums. What was apparently called "folk" art in other European building cultures was Norway's primary form of expression and was being produced even as late as 1900.

Farm Building Patterns

The two most important buildings on any farm were the dwelling house, or *stue*, and the storage house, or *loft*. In them, one sees best the way of life in the country and the influence of deep-rooted building traditions. They defined the premise, the purpose, of a farm; the *tun*, or courtyard, revolved around these "centerpieces." The farm itself can be perceived as an object in the landscape, a complete unit derived from a larger whole. The same is true for the *tun*'s buildings. A *loft* torn from its surroundings does not have the same meaning as when one becomes aware of the inner *tun*'s context, and the simple outhouses obtain their real meaning in relationship to their architecturally richer neighbors.[8]

In the same way, the juxtaposition of modest cottages next to exuberant *loft* serves to re-emphasize each other's message. The *stue* can be described as an introverted building, hugging the ground, with its expression found in the interior— it was the family's private room. The *loft*, in contrast, was an extroverted building, its gallery rising over the other farm structures; the pride of a farmer, it was where he gathered the riches of his work. Its interior might be plain, but its exterior was flamboyantly expressed.

Both buildings fulfilled the simple, functional needs of the farmer and his family. A sturdy, well-protected building was required to store his goods for the long winter. A dwelling had to provide sleeping quarters and a place to prepare meals. Log construction, combined with secondary stave work, were the means to these ends. The buildings were strong and warm, their shapes dictated by the properties of log building.

For each structure on the farm, a building type evolved and its pattern was perfected by later generations. Perhaps the joining technique was improved, a gallery surrounded not two, but three sides of a *loft* or encompassed a lower porch, stairs were moved, or doors changed positions. In this manner, a pattern crystallized through continuous use. It required generations of experience, a true knowledge of a building material, and a way of life that was handed down through centuries in familiar terrain.

The *Stue*

A house reveals more about a culture than any other type of building: how the people live, what acts they need to perform in their daily routine, what is most important to them, what objects surround them every day. In Norway, the *stue* reflects how families dwelled in their particular landscape. In fact, the word "*stue*" is related to the English "stove," which indicates that the dwelling was primarily conceived as a *heated* place in this subarctic environment.[9]

The organic character of wood gave rise to houses that suited the Norwegian world: in addition to physical shelter, their interiors offered psychological protection from the Nordic climate where the long winters and the summer sun were not always welcome. The northern light never comes from above in this part of the world and the low sun casts long shadows. The feeling of general luminosity is different from the experience of the concentrated sunlight found in southern Europe,

Fig. 3.8. The restored stue *room, or main living room, of Raulandstua, ca. 1300, from Uvdal, Numedal, now at the Norwegian Folk Museum, Oslo. This building is an early example of the three-room* stue *type.*

Fig. 3.9. The central hearth in Mølster Farm, 1680, Voss, Sogn. This is one of the oldest existing hearths and was used until 1730 when the chimney stove was introduced to this conservative region.

Fig. 3.10. Vigastua, 1780, from Oppdal, Trøndelag, now at the Trøndelag Folk Museum, Trondheim. The corner chimney allowed more living space in the stue *room, and the doors led to two-story bed-chambers in the* akershus *arrangement.*

Fig. 3.11. Schematic floor plans of stue *types.*

and the early, windowless houses of Norway were a natural response to this quality of light.

Not many houses are preserved from the Middle Ages, but the few that are reveal the basic patterns for developments of the sixteenth century onward (fig. 3.11). The earliest cottages, or *stuer*, were of the *megaron* type, which consisted of one story—a single room with the door in the gable wall. A central hearth dominated the room, and a smoke outlet above provided the only source of light. This outlet could be covered with a transparent animal hide to shut out light when necessary. The floor of the house was made of tamped earth, and along three of the house's walls ran wooden benches filled with earth for insulation.

An open protective porch was added to the entrance, which eventually was filled in to become two separate rooms: an entry hall and a small bedchamber. Gradually, this type of *stue* became a three-room, squarish building with the door in the long wall leading through the entrance hall to the main room and bedchamber. The Raulandstua is a rare preserved central hearth cottage, or *årestue*, from the Middle Ages (fig. 3.8). The central space, with its earth-packed floor surrounded by benches, served as the main living room, or *stue* room as it became known. This three-room plan is the basic kernel of all the consequent variations of the building type.

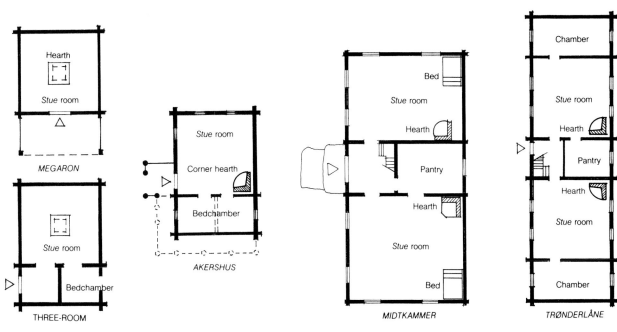

MEGARON

THREE-ROOM

AKERSHUS

Hearth

Stue room

Stue room

Bedchamber

Stue room

Corner hearth

Bedchamber

MIDTKAMMER

Bed

Stue room

Hearth

Pantry

Hearth

Stue room

Bed

TRØNDERLÅNE

Chamber

Stue room

Hearth

Pantry

Hearth

Stue room

Chamber

In some regions, the need for more living space forced the entry hall to serve as a second bedchamber. Rather than enter the house through this second bedchamber, the door of the *stue* was later relocated so that it led directly into the main living room, providing more privacy and a functionally better relationship and orientation to the outdoor *tun*. While the core of a *stue* always remained of log construction, the entry was usually enclosed with a long, half-open, protective staved gallery, a *svalgang*, as in an *årestue*, or with an entrance porch, as in a ridge-pole *stue*. The entries provided a transition between the *tun* and the *stue* room. This is the simplest offshoot of the three-room plan and is known as the *akershus* type. A beautiful example is found in the Aamli *årestue* (fig. 3.4; pl. 12).

The introduction of the corner hearth, at different times in various areas, resulted in the rearrangement of the basic *stue* plan from the Middle Ages. The corner location, with or without a chimney, replaced the central hearth and freed the floor plan for more specialized uses of the living room. Though the corner hearth is known from the sixteenth century, it is believed to have been in use even earlier. It was only in the seventeenth and eighteenth centuries that actual chimneys with flues became common, however. In fact, as late as the eighteenth century, central and corner hearths with the old central smoke outlets could be found in the western and southern regions of Norway.

After the appearance of corner hearths, one-story *stuer* were mostly improved with built-in furniture and windows. Furniture was rearranged along the walls, allowing for more space, and windows, which began as small and colored, were later enlarged and composed of small, clear panes of glass.

Tied inherently to the development of the corner hearth, roof construction in Norway's *stuer* and other buildings varied from region to region. The *rafter roof* had rafter beams, which began at the long walls and met in a ridge. This roof type was common in western Norway because of the continued use of the central hearth, as the smoke outlets needed to be placed between rafters. A feature of these roofs was a crossbeam that spanned the long walls in the interior and supported kettles over the hearths.

When the chimney was finally adopted in western Norway, the use of *purlin roofs* spread there from the richly forested eastern regions. This roof type consisted of full-size, uncut logs that stretched from gable to gable. A combination of the rafter and purlin roofs, the *ridge-beam roof*, is found in the border zones between eastern and western parts of Norway. This roof had one large, strong ridge beam spanning the gabled walls, with smaller rafters extending to the long walls.

Norwegians typically placed several layers of bark covered by a layer of sod on the tops of important buildings, such as their *loft* and *stuer*. The sod not only provided a protective mantle for the bark covering but was also an effective shield against the winter cold and the heat of the summer. By providing a carpet of vibrant greenery atop the buildings, the sod gave these structures the appearance of living, growing, and somehow, friendly creatures.

Sod-covered roofs required a gentle pitch to prevent the sod from sliding. Depending on the type of roof framing employed, distinctive eaves and bargeboards were created throughout Norway, and Scandinavia in general, to retain the sod. Planked roofs, shingle roofs, and roofs made of tamped thatching were also used, held in place by various means such as rocks, saddle poles, and pegs.

The development of the two-story *stue* was a direct result of the use of a chimney, which first became common in the richer and larger farming communities in eastern and northern Norway, sometime in the late 1600s or early 1700s. Its

Fig. 3.12. Cross-sections of roof types. RAFTER ROOF: The interior of Aamli stue *(late seventeenth century, from Valle, Setesdal, now at the Norwegian Folk Museum, Oslo) is typical of open-hearth cottages with their rafter roofs; the opening above the hearth allowed smoke to exit and light to enter the room. PURLIN ROOF: Løkre* stue, *ca. 1760, from Sjåk, Gudbrandsdal, now at the Maihaugen Folk Museum, Lillehammer. In buildings with chimneys, the purlin roof replaced the traditional rafter construction. RIDGE-BEAM ROOF: Hjeltar* stue, *ca. 1760, Sjåk, Gudbrandsdal, now at the Maihaugen Folk Museum, Lillehammer. The ridge-beam method combined purlin with rafter roof types.*

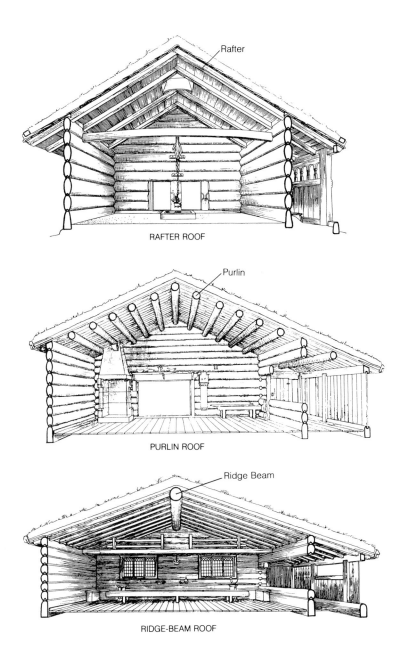

Rafter

RAFTER ROOF

Purlin

PURLIN ROOF

Ridge Beam

RIDGE-BEAM ROOF

effect inspired builders to rearrange their traditional roof structures for the extra space above the *stue* room. If a farmer had the means, he added a few more beams, and the upper space could then be used for sleeping since it was a high and, therefore, warm place to rest. The *akershus* plan provided the starting point for these larger cottages. Once the two-story *stue* became popular, many variations appeared according to individual dwelling requirements, and they can be seen as a desire to combine the functions of the *stue* with those of the *loft*.

According to Gunnar Bugge and Christian Norberg-Schulz, "The transition from one- to two-story *stuer* can be seen in types such as the *oppstua* from Trøndelag or the *ramloft* cottage from Gudbrandsdal where bedchambers were added to the large main rooms in two full stories. In eastern regions a two-story *loft* was joined directly to the cottage and protected the entrance and was known as the *barfrø* type."[10] As building customs from the cities took over and *stuer* became longer and taller in the eighteenth century, the one- and two-story *stuer* were transformed into

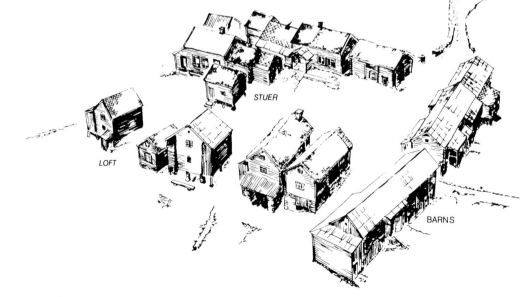

LOFT

STUER

BARNS

buildings with two completely separate floors. In Trøndelag, a second main living room was added to each side of the entrance with a second floor above, and the large *stuer* were known as *trønderlåner*.

Building descriptions do not adequately convey the variations in character from place to place that are the result of a spatial pattern or *tun* configuration. They do not explain why certain *stuer* were repeatedly used throughout an area because of special activities nor how their developments were related to the different types of *loft*. Because such descriptions cannot translate the harmony that exists among the buildings themselves and the *tun* forms from which they arose, an examination of these buildings by region is useful to provide a sense of their order. One can see, then, as Gisle Midttun once said, a wonderful chaos, a pattern, a whole in the variety.[11]

Western, Southern, and Border Zones. The one- and two-story *stuer* in the border zones between the eastern and western parts of Norway, in the southern zones, and in the coastal districts are very different from those in the east and north. The multi-structured landscape demanded more open and irregular courtyards in these regions and, as a result, led to the development of freestanding buildings. In these areas, also, the one-story *stuer* remained in use longer than in other parts of the country, perhaps because of the families' scant resources or because the two-story *loft* was always larger, and more dominant architecturally, than the other buildings in the *tun*.

In the haphazard cluster courtyards found in the west, *stuer* retained the centralized, three-room hearth plan the longest. People here held on to customs—building traditions in particular—longer than in the eastern or northern regions, and they incorporated the chimney latest, sometime in the eighteenth century.

In the southern regions of Telemark and Setesdal, where the row-type courtyard is typical, the one-story *årestue*, or hearth cottage, can be found. This three-room type of *stue*, with its dominant central hearth and smoke outlet, is exemplified by Aamli *årestue* (pl. 12). The exterior stave gallery of an *akershus* plan is tucked into large roof rafters along the *stue*'s entire long wall. The long *svalgang*, or porch, of such a *stue* echoed and emphasized the streetlike *tun*.

In Setesdal, when chimneys were adopted in the late 1700s, new *stuer* were built adjacent to the old, one-story *årestuer*. The desire to match the large *loft* inspired builders to raise the height of the new *stuer*, and sometimes they were built with two large floors. If a new *loft* was also added or rebuilt, perhaps the old, one-story *akershus stue* was heightened to continue the massive row façade.

Other times, as at the Gardsjord row farm in Telemark, the old *årestue* can be found unaltered with a new, similar *stue* attached directly to it (figs. 3.15, 3.19). In Telemark's irregular row *tun*, *stuer* were embellished with elaborate staved porches to form distinct faces in the midst of chaotic building placements. The long galleries with decorated posts pulled the row *tun* together.

In the more centralized or irregular square *tun*, the one-story ridge-pole *stue* was common in the southern and border zones of Telemark and Numedal. In contrast to the linear *årestue*, the entrance porch of the ridge-pole *stue* was marked by two large, richly carved corner posts that jutted into the *tun* (figs. 3.16, 3.17, 3.18). This entry provided a focal point for the yard and centered, or anchored, the doorway in an otherwise loosely formed *tun*. Furthermore, in Numedal's regular square *tun*, ridge-pole *stuer* were larger than Telemark's to mirror the monumental character of their larger *loft*. Sometimes *stuer* were attached directly to *loft* and were almost as richly decorated, which further emphasized the regular *tun* form.

Fig. 3.13. Helle Uppigard Farm, 1582, Helle, Setesdal. The later *stue* (seventeenth century), seen at the left, was built in two stories to match the height of the loft *and was attached to it in what remains of a row-type tun. The stue was modernized in this century.*

Fig. 3.14. Perspective sketch of the one-story cottages and two-story loft *at Mølster Farm, sixteenth century, Voss, Sogn. It was not until the second half of the nineteenth century that the cottages in these isolated regions received chimneys and second-story sleeping quarters.*

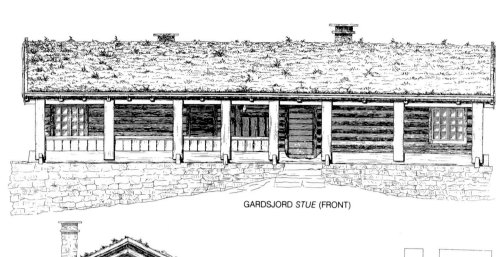

GARDSJORD *STUE* (FRONT)

GARDSJORD *STUE* (SIDE)

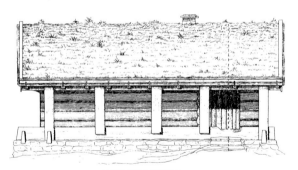

BRUE *STUE* (FRONT)

DETAIL OF GALLERY STAVE
FROM GARDSJORD *STUE*

BRUE *STUE* (SIDE)

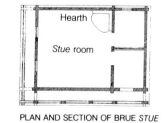

Hearth

Stue room

PLAN AND SECTION OF BRUE *STUE*

0   5   10   20 FT.

3.18

3.19

Fig. 3.15. Above: Gardsjord stue, late seventeenth century, Rauland, Telemark. The original årestue is to the right; an addition for guests (to the left) was built ca. 1760 following a medieval custom; both stuer were modernized with hearths and windows at the time of the expansion. Below: Brue stue, ca. 1704, Vinje, Telemark. A hearth cottage similar to the Aamli stue, Brue's windows were added later; the corner hearth shown in the drawing may not be accurate considering the early date and location of this building.

Fig. 3.16. Sør Hov cottage, a ridge-pole stue, late seventeenth century, from Rollag, Numedal, now at the Kongsberg Folk Museum.

Fig. 3.17. Rear and side view of Sør Hov stue.

Fig. 3.18. Corner posts at the entrance porch to Sør Hov stue.

Fig. 3.19. Gardsjord stue. When an addition was built onto the hearth cottage ca. 1760, the new and old parts were unified by the extension of this long porch with its richly decorated posts.

Fig. 3.20. Two-story
dwelling house, ca.
1775–1825, from
Telemark, now at the
Skien Folk Museum.

Fig. 3.21. Entrance porch
to the dwelling house
above. The heavy corner
posts of these later stuer
were influenced by those
used on earlier one-story
ridge-pole stuer.

Fig. 3.22. Hande loftstue,
from Hol, Valdres, ca.
1775, now at the
Fagernes Folk Museum.
The desire to combine
loft and stue functions
in this building was
also expressed in the
ramloft and oppstua
from eastern and
northern regions and the
much earlier medieval
"long loft" of Numedal.

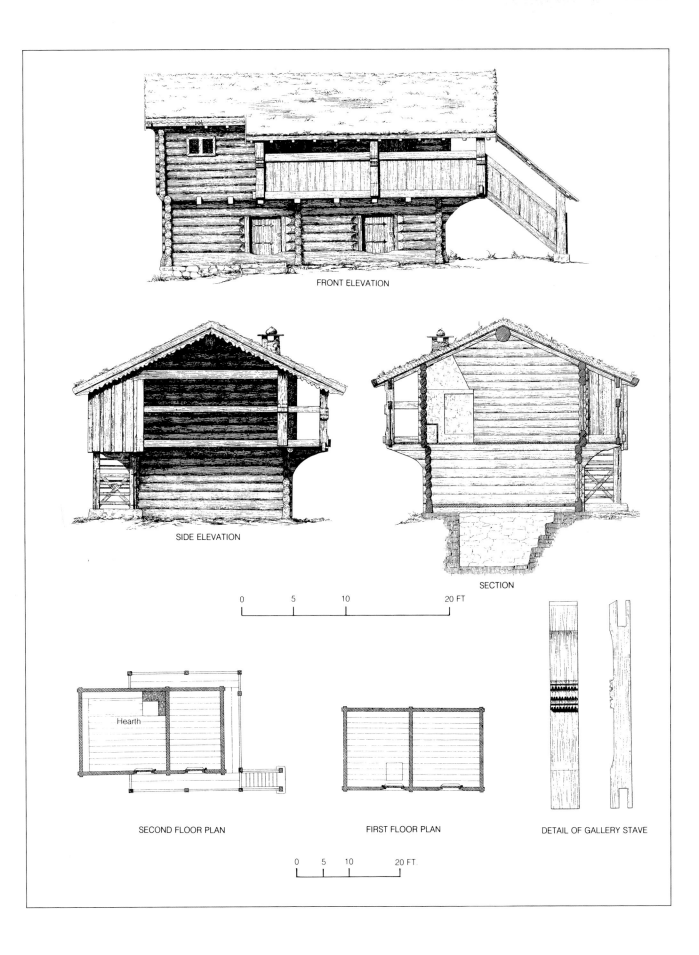

FRONT ELEVATION

SIDE ELEVATION

SECTION

0   5   10   20 FT

Hearth

SECOND FLOOR PLAN

FIRST FLOOR PLAN

DETAIL OF GALLERY STAVE

0   5   10   20 FT.

In most parts of Numedal and Telemark, the *loft* retained its importance by remaining a freestanding structure. Despite this, in the late eighteenth century the two-story *stue* gained acceptance among the wealthier farmers in these steadfast and conservative regions, and it began to dominate the *tun*. With the introduction of the chimney, a second story was added to the original *stue*. Often a completely new *stue* was built with two full stories, and some functions of the *loft* were relegated to the *stue*. The new *stuer* were quite popular in many parts of eastern Telemark, and the sensitive combination of stave and log work typical of this region characterizes the buildings. The posts of the stave work carry the gable and recall the ridge-pole *stue*. As the building pattern developed, the porch and gallery were shortened to allow light to enter through the new windows.

In Hallingdal and Valdres, northern zones that border eastern and western Norway, a monumental type of *stue* combined with the *loft* was commonly built. Called a *loftstue*, it had two or three rooms on each floor: the living rooms were downstairs while the upper floors served guests. The *loftstue* typically dominated the open-square, regular *tun* common to the region (fig. 3.22).

Eastern and Northern Regions. The larger, two-story *stue* types—all variations of the *akershus* plan—are found most commonly in Norway's eastern and northern regions. In these areas, which displayed both open- and closed-square courtyards, the farms were larger than in the southern or western parts of Norway and so, consequently, were the buildings. Buildings in these regions were usually placed right next to one another, forming two-story elevations that defined the precise geometric *tun*. No one particular building stood out, with the possible exception of the *stue*. The *stue* itself was bigger than the other structures on a farm, and it generally was the focus of more attention than was the *loft*.

Several rather elaborate *stue* types were typical in these regions. The *ramloft* and *barfrø stuer* were attempts to combine the functions of the *stue* and *loft* (figs. 3.23, 3.26). The early *ramloft*, with a second story only over the living chamber, may date from the Middle Ages, when the open hearth was common. The *ram*—the attic room, or *loft* space—was added in two stories over the end of the building, opposite the hearth. The *ramloft* was found typically in Gudbrandsdal, and in the eighteenth century it was enlarged to incorporate two separate floors. These large cottages featured intricately carved galleries on their front façades on both upper and lower floors. All the inhouses in Gudbrandsdal's double-square *tun* were blended by the extensive use of such galleries constructed of light, skeletal stavework in the family *tun*, while the outhouses were left unadorned in the animal *tun*. Often, the only element that penetrated an otherwise completely square *tun* was the *stue*'s entrance porch. Many had domelike "onion" profiles reminiscent of the motif found in many log buildings of eastern countries.

Common primarily in Østerdal, the *barfrø stue*, with a small *loftstue* over the entry hall, was known in Norway perhaps as early as 1600 and was widely used in eastern valleys throughout the seventeenth and eighteenth centuries. It was also popular in other parts of northern Europe. The word *barfrø* comes from the German *Bergfried*, a small tower or stairwell. In the Norwegian buildings, the *loftstue* had the appearance of a tower and served as a bedchamber. Two-story *stuer* took over in the nineteenth century and replaced the early *barfrø* types with typically larger structures.

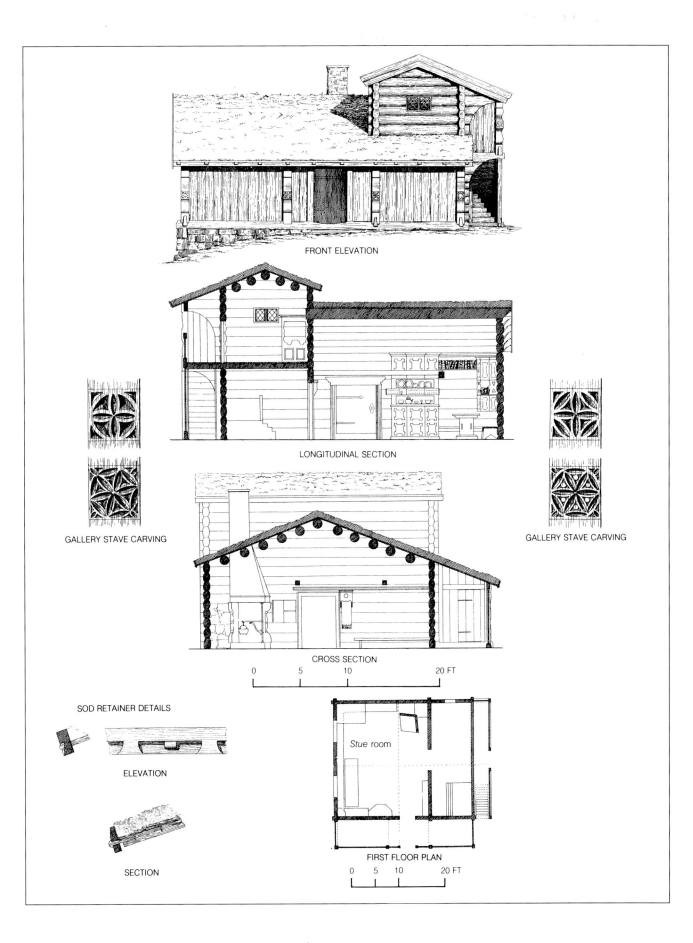

FRONT ELEVATION

LONGITUDINAL SECTION

GALLERY STAVE CARVING

GALLERY STAVE CARVING

CROSS SECTION

0   5   10   20 FT

SOD RETAINER DETAILS

ELEVATION

SECTION

Stue room

FIRST FLOOR PLAN

0   5   10   20 FT

Fig. 3.24. A large, two-story stue, late eighteenth century, from the Søndre Harildstad Farm, Heidal, Gudbrandsdal. Both floors of the stue were based on the simple, three-room akershus plan. This building type was fairly common in Gudbrandsdal's valleys.

Fig. 3.25. Sandbu Farm, ca. 1882, Heidal, Gudbrandsdal. Compared to the elaborate stue, the outhouses in the animal tun were rather plain.

Fig. 3.26. Derived from Bergfried, German for tower, the barfrø stue had bedchambers built above the entry hall, so that the structures resembled small towers. This eighteenth-century barfrø cottage from Trønnes, Østerdal, is an early and unusual variation of the barfrø type: it has the typical second-story bedchamber tower above the main entry hall with the stue room to the right (in plan); but later, two single-story rooms were added, with an additional entry porch, to the left (in plan) of the original barfrø entry tower.

FRONT ELEVATION

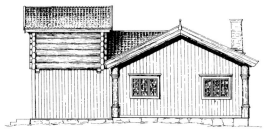

SIDE ELEVATION OF *STUE* ROOM AND ENTRY

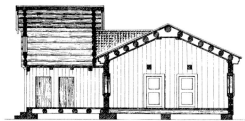

SECTION THROUGH *STUE* ROOM AND ENTRY

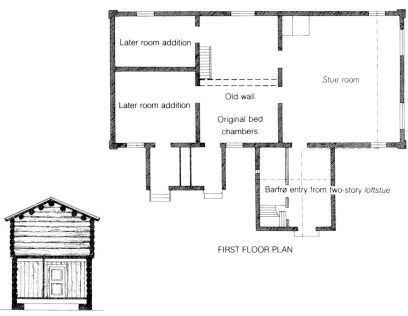

Later room addition

Old wall

Later room addition

Original bed chambers

Stue room

Barfrø entry from two-story *loftstue*

FIRST FLOOR PLAN

SECTION THROUGH ENTRY

0   10   20   40 FT

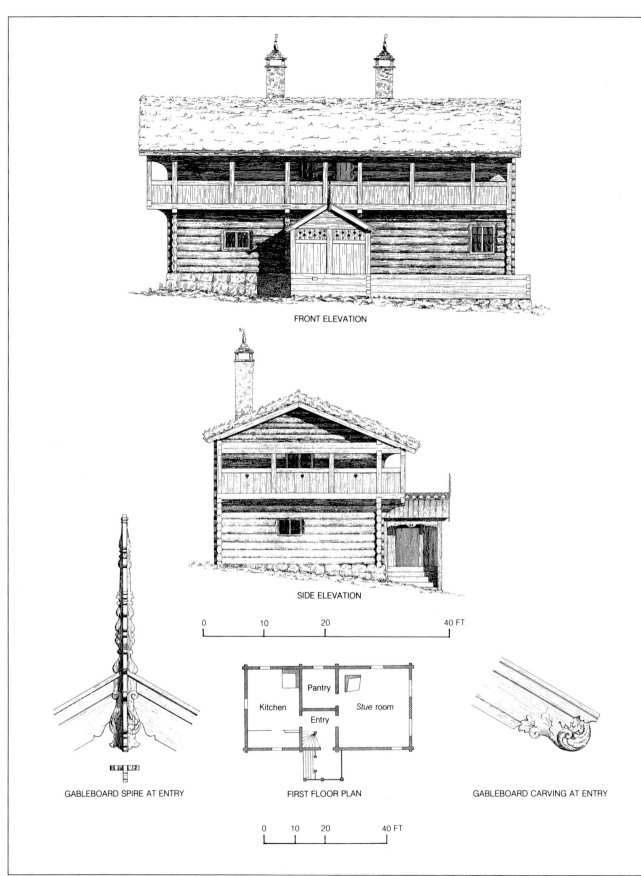

FRONT ELEVATION

SIDE ELEVATION

0   10   20   40 FT.

GABLEBOARD SPIRE AT ENTRY

Kitchen   Pantry

Stue room

Entry

FIRST FLOOR PLAN

GABLEBOARD CARVING AT ENTRY

0   10   20   40 FT.

3.27

The *midtkammer stue* was also common in eastern valleys, especially in Øs-terdal, but it can be found in some central valleys as well. The *midtkammer stuer* were an eighteenth-century development on Norway's farmsteads, featuring an en-trance in the middle of the building with a pantry behind it and a *stue* room to either side. One was the "best" *stue*, akin to a parlor, and the other was for working and eating. Later in the eighteenth century this latter room became the kitchen. Originally, the type was a one-story structure, but as larger *stuer* became customary, it easily developed into two stories (fig. 3.27). The later *midtkammer* houses were quite popular in eastern Norway, and from there they spread north, providing a basis for the *trønderlåner* houses characteristic of Trøndelag.

In the northern regions of Norway *stuer* were also quite large, but their expres-sion was much different than that of their eastern counterparts. The transition from one- to two-story *stuer* can be seen in the *oppstua*, a small version of the *ramloft* (fig. 3.28). Typical of Trøndelag, it had its attic space over the entry room on one side of the building, adjacent to the stairs.

In contrast to the *oppstua*, the centralized and monumental effect of Trøndelag's large, closed-square farms is epitomized in the *trønderlåne stue*, a version of the *midtkammer* plan (figs. 3.29, 3.30). The fully developed *trønderlåner stuer* were long, and their completely symmetrical plans on both floors emphasized the rigid, closed-square *tun*. The landscape's clear disposition allowed for the addition of small rooms in linear fashion to either side of a large central stairway.

In these buildings chamber rooms were periodically added to each end of the structure rather than adding separate buildings to the formal *tun*. The sides and face of the *stue*'s solid log walls were often paneled and were only broken up by symmetrically placed windows. Perhaps only the front elevation would receive such boarding, but it covered up the distinctive articulation of log building. Though

Fig. 3.27. A two-story midtkammer *cottage from the Sandbu Farm, Heidal, Gudbrandsdal, as it appeared ca. 1882. The entrances of the* midtkammer stuer *were in the middle of the buildings, and they were flanked inside by two* stue *rooms. The stavework on the exterior galleries of this cottage was characteristic of Gudbrandsdal.*

Fig. 3.28. A two-story oppstua *from the Engelsjord Farm, ca. 1800, Oppdal, Trøndelag, now at the Trøndelag Folk Museum, Trondheim. The* oppstua *marked the transition from a one- to two-story cottage in northern Norway, and featured a small attic space over the entrance, similar to the larger* ramloft.

oriented frontally, the effect is not like that of the similarly large houses in eastern Norway or Sweden. As opposed to the light frontal stave work found in Gudbrandsdal, in northern Norway, these *stuer* were actually more massive and closed in their expression.

Stuer Interiors

A *stue*'s primary expression is found in its interior. Here, the family sat around the warm hearth on a winter night, where many intimate hours were spent in work and play. Based on the customs of the family, the arrangement and furnishings of each room in a *stue* were directly connected to the activities that took place within. There was always a precise order in the location of these familiar objects because they reflected daily life, which revolved around certain predictable events.

The *stue* is probably the building that changes most from place to place, from one social milieu to another. But to anyone not familiar with the old, rulebound farming communities, their interior arrangements appear surprisingly consistent within a given region. If one enters a traditional *stue* in Telemark, one can be certain to find the bed to the right, next to the door, and the large cupboard against the opposite long wall. One may also find the *loft* placed in direct view of the *stue*'s main window, depending on the shape of the *tun*. In Hallingdal one can be just as certain that the bed is placed in the corner, diagonally across from the door. The long table is always found against the gable wall with the high seat at one end, close to the hearth.[12]

The strongest and earliest deviation from the typical *stue*'s function occurred where social differences were greatest, or where wealthy farmers lived. In the larger houses the three-room arrangement was modified by more than just the addition of new hearths and windows. A second floor was added to take over the guest-house functions of the *loft*, and these finely furnished guest floors sometimes contained their own fireplaces as well. In the eastern valleys the bed was moved completely out of the *stue*, since there was enough room for it in the upper *loft*. The kitchen had its own room and was the center of a greater number of activities, and larger and newer furniture was imported from the cities. As furniture became locally produced, a new class of cabinetmakers developed in response to the needs of these *stuer*. In eastern and northern farming communities, new customs were gleaned from urban centers, and these had almost completely taken over by the end of the 1800s. Kitchens were enlarged, as were the bedchambers, and guests had their own sleeping quarters. But such extravagances were slower to come to the southeastern mountain valleys of Telemark, Numedal, and Setesdal, or the western coastal areas which were, historically, the last to experience change.

Despite all the variations of the basic *stue* form, it is clear that most families gathered around three important focal areas: the long table, the hearth, and the bed. Earth's bounties, nurtured by rain and sun, were brought together at the long dining table; the fireplace invited meditation and imagination; while the bed marked the beginning and end of daily life.[13]

Naturally, such important functions were emphasized in a *stue*, and their familiar furnishings were distinguished with special detailing: the hearth was generally sculpted from soft soapstone, the long table was carefully carved, and the small beds were always cheerfully painted and chiseled. The walls and furniture of the *stuer* were also painted with bright flowers in primary colors (figs. 3.31, 3.32; pl. 13).

Fig. 3.29. Four trønderlåner stuer, nineteenth century, Østgardsgrend, Trøndelag. The large buildings reemphasize the rigid, precise geometry of their closed-square tun.

Fig. 3.30. A trønderlåne stue, nineteenth century, from the Nesset Farm, Meråker, Trøndelag, now at the Trøndelag Folk Museum, Trondheim.

Fig. 3.31. The long table, or dining table, of Vigastua, 1780, from Oppdal, Trøndelag, now at the Trøndelag Folk Museum, Trondheim.

Fig. 3.32. A finely crafted bed from the Ramberg stua, ca. 1790, Heddal, Telemark. The well-made bed is typical of Norwegian stuer, as is the rosemaling on the ceiling, done here by Ola Hansson, one of the most renowned artists who painted in this tradition.

Interior painting, the art of *rosemaling* ("rose-painting"), was made possible when the smoke ovens in the old central-hearth cottages were eliminated. It quickly became a popular art form in the eighteenth century, a way to brighten the long, dark winters with the memory of summer colors.

The interiors of the *stuer* also have a deeper meaning in that they represent human activities in a definite place. When one enters a *stue*, with its flickering hearth reflected on rose-painted walls, a warmth is apparent in its order, in contrast to the wild, unruly nature outside. Norway's harsh winter forced many activities to take place inside and, therefore, these buildings reveal a great deal more about dwelling in such a world. In the words of Gaston Bachelard, "Because of the diminished outside world, the quality of intimacy is experienced with increased intensity."[14] For this culture, the *stue*'s intimacy was a psychological necessity.

The *Loft*

The Norwegian *loft* was a building type known throughout the northern and eastern regions of Europe and is thought to be of Germanic origin. After the stave churches, the *loft* represent some of the finest examples of Norwegian wooden architecture from the Middle Ages, illustrating the high level of secular buildings that could be found on early kings' farms and their larger landholdings. With the passage of time, the *loft* were transformed into the beautifully articulated buildings constructed in the 1600s and 1700s in all parts of Norway. Today they are regarded as national symbols of Norwegian culture.

A *loft* was the opposite of a *stue* in every way. It was a two-story structure whose main function was purely practical: the storage of food and clothes rather than the sheltering of life. As a result, its simple plan was not as varied as the *stue*'s. But its presence on a farm was important psychologically, almost more so than the *stue*'s; it was the "treasury" of a farm.

Upon entering a *tun*, the *loft* is the first building one notices, with its focal position and abundant wood carving. Even on the poorest farms, a farmer built a *loft*. It symbolized what a farmer had, who he was, what he could do. It rose up over the other buildings, proclaiming its dominance, the central image on all farms. Counterparts exist in other traditional cultures, where one finds similar, well-adorned storage structures.

The *loft* had a secondary function during the summer months when the need for storage was not so great and the days were warmer: the top story became sleeping quarters, especially for guests. On wealthier farms, a smaller, one-story building known as a *bur* was placed next to the *loft*, and sometimes, as in Setesdal, even this building could be constructed with two floors. The *bur* was used for additional storage space and was usually built to match its neighbor.

Sometime in the Middle Ages, the Norwegians combined stave and log construction. This refined system became known as *reisverk*, or "raised work," and it was traditionally used in *loft* construction. The system is believed to have been refined as techniques from stave churches became widespread, but much remains to be discovered about the origins and influences of *reisverk*. While it seems natural to assume staved, frame construction was of westerly origins and related to church structures, and that log construction was of easterly origins and related to secular houses, archaeological evidence has not ascertained such influences. Furthermore, it is not clear how the actual synthesis of the techniques occurred in Norway's early

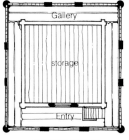

SECOND FLOOR

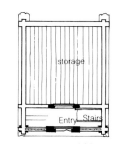

FIRST FLOOR
(with enclosed lower porch)

Fig. 3.33. Floor plan of the Kleivi loft, ca. 1783, Åmotsdal, Telemark, showing storage rooms on both levels.

history (similar systems also developed in other European wood cultures), and early documentation of Scandinavia is too scant to pinpoint the exact origins of their masterly system[15]

Reisverk combined the geometric, square core of a log building with over-hanging galleries of lighter stave members in a wooden frame. A good example of how the two techniques function together is the simple *loft* with one room on each floor. The reconstruction drawing of the large Lydva *loft* from Voss, Sogn, represents the type common to western districts although the system was relatively consistent from farm to farm (fig. 3.34).

The *loft*'s storage area on the first and second floors was heavily protected by log walls, for winter survival depended on these stores. The lighter form of stave construction on the second-story gallery was needed because of the gallery's can-tilevered position. The area, somewhat enclosed, was where fish, meats, and other foods were dried. Originally, it was probably only the transition zone between the first and second stories, however, as the building pattern developed in the Middle Ages, it became well suited for curing processes.

The upper gallery also protected the log-built core below, and because of its location, it bore the brunt of severe weather; consequently, it deteriorated more quickly. As staves were easier to maintain and replace than logs, they were logically placed here. The protected log structure was thus preserved almost into eternity with this type of replaceable and interchangeable system.

In the Middle Ages, the *loft* stood on the ground. With the influence of stave-church foundation work, these buildings were raised on a chassislike framework of four or more wood stumps to prevent moisture and mice from entering. This practice first appeared sometime in the seventeenth century when many new *loft* were built, and the resultant buildings became known as *stabbur*. The *loft* from Kviteseid illustrates this technique (pl. 8).

The *reisverk* of log cores and overhanging galleries did not change much for 600 years, from the Middle Ages through the nineteenth century. Besides the foun-dation work, the only real modification of the structure occurred in the southern regions of Norway. There, the ground-floor porch was enclosed with stave work, which transformed the front of the building into a two-story, unbroken façade, as the Kviteseid *loft* exemplifies. The lower enclosed porches first appeared in the seventeenth century. Often, a medieval log building was renovated with only a new gallery; that is why many inner doors on these buildings retain their old shapes in spite of the later stylistic forms and carvings on the galleries.

Just as the character of the *stue* changed from region to region, so did that of the *loft*. The individual forms were derived from a general type, which was repeated and modified as a particular place required. The unique character of every *loft* was simply the reflection of the differences that existed from farm to farm.

Western Regions. The *loft* in these regions are less differentiated from each other, more homogeneous than in other parts of the country. Typically, protective board-ing was applied over their log walls because of the extremely damp climate. This boarding acted as a blanket and concealed the characteristic differences between buildings.

At the Nesheim and Mølster farms in Voss, the *loft* were not really distinguished from their neighboring cottages and had the same geometric form as the other farm buildings (fig. 3.37; pl. 1). Yet, the *loft* found here are larger than in other regions.

Fig. 3.34. The Lydva loft, *in Voss, Sogn, was erected ca. 1250, then removed from its original* tun *and reconstructed in 1909. This drawing of the original* loft, *as it looked in 1880, was made by the Norwegian historian Arne Berg.*

Fig. 3.35, 3.36. Front and rear elevations of Finnes loft, *ca. 1250, restored after 1890, Voss, Sogn. This type of large* loft *is found on the west coast and can be traced back to the Viking era, when it probably served as headquarters for a Viking chief. It has two storage rooms on the ground floor; on the second floor it contains one great hall and a smaller entry hall. Atypically, the Finnes* loft's *upper story is constructed entirely of staved walls, rather than log walls and its staved galleries only encompass the two long walls. As a result, its finely crafted stave work resembles that of a church.*

Fig. 3.37. The eighteenth-century loft *of Nesheim Farm in Voss, Sogn, is larger than the neighboring* stue *and farm buildings but not otherwise distinguished from them, in an integrated fashion characteristic of western regions.*

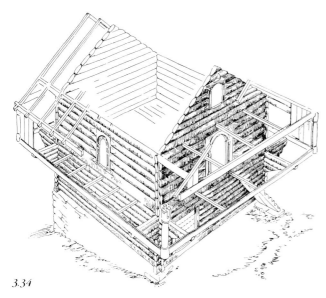

3.34

3.36

3.37

Fig. 3.38. Helle Uppigard loft, 1582, Helle, Setesdal.

Fig. 3.39. Helle Haugo loft, seventeenth century, Helle, Setesdal.

Fig. 3.40. The first loft built in 1591 at Rygnestad Farm, Rygnestad, Setesdal, is attached to the old two-story cottage, forming a row. This cottage was raised a story to match the height of the monumental loft.

This tendency might have been influenced initially by the large hall-like *loft* built by the Vikings, but it persisted because it was the only way to allow the important *loft* to emerge from the apparent jumble of similar shapes in the cluster *tun* common to western Norway.

Southern Regions. In the richer southern zones of Telemark and Setesdal, the building type is unique and more expressive than that found in the west. The upper galleries of a *loft* were constructed to surround all four sides of its timbered core and the stave work of the galleries was usually highlighted. Because the open *tun* in these regions generated freestanding buildings, all four sides of a *loft* were important for its expression. In addition, more stave work was used on these buildings than in the eastern or northern areas of Norway because of the regions' often rainy climate. This may also be an influence from the western coastal regions, where stave work persisted because of a dearth of wood and the coastal climate.

In Setesdal, at one end or the other of a row *tun*, the huge *loft* invariably rises above the other inhouses, and greets one as one enters the *tun*. Setesdal is known for the large logs of which its structures are built, which give a distinct character

to their strong *loft*. The large dimensions of the logs are indeed remarkable on these buildings, and they re-emphasize the size of the *loft* themselves. The *loft* anchor or end the row *tun*, and an example of the powerful feeling these structures convey can be found in the *loft* from the Rygnestad Farm—especially in the second, free-standing *loft* built later on the farm (fig. 3.41; pl.7). The Ose *bur* is also a fine example from the region (fig. 3.42). In fact, it is in this region that the rare three-story *loft* developed, a type that clearly conveys a monumental effect; the Brottveit *loft* is an example of such a structure (fig. 3.4). According to regional tradition, the ground story was for sleeping, the middle was for dancing, and the upper floor was for drinking.

Telemark is a region renowned for its *loft*. The Havsten *loft*, with its dominant galleries, is a classic example of the region's finesse with the building type (pl. 6). Each elevation reveals exquisite proportions and detailing and the overall quality of woodworking is exceptional. The *loft* in this part of Norway seem to stand out like individual pieces of sculpture, struggling for attention in their *tun*, whose irregular shapes are dictated by the complex topography. Because of this struggle, the *stue* and especially the *loft* attained their most refined and ornamental expression here, each face trying to define the *tun*.

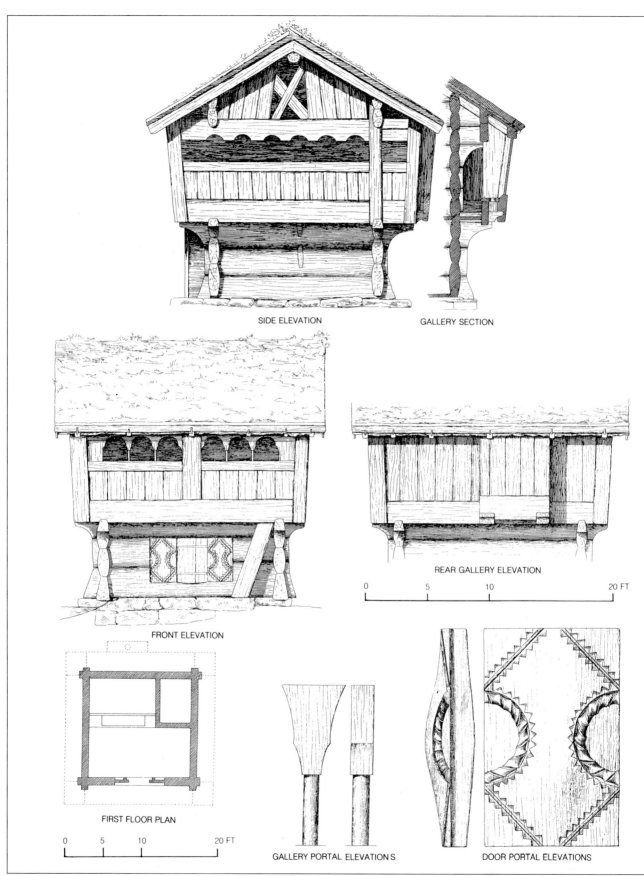

SIDE ELEVATION

GALLERY SECTION

REAR GALLERY ELEVATION

0   5   10   20 FT.

FRONT ELEVATION

FIRST FLOOR PLAN

0   5   10   20 FT.

GALLERY PORTAL ELEVATIONS

DOOR PORTAL ELEVATIONS

3.41

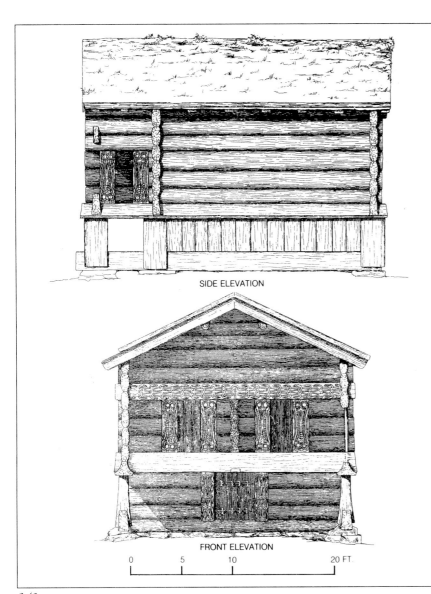

SIDE ELEVATION

FRONT ELEVATION

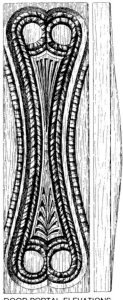

DOOR PORTAL ELEVATIONS

0   5   10   20 FT.

3.42

Fig. 3.41. The second freestanding loft, ca. 1600, at Rygnestad Farm. The carving on the door portals is medieval in origin; the incline of the staved gallery helped deflect rain and offset the settling of the log walls.

Fig. 3.42. The large bur from the Ose Farm, ca. 1700, Ose, Setesdal (now at the Norwegian Folk Museum, Oslo), as it appeared in the nineteenth century. To match its companion loft, the large logs of the bur (an additional storage house) dominate the building's form. The

height of the lower door is determined by only two log courses and the upper doors are framed with huge medieval posts. Typically, in other regions of Norway, bur were one-story structures.

Fig. 3.43. Suigard Berdal loft, 1749, from Vinje, Telemark, now at the Norwegian Folk Museum, Oslo. Finely detailed on all sides, the loft received the most attention on its front façade, which was further accentuated by an enclosed porch on the ground floor.

3.43

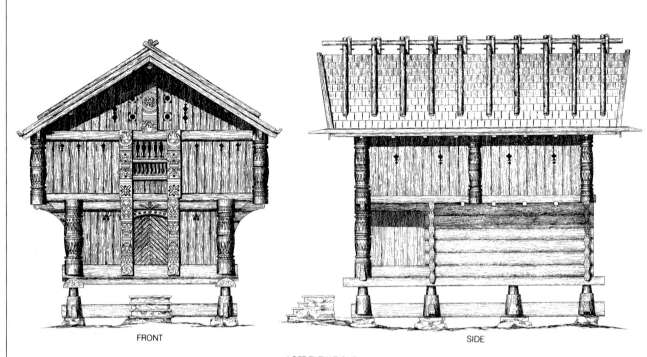

FRONT   SIDE

LOFT ELEVATIONS

0   5   10   20 FT.

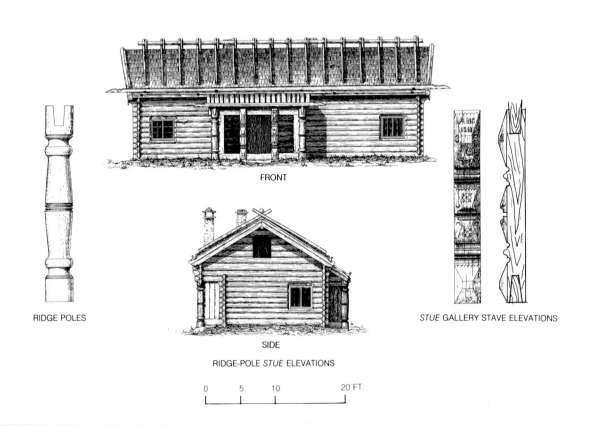

FRONT

RIDGE POLES

SIDE

RIDGE-POLE *STUE* ELEVATIONS

STUE GALLERY STAVE ELEVATIONS

0   5   10   20 FT

In parts of Telemark and in Numedal an enclosed lower porch was added to the *loft* sometime in the 1600s, allowing for more storage space. In Telemark, this gave the somewhat haphazard *tun* a larger elevation upon which to focus. Since the buildings could not stand together in their scattered *tun*, the task of ordering fell to individual façades. When one looks at these structures, one's eye moves from one articulate building to the next in succession, forming the *tun*'s complete inner façade and justifying the *loft*'s additional expanse.

A beautiful example can be found in the Kleivi *loft* (pl. 9); although the building was finely detailed on all four sides, the front received the most attention as it was to serve as the *tun*'s focal point. In Telemark, the impression one gets is not of well-ordered farms but rather of well-ordered buildings, where even individual building elements were highly articulated. In this way, a *tun* determined whether buildings were to be distinguished from one another or blended together.

Border Zones. In the border zones between eastern and western Norway, the *loft* are not as individualized as Telemark's. Although the buildings stand apart, the coherent *tun* form allowed the builders in these districts to blend the different buildings and their individual components. The buildings as a whole have a technical, regular appearance, as do their details. These *loft* offer valuable alternatives to the two extreme *loft* types of Telemark and Gudbrandsdal.

The *loft* in these regions are larger than Telemark's and have galleries on only three sides, giving the buildings a more frontal expression. These almost brutal fronts are often inclined outward in the gable wall to emphasize this effect, and the *loft* are sometimes connected to their companion *stuer*, which helps to strengthen the square *tun* space. The Stærnes *loft* is an excellent example of the integrated refinement the region attains with its buildings (figs. 3.44, 3.45, 3.46). The ridge-pole *stuer* typical of the region generally had heavy corner posts to match their *loft*. Occasionally the *loft* had two or three rooms on each floor, which was unusual for the building type but probably led to the development of the large *loftstue*.

The *loft* seem more technical then Telemark's in that their expressive qualities manifest themselves on the primary functional members, such as the stave posts at the gallery corners. The Parsonage *loft* is one of the larger remaining examples of this type (fig. 3.47). Both the Stærnes and Parsonage *loft* exhibit two-story, enclosed

Fig. 3.44. Loft and stue *from Stærnes Farm, ca. 1725, Rollag, Numedal, as they appeared in the nineteenth century. The saddle poles and bargeboards on the roofs, as well as the inclined gable eaves, gave the buildings distinctive profiles, emphasizing their frontal appearance. The integrated, wholistic character typical of Numedal farms is well represented in these buildings.*

Fig. 3.45. The massive proportions of the Stærnes loft *are beautifully integrated by careful workmanship, making this building probably the best of its kind in Numedal.*

Fig. 3.46. Side view of the Stærnes loft, *showing the precisely matched posts of the upper and lower galleries.*

Fig. 3.47. Parsonage loft, *1719, Rollag, Numedal. The* loft *in Numedal have particularly strong frontal dispositions; the massive front façade of this one reflects the medieval character typical of isolated valley regions.*

porches on their front elevations, but in contrast to Telemark's *loft*, these expansive façades serve only to reinforce their regular *tun* and are always integrated with their *stuer*.

Larger variations of *loft* also appear in these regions. The architectonic long *loft*, with more than one room on each floor, is found in Numedal, and the huge stave *loft* is found in Hallingdal (figs. 3.48, 3.49). The strong medieval character of these structures was passed down through generations as a result of the relative isolation of these valleys and their steadfast traditions. Their massive and ordered appearance recalls the days of Viking halls, and indeed, many Viking kings resided in this part of the country. The large *loftstue*, which combined both a *loft* and *stue*, was probably inspired by such buildings.

Eastern Regions. In the eastern valleys of Norway, the *loft* began to lose their individuality and were usually not as extravagant as the *stuer*. They were given less distinctive treatment and were more integrated into the whole farm. Farm buildings were gathered neatly around a large, square *tun*, with a *loft* to one side and a *stue* to the other—as opposed to the haphazard arrangement of farmsteads from Telemark. The clear form of eastern valleys led to well-ordered *tun* and, consequently, subservient buildings. The open- and double-square farms have buildings that bow to the overall geometry: no one structure stands out, with the exception of the large *stue*. In Gudbrandsdal, the double *tun* best exemplifies the ordered effect. The landscape allowed for two completely square courtyards, separated only by a symmetrical and central horse stable. The buildings did not receive the individual attention Telemark's did; only the skeletal façades received such detail. In this

Fig. 3.48. Sevle loft, ca. 1632, Nore, Numedal, side view. The façade of this "long loft" is on the long, rather than the gable, side of the building. With two rooms on each floor, this type of building dates back to the Viking long halls, whose floors were also divided into separate rooms—similar to the Finnes loft. The inclined gables of this building have an imposing effect which adds to its grandeur. The only existing loft of this kind were built before 1600.

Fig. 3.49. Stave loft, ca. 1250, from Ål, Hallingdal, now at the Hallingdal Folk Museum, Nesbyen. Another variation of the Numedal loft, this medieval loft's extremely large timber core, with widely over-hanging galleries, resembles those found in coastal districts. It shows the almost brutal character such a building could convey.

Fig. 3.50. Kruke Farm,
ca. 1550–1686, Heidal,
Gudbrandsdal. The two-
story stue *to the right,*
and its companion loft
to the left, have identical
galleries and reflect the
homogeneous character
of double-square tun
common to the region.

fashion, the structures were blended together: the individual buildings and their components were not as important as the total effect. In fact, sometimes even the notching of the logs was of poor quality compared to the care exerted in the gallery work. The attention that was directed to the surface ornamentation of these farms and their *loft* did not extend beyond the façades.

As a general result, the *loft* in these regions had only one staved gallery on the gable wall, which faced the square *tun*. The other three walls consisted primarily of log work, as can be seen in the *loft* at the Kruke Farm (fig. 3.50). As logs were more abundant in eastern regions, they were used more extensively in the *loft*. The eastern *loft* resemble their Finnish and Swedish counterparts, which were often solid, yet rather plain buildings.

Northern Regions. The *loft* a little farther north, in Trøndelag, echo the stern quality of the *stuer* in their completely closed and regulated square *tun*. They are generally of the same geometric shape as in eastern regions, featuring two stories and a one-sided gallery porch. But, unlike eastern *loft*, northern *loft* rarely received any special ornamentation. As can be seen on the Nesset and Lillebuan *loft*, only a log wall formed the gallery; it was not staved and it did not have any openings, again recalling Swedish *loft* (figs. 3.51, 3.52). All the buildings were perceived as pure geometric forms in a precise *tun*: the individual buildings were not as important as their total effect. Thus, they stood symmetrically against the dark, northern landscape.

Each region of Norway manifests architectural variations in its farm-building patterns. Yet within all the rich variety, and within each area, a coherent structure is apparent that reveals what it meant to live in a certain place. The beauty of the Norwegian building patterns lies in how they were made to illuminate the geometry of a particular world.

Fig. 3.51. Loft *from the Lillebuan Farm, nineteenth century, from Meldal, Trøndelag, now at the Trøndelag Folk Museum, Trondheim. The plain, log building is not articulated with any special detailing or stave work, as was characteristic of the region.*

Fig. 3.52. An unadorned loft *from the Nesset Farm, nineteenth century, from Meråker, Trøndelag, now at the Trøndelag Folk Museum, Trondheim.*

Churches

History was embodied in the stave church's construction, while the idea of the church flowed to all places. The horizon was the embodiment of nature and the tower was the means to conquer it. The symbol a stave church represented could reach beyond the horizon—the borderline of the unknown.
—Sverre Fehn

To approach a Norwegian stave church for the first time is to be overwhelmed by the feeling that the structure is alive. Rising out of an often dark and forbidding landscape, the church conveys power, much like the serpent-dragon of Viking tales rising from the sea. The building itself is almost as arresting—and even frightening—as the natural world that surrounds it; in contrast, the interior is serene, protected, an oasis of candlelight in which the spirit of the forests live peacefully.

The stave church is a monument to the eleventh-century transition of the Norwegian people from animism and pagan worship to Christianity. Formidable and remote authorities developed in the form of church and state and they interfered with matters previously under family or local control. Yet, rooted in a tradition that was deeply connected to nature, the medieval Norwegian culture did not experience irreconcilable conflict between the old mythology and Christian concepts but instead grew into Christianity. According to Dan Lindholm and Walther Roggenkamp, the Norwegians did this not through the teachings of the church but through the physical act of the holy ritual, through the magical feelings called forth by every service.[16] Pagan beliefs were never formal concepts; they were practices continuously being developed, and the Norwegians easily substituted the excitement of mass worshippings with Christian services. Gradually, Christ was considered the more powerful deity although old gods still existed in popular belief and superstition.

Worship of a single god was a new element in Norwegian daily life and pagan meetings were probably continued outside the church, whereas Christian services were held inside, in "Christ's house." At its outset, Christianity posed certain difficulties: How did rural communities gather together under one roof to give tribute to this almighty Savior? What resources did a small country such as Norway, known more for its warriors than for any kind of religion, use to create the necessary structures?

In general, the kings and farmers had no real monumental architecture as a model for their new church buildings, and in the beginning of the eleventh century, only a scanty notion of Christianity itself. The state of technology reached during the Viking period indicates that much was known about wood construction. Even without precise knowledge of the building type, the Norwegians had been using wood with dexterity long before an expansive church-building program began. Additionally, through their Viking travels, many yeomen of this initial transitory period had an idea of what a church was and perhaps of what it should look like.

Fig. 3.53. Urnes Church, ca. 1130, Lusterfjord, Sogn. While the present church on this site is from the twelfth century, parts of it can be dated to 1030. The church was stripped of some of its medieval exterior embellishments and much altered in the past; its front porch is what remains of the ambulatory.

The Christian religion was relatively slower to reach Norway than it was to reach the rest of continental Europe. The earliest attempt to introduce it into Norway was the result of a collaboration between Viking kings and English royalty. The first Norwegian king to transport Christianity from the Anglo-Saxon world was Haakon the Good, who ruled in the tenth century. Resistance to the new religion was combined with resistance to royal authority, but in spite of many bloody battles that followed, Haakon had three churches built in the Møre district, a region in northern Trøndelag. These churches were soon burned, and the priests Haakon had transported from England during his pirate expeditions were killed. The missionary efforts of two later kings, Olav Tryggvason and Olav Haraldsson (Saint Olav), were also fiercely resisted.

It was not until the reign of Olav Kyrre (Olav the Peaceful), which extended from A.D. 1066 to 1093, that a lasting, official Norwegian church was established. Olav set up Episcopal sees at Trondheim, Bergen, and Oslo and probably instituted the first program of church building in these market towns. It is also significant that by this time Vikings and chieftans had returned from abroad where they had been christened. The first patrons of the religion, in the early period before the church achieved economic and administrative independence, were such kings. As these leaders settled back onto their farms, Christianity slowly penetrated society from its rulers down.

The role of kings was quite important to the initial church-building program. They were the first to decree that churches be raised and, in fact, the conversion of Norway to Christianity was not the result of cleric missionaries but of kings leading their people from pagan priests. The kings and the church were especially close in Norway, more so than in other Scandinavian countries. The result was that until the middle of the twelfth century, the highest clerical authorities were tied to a milieu saturated with native lore, one in which modern Christian concepts—for example, canonical rules on church building and iconography—were only gradually penetrating.[17]

Skaldic poets, who held positions in the royal courts and were highly esteemed and praised by their kings, also directly affected the character of Norwegian church buildings. These poets were the only source of royal history and became influential when King Tryggvason used them for promoting the new religion. Medieval theology, as a result, was created in an environment in which ancient Norse imagery was used to express Christian ideas. A story from the eleventh century is illustrative of the period's dilemma: a skald, who was being christened, was called upon to abjure the heathen gods; he was very reluctant, saying that as a skald, he could not fulfill his task without the old gods.[18]

During the reign of the "Brother Kings," Sigurd and Eystein Magnusson, from 1103 to 1130, old regional laws were recorded in the Old Norse language. By the end of the twelfth century, these laws were considered valid and protected by God and the church. Initially, the laws dictated that it was the communities' obligation to build churches, and many kings and wealthy farmers provided the first wooden churches, during what the historian Peter Anker calls the missionary period, between 1050 and 1125. At a time when no independent clerical authority yet existed, the kings' wooden palace churches provided a model for the first community churches.

In approximately 1120, the introduction of tithes by King Sigurd Magnusson helped the expansion of church building and provided the church with the beginnings of a solid financial basis. The country was actually too poor and sparsely populated for its ambitious program of church building. Although canonical law required stone for houses of worship, the native material of wood provided an acceptable alternative in Norway. According to Peter Anker, "The discovery of primitive wooden churches all over Scandinavia in the early Middle Ages is not surprising in such a huge forest belt. Until the end of the Middle Ages, all its secular architecture was of wood. Missionaries in Scandinavia encountered vast regions where no tradition of stone building existed and, as a result, their churches were initially constructed of wood."[19]

Although skilled stonemasons would have to be imported from southern countries, priests did eventually intend to have stone churches built. Consequently, Denmark and Sweden began to use stone for their churches and other important buildings early in the Middle Ages. In Norway, however, these stone churches were rarely executed. Norway's traditional wooden architecture was technically more advanced than the stone building of Scandinavia's missionary period, and it had sufficient comparable qualities for clerical authorities to accept it: durability, size, and a suitably impressive appearance. Furthermore, the wooden edifices were cheaper, required only a skilled master builder and local carpenters, and provided carved decoration on a large scale.[20]

If one looks at the distribution of churches in Norway, one finds that stone churches were, in fact, built in the wealthy eastern valley parishes and along productive western fjords. The early private churches built by kings and the wooden churches built in towns were also eventually replaced by stone structures. But throughout most of Norway, in its less populous districts, churches were constructed of wood. Stone building did increase in Norway's Middle Ages, but during its greatest period of expansion, the stave-church period, the country lacked the resources to build in stone.

Because of King Magnusson's tithes, by the mid-twelfth century, the church was well established and had acquired enough wealth to become an independent authority alongside the aristocracy. In approximately 1135 the last palace church was built by a king, and at this time, clerical authorities began to influence the layout of churches. Their demands are reflected in the large number of churches built between 1150 and 1250, which represent mature, fully developed stave-church construction. The form of these churches was certainly predicated on the priests' acceptance of Norway's early wooden churches. Yet, even after the church was established and organized throughout Norway, stave churches were still constructed of wood. By the end of the Middle Ages the church owned half the land on which the parish churches were built, and between 1250 and 1350, the wooden churches were only embellished with features such as galleries and turrets, which further enhanced their native construction.

In 1350, when the number of stave churches was at its peak, the bubonic plague struck Norway as it did the rest of Europe. The population was depleted and church construction stopped. When it began again, it was under the new Lutheran religion, which was forced upon Norway by Denmark, against violent opposition, in 1536— when, because of the lack of unity among Norway's leaders, Danish nobility formally took over Norway's rule, remaining in control for the next 300 years. As the new religion grew, the Lutherans considered stave churches too small, dark, and cold for religious purposes, and they demanded new buildings. Many churches were severely modified or torn down altogether or were simply left to decay. In the seventeenth and eighteenth centuries, cruciform plans were popular, and some stave churches, especially in eastern regions, were remodeled with transepts of log construction. Lom is a good example of such a church (fig. 3.79).

Fig. 3.54. The interior of
Kaupanger Church, ca.
1190, Kaupanger, Sogn,
showing the upper
clerestory windows,
which allow only a
glimmer of light to enter
the nave.

In 1851 a law was passed requiring all churches to be able to hold 60 percent of their congregations, and many older churches, again including a number of extant stave churches, were consequently torn down. Toward the turn of the century, a revived interest in the country's cultural heritage gave strength to the newly formed Society for the Preservation of Ancient Monuments. Because of the Society, most of the remaining stave churches were somewhat protected; but today certain jurisdictions in Norway still retain local authority over a small number of churches. The few churches that have survived are heavily modified or have been moved to new sites. However, they offer enduring evidence of a time of grandeur when Norwegians built with human proportions and a sure sense of their native wood.

Stave Church Building Patterns

Some regional patterns among churches can be discerned, as among the farm complexes: simple, rectangular churches are found in Trøndelag; central-mast churches are common in Nes and Uvdal; and the apse form is found in eastern regions, but not in western areas, where many-masted churches were constructed.[21] These variations, however, are overshadowed by the universal nature of church structures. This is most evident in the interiors of stave churches, all of which have a common characteristic: they reflect the eternal qualities of Norway's landscape.

In Norway, the bleak countryside is often mirrored in a gray sky. Similarly, the dark interior of a typical stave church, lit only by candles, has a definite character-shaping quality; it reminds one of the dark heavens above. Small holes cut into the upper clerestories were probably used only for ventilation rather than for lighting,

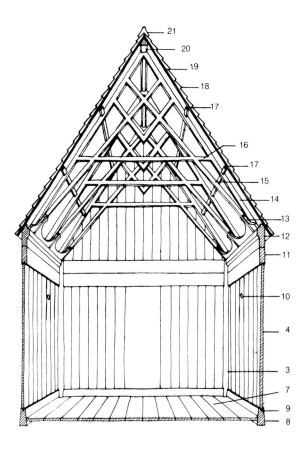

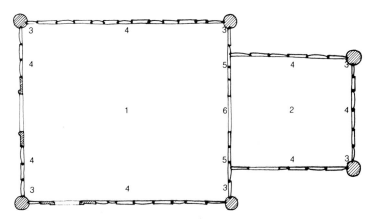

1. Nave
2. Chancel or choir
3. Corner column or stave
4. Wall planks
5. Choir partition
6. Choir opening
7. Floor planks
8. Ground-sill beam or plate
9. Drain hole
10. Window plank or porthole
11. Wall plate, lower member
12. Wall plate, upper member
13. Quadrant bracket
14. Truss rafter
15. Truss strut
16. Nave collar beam
17. Purlin
18. Shingle roofing
19. Roof boarding
20. Nave ridge beam
21. Ridge keel (ridgeboard)

a natural response to the dearth of sunlight and the long Norwegian winters. While the weak light filtered in from above, Norwegians paid quiet homage to the higher forces that shaped their land. The interiors of these churches are stark yet serene, although this might not have been their intended state. The intricate original wall planks and posts at Urnes Church, for example, suggest the existence of a once highly decorative interior (figs. 4.51, 4.74). During the Lutheran Reformation church interiors were probably modified to accommodate the stricter religion.

It can be assumed that early missionaries from England brought their concepts of ideal church structures to Norway, but they certainly lacked experience for building in such a snow-filled, mountainous landscape. Although some English churches were built of wood, and although numerous excavations of postholes in England reveal that churches, contemporary halls, and houses employed vertical timber, or palisade, techniques, it is doubtful that priests brought the actual skills or knowledge to erect Norway's stave churches. Furthermore, England's largest churches were generally built of stone, and Norway's buildings had always been of wood.

In order to promote Christianity in Norway without alienating potential followers, it was in the interest of the kings and their royal courts to use images and buildings that were familiar to people. The model most easily adapted to Norwegian circumstances was the simple Anglo-Saxon church with a square chancel at the east end and an entrance on the west end. Whether the building type was previously in existence in Norway is unknown.

As with the farms, this standard model provided the starting point for all the later variations of stave churches. The first eleventh-century churches consisted of a small meeting hall with a chancel. Considered to be one of the oldest churches

Fig. 3.55. Sectional perspective and plan of Holtålen Church, ca. 1050, from Gauldalen, Trøndelag, now at the Trøndelag Folk Museum, Trondheim.

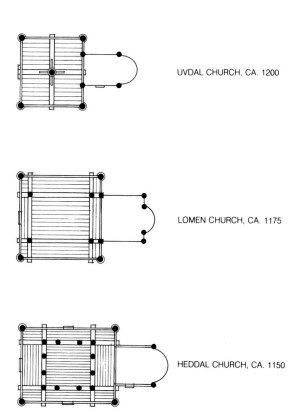

UVDAL CHURCH, CA. 1200

LOMEN CHURCH, CA. 1175

HEDDAL CHURCH, CA. 1150

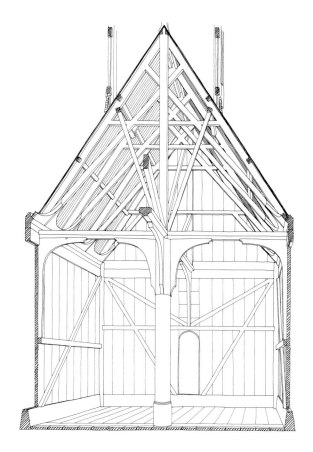

Fig. 3.56. Plans of church patterns comparing early columns integrated at walls, and later, separated from walls.

Fig. 3.57. Reconstruction drawing of Nes Church from Nes, Hallingdal, the largest central post church in Norway. The central nave was probably built at the end of the thirteenth century, but its contruction resembled earlier nave- and- chancel types, such as the eleventh-century Holtålen Church. The central post and lower turret were medieval, but the apse and transepts were added sometime after the thirteenth century. The church was demolished in 1864.

in Norway, Holtålen Church (ca. 1050) exemplifies this type (fig. 3.55; pls. 16, 17, 18). In this plan the nave provided room for the congregation to stand during the Latin mass, while the chancel was allotted to the altar and clergy.

The Norwegian kings employed the ancient palisade technique for their early churches. The distinct difference between this ancient method and traditional Norwegian construction was that the wall planks no longer rested in the ground but on a raised sill beam above the ground, although all the vertical wall members still structurally enclosed the building. The structural framing posts were either placed in the four corners, which were supported by the horizontal sills, or, as in the earliest churches, embedded directly into the earth. There were no interior, freestanding posts and the roof trusses were rigid and did not require any transverse tension members. Early examples of similar churches were known to have existed at the present sites of Urnes and Kaupanger churches. During excavations of the extant churches, postholes were discovered in the ground from earlier structures dating from the eleventh and twelfth centuries, respectively. The wall planks, set between the posts either vertically or horizontally, are believed to have rested on sills above the ground.

A further development of the nave-and-chancel-type building during the middle to late twelfth century was the central-mast church. The purpose of the central and single freestanding pole was to carry a spire, as the fragile buildings needed additional support for this element, whose weight was transmitted directly to the foundation rafters. The sill beams, like those in nave-and-chancel churches, carried only the weight of the walls and were supported by the foundation rafter beams as well. Only two examples of central-mast churches remain, at Nore and Uvdal, Nes having been torn down (figs. 3.56, 3.57).

Toward the end of the eleventh century, kings no longer built their own sanctuaries, and priests began to organize Norway's church-building program. A phase of building began in which master builders were dominated by the independent demands of clergy. In general, the priests wanted Norwegian churches to resemble more traditional religious structures. This implies that native wooden churches had already been accepted by the clergy and that they provided a satisfactory building form. The master builders had only to augment their traditional churches with additional elements and this meant that construction techniques were advanced enough to comply with such wishes. Sometime in the early twelfth century, perhaps as a result of the priests' influence or perhaps as a natural consequence of more developed techniques, framing members were separated from enclosing members, and each functioned independently of the other (fig. 3.58). Once this construction principle became common, in combination with sills placed above the ground, builders had the means to expand their church-building patterns. It was possible for a building's nave to be lengthened and its walls raised to allow for a clerestory. However, the actual building model the Norwegians used for their later structures is uncertain, and it is equally unclear what kind of building the priests promoted, or if they promoted a specific type at all.

Nevertheless, the resultant group of churches built at the turn of the twelfth century comprise the largest number of stave churches in Norway and are more complicated than the nave-and-chancel structures. They employed a system of four, eight, twelve, sixteen, or even twenty freestanding interior posts, which defined a lofty central space (fig. 3.62). The group represents the high point of stave-church building, and the advanced structures can be defined as a system of interlocking frames, all working to offset the forces of nature. In many cases, older churches

PERSPECTIVE OF NORTH WALL

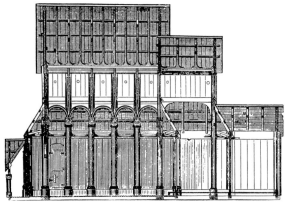

LONGITUDINAL SECTION

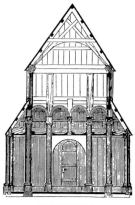

CROSS SECTION

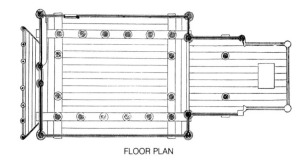

FLOOR PLAN

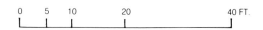

0   5   10   20   40 FT.

Fig. 3.59. Urnes Church, ca. 1130, Lusterfjord, Sogn; painting by J.C. Dahl, ca. 1840; plan and sections after Lorentz Dietrichson, 1892. The elongated nave with a central clerestory, defined by freestanding columns and aisles terminating at a square chancel, was the structural system typically used in the twelfth century. Urnes is the oldest existing church made with this system and has sixteen freestanding columns defining its clerestory.

Fig. 3.60. Borgund Church, ca. 1150, near Lærdal, Sogn. One of the most unaltered of existing churches, Borgund represents a transition from the elongated clerestory churches found in western Norway, such as Urnes, to the more centralized churches of eastern valleys, such as Gol and Lomen. The nave reveals fourteen freestanding columns, but only twelve of them extend to the floor.

were dismantled in order to erect the newer type, or if a church burned down, it was replaced with a structure using the refined framing method.

In general, these later churches with long naves and clerestories could be said to resemble traditional basilicas, and the form was typically found in the western regions of Norway. The existing church at Urnes from 1130 illustrates the type, with sixteen interior freestanding posts decorated very much in the manner of Romanesque stone architecture (fig. 3.59).

In the eastern and border regions, church plans emphasized the square nature of nave-and-chancel buildings. The buildings recall a centralized Byzantine expression, and perhaps their form was influenced by eastern parts of the world. The four corner posts of the nave were separated from their walls, and others were added, but rather than elongating the nave, the builders maintained a somewhat square space. Developing parallel to the long-naved churches, the type is best seen in the Borgund (ca. 1150) and Gol (ca. 1170) churches (figs. 3.60, 3.61, 3.62; pls. 21, 22). In Gol Church, the eight freestanding stave posts define a nave configuration different in character from that of Urnes Church. Later in the thirteenth century, ambulatories were added to both churches, giving them a more Gothic appearance.

The centralized expression of such churches is also related to the weak construction of their chancels, although similar weaknesses are also common in some long-naved buildings. Variations in the different structural members of the chancel from church to church indicate that an accepted solution to this construction

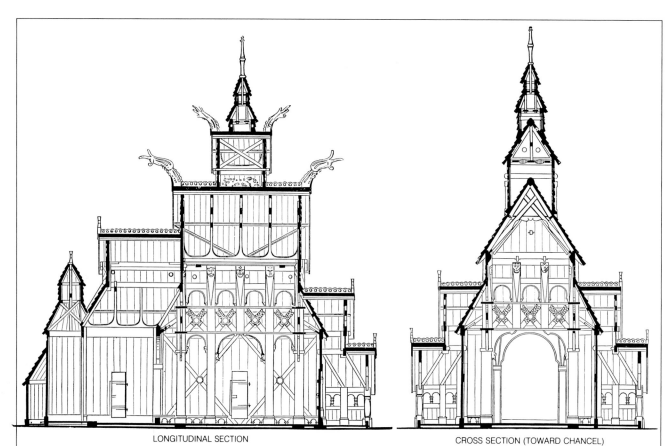

LONGITUDINAL SECTION

CROSS SECTION (TOWARD CHANCEL)

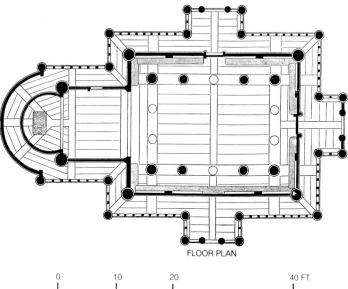

FLOOR PLAN

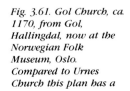

0   10   20   40 FT

Fig. 3.61. Gol Church, ca. 1170, from Gol, Hallingdal, now at the Norwegian Folk Museum, Oslo. Compared to Urnes Church this plan has a less rectangular character with four large corner posts. The nave contains fourteen columns, but only eight extend to the floor in the triforium.

WEST ELEVATION

Pl. 15. Urnes Church, ca.
1030–1130, Lusterfjord,
Sogn.

*Pl. 16. Holtålen Church,
ca. 1050, from
Gauldalen, Trøndelag,
now at the Trøndelag
Folk Museum,
Trondheim.*

*Pl. 17. Side elevation of
Holtålen Church.*

*Pl. 18. Corner columns
of Holtålen Church.*

*Pl. 19. Lomen Church,
ca. 1175, Vestre Slidre,
Valdres.*

*Pl. 20. Øye Church, ca.
1175–1200, Øye,
Valdres, recently rebuilt
near its original
location on Vangs Lake.*

22

23

Pl. 21. Gol Church, ca. 1170, from Gol, Hallingdal, now at the Norwegian Folk Museum, Oslo.

Pl. 22. Borgund Church, ca. 1150, near Lærdal, Sogn.

Pl. 23. Hedal Church, ca. 1175, Hedalen, Valdres.

Pl. 24. Gol Church.

Pl. 25. Eidsborg Church,
ca. 1200, Eidsborg,
Telemark.

problem was never achieved in Norway in the Middle Ages. Compared to the nave, where structural elements were relatively consistent in churches, the chancel, one can assume, was an independent building task, given its irregular configuration.

By the end of the twelfth century, a whole school of clerestory building techniques had evolved into common practice. Churches had grown taller and these structural inventions produced new building expressions. The development and separation of elements such as masts, staves, and beams illustrate how well the Norwegians adapted their framing methods to church buildings and also illustrates how adept the builders were in solving the particular problems posed by taller structures. Builders were still following the direction of clergy, but their advanced techniques gave their churches a unique expression unparalleled in the Christian world.

The precise categorization of church types into related periods is complex and uneven given the absence of archaeological evidence and the overlapping of influences from Norway's many different regions. In addition, churches were continually modified throughout the Middle Ages, dates are uncertain, and historians can only hypothesize about certain developments. The only certainty is that the twelfth-century stave church was an original architectural creation for which a native tradition was a prerequisite. In a country in which wooden churches were erected in spite of canonical law, it is understandable that the Norwegian church was as unlikely to follow the established ecclesiastical customs as it was to follow the international model in expressing its form.[22]

The freedom and skill with which the Norwegians blended European traditions with their own rich, zoomorphic Viking art gave the churches their unique ambience: it allowed the builders to match their creations precisely to the vision and forces of their own world. But if one considers that a builder had first and foremost to construct a church, it is evident that he had to adapt traditional building techniques to make such a building and that certain constructive elements were more important for a church's expression than any particular style. Furthermore, the active role that the clerical authorities played in laying down specific liturgical requirements for a place of worship affected the builders' choices.

A builder could modify certain features from whatever existed of the ancient *hov*, the supposed Viking ritual grounds, or other forms of secular building, but he could not duplicate a pagan temple. According to Peter Anker, "He invented or combined structural features as needed and the results were monumental structures and spatial effects hitherto unachieved in wood. The structure a builder raised had to look like a Christian church and in the broad outline, it had to follow some convention. In some instances, a builder would allude to characteristics of a stone basilica such as arcades or cushion capitals, as in Borgund and Urnes, while in others he could omit decorative features or transform the design and adapt a square, more centralized church plan, as in Kaupanger and Gol."[23]

The rising influence of clerical authority during the twelfth century and the growing contact between Europe and Norway began to affect the form of churches and hastened the development of Christian practices. Once they had become familiar with the structure of the church as a building type, and the events and images its walls housed, the Norwegians began to refine their churches. The central hall with its four marked corners became embellished with traditional Christian images; the pilgrimage route was transformed into side aisles; and ceiling heights began to rise, reaching up to a more familiar heaven.

Sometime during the early thirteenth century, altars acquired barrel-vaulted

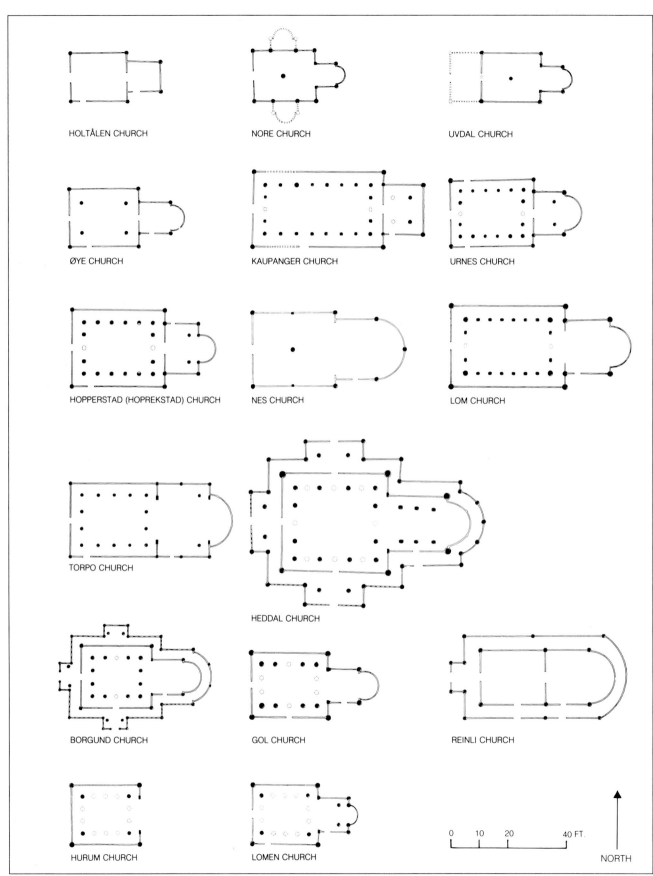

HOLTÅLEN CHURCH

NORE CHURCH

UVDAL CHURCH

ØYE CHURCH

KAUPANGER CHURCH

URNES CHURCH

HOPPERSTAD (HOPREKSTAD) CHURCH

NES CHURCH

LOM CHURCH

TORPO CHURCH

HEDDAL CHURCH

BORGUND CHURCH

GOL CHURCH

REINLI CHURCH

HURUM CHURCH

LOMEN CHURCH

0   10   20   40 FT.

NORTH

3.62

canopies and painted frontal panels, called *antemensaler*. Both marked the priest's traditional domain and distinguished the altar from the nave. These jubilantly colored structures contrasted with the surrounding unadorned wood. Spain is the only other country in which similar oil-painted wooden objects are found from such an early period. European miniatures are believed to have been the source of inspiration for the *antemensaler*, since Norwegians had no ancient traditions to follow in this regard. The early church paintings indicate that influences from abroad were welcomed, especially for sculptures, crucifixes, and saints' images (fig. 3.63).

The further evolution of church patterns at the turn of the twelfth century developed naturally. Lomen and Hurum churches, ca. 1175, represent a culmination of the eastern-valley tradition represented by Gol Church. In Lomen Church, only four of the many columns reach the ground to define the square nave (fig. 3.64; pl. 19). Kaupanger Church dates from approximately 1190, and it is the high point in the tradition of long-naved, basilicalike churches from the western regions that began with Urnes Church (figs. 3.65, 3.71). Although the original nave contained only sixteen freestanding posts, it was extended sometime in the thirteenth century to feature twenty such staves and conveys a truly Gothic expression. The climax of both long-naved and centralized types is found in Heddal Church, one of the few long-naved churches built in Telemark, from approximately 1248 (fig. 3.66). Its grandiose expression, with twelve interior staves, was actually a result of much modification and also represented a desire to outshine other churches in size and

Fig. 3.62. Comparative plans of stave churches.

Fig. 3.63. Interior of Torpo Church, ca. 1150–1175, Ål, Hallingdal, showing the barrel-vaulted canopy at the altar. The painting represents the legend of Saint Margaret; the remains of the original square chancel and apse can be glimpsed behind the canopy.

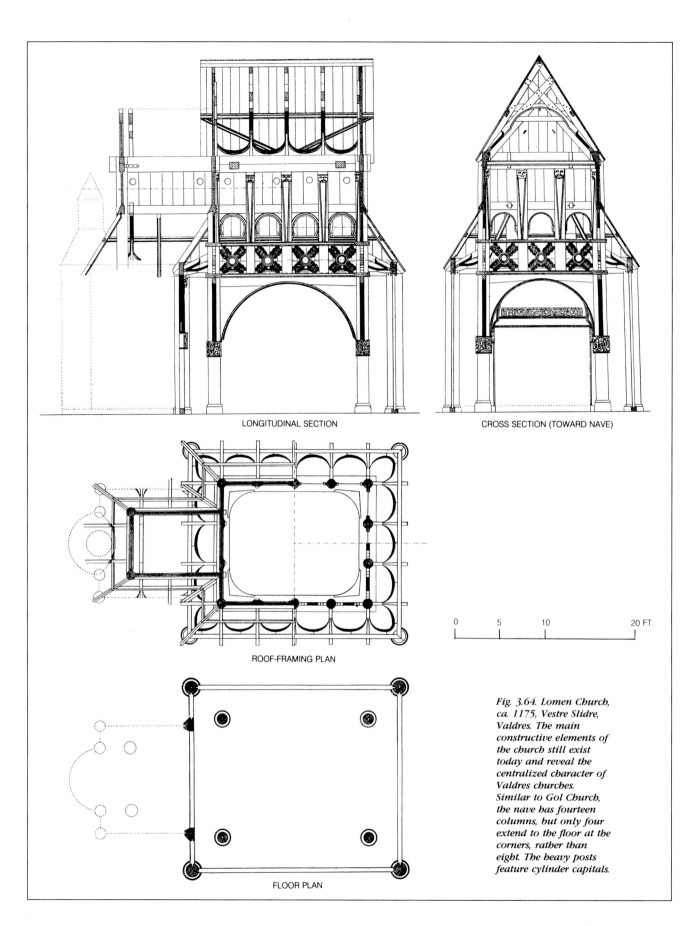

LONGITUDINAL SECTION

CROSS SECTION (TOWARD NAVE)

ROOF-FRAMING PLAN

0   5   10   20 FT.

FLOOR PLAN

Fig. 3.64. Lomen Church,
ca. 1175, Vestre Slidre,
Valdres. The main
constructive elements of
the church still exist
today and reveal the
centralized character of
Valdres churches.
Similar to Gol Church,
the nave has fourteen
columns, but only four
extend to the floor at the
corners, rather than
eight. The heavy posts
feature cylinder capitals.

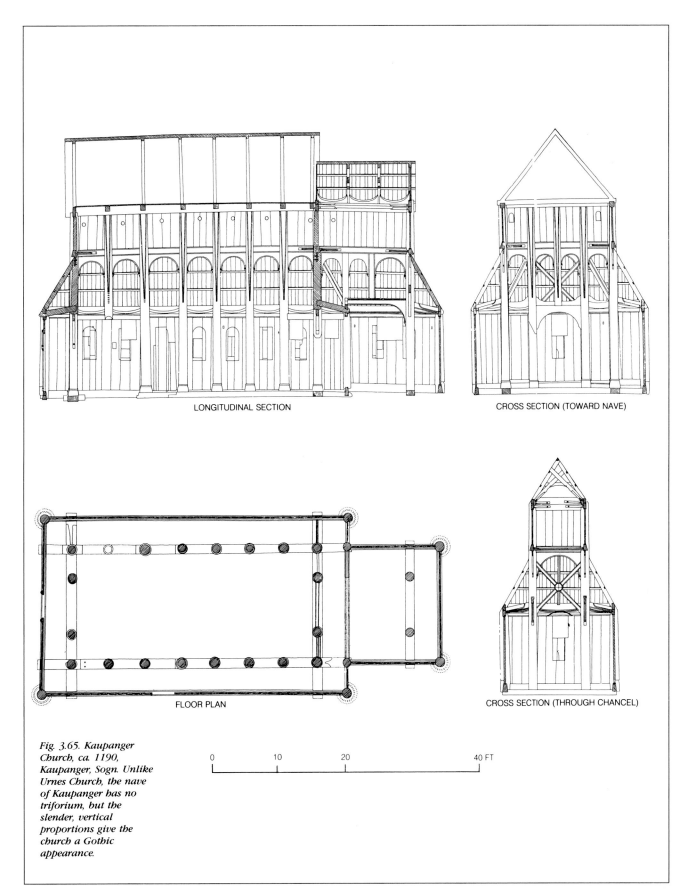

LONGITUDINAL SECTION

CROSS SECTION (TOWARD NAVE)

FLOOR PLAN

CROSS SECTION (THROUGH CHANCEL)

Fig. 3.65. Kaupanger Church, ca. 1190, Kaupanger, Sogn. Unlike Urnes Church, the nave of Kaupanger has no triforium, but the slender, vertical proportions give the church a Gothic appearance.

0   10   20   40 FT

WEST ELEVATION

SOUTH ELEVATION

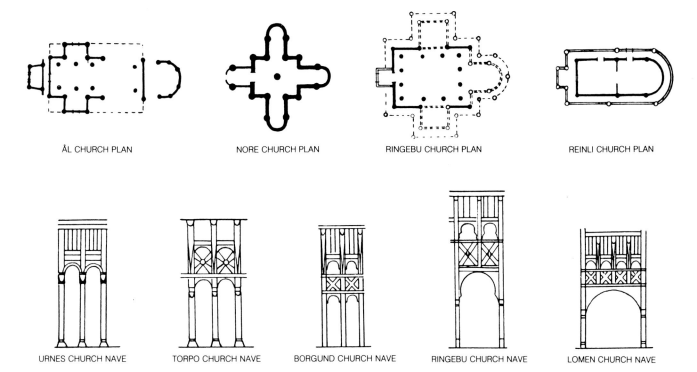

ÅL CHURCH PLAN   NORE CHURCH PLAN   RINGEBU CHURCH PLAN   REINLI CHURCH PLAN

URNES CHURCH NAVE   TORPO CHURCH NAVE   BORGUND CHURCH NAVE   RINGEBU CHURCH NAVE   LOMEN CHURCH NAVE

effect. According to Peter Anker, "The terminal point in the development of basilican stave churches is Heddal, the final result and the culmination of a hundred years' architectural tradition. Whether such buildings were erected in later periods is open to question."[24]

Later church developments should be regarded in light of the large number of clergy attached to the church at this time. Ecclesiastical movements were becoming stronger, encompassing a wider range of influences and resources, and the priests naturally brought their experiences to the churches they were responsible for erecting. The last period of stave-church building, lasting from approximately 1250 to 1350, combined a number of traditional techniques with new forms.

In Reinli Church, for example, built around 1250, a rounded apse dominated the nave, an unusual feature, as even the typical chancel was never an integral part of most stave churches (figs. 3.68, 3.69, 3.70). In addition, the rounded form of the apse was unnatural given the required wooden foundation beam. Another new element is found in Hedal Church, built in Hedalen, Valdres, about 1200, where a transept was added sometime in the late thirteenth century (pl. 23).Very few stave churches exhibit cruciforms, and it is difficult to ascertain the origins of those that do exist. Most likely it was a form realized in combination with timber, or log, construction after the Middle Ages.

As these newer patterns of construction become more familiar and more responsive to religious practices, the builders developed more refined features, and many existing churches were modified to incorporate them, as illustrated by Heddal Church. From the late thirteenth century onward, churches were embellished with more formal apses and protective ambulatories, they received lantern and saddleback turrets, and they were given accompanying bell towers. The buildings reached ever

Fig. 3.66. Heddal Church, ca. 1248, Heddal, Telemark; paintings of the church as it appeared mid-nineteenth century, after drawings by Schiertz, 1837. The nave dates from ca. 1150, while elements such as gables and turrets were added later to achieve the vertical, Gothic appearance that gives the church an almost oriental character. The church as it stands today reflects many generations of changes, from the seventeenth, nineteenth, and twentieth centuries.

Fig. 3.67. Church plans and comparative elevations showing thirteenth-century modifications.

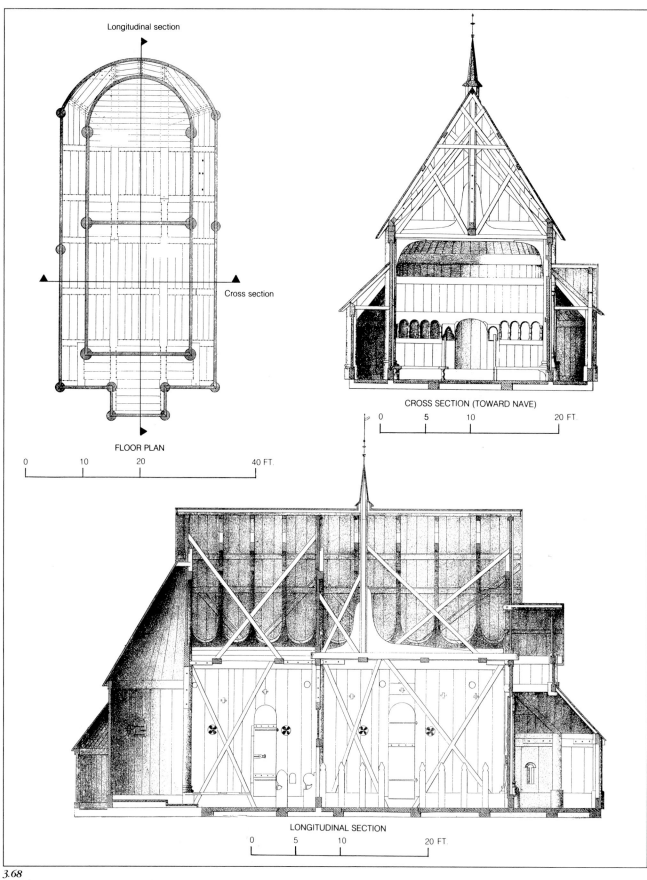

Longitudinal section

Cross section

FLOOR PLAN

0   10   20   40 FT.

CROSS SECTION (TOWARD NAVE)

0   5   10   20 FT.

LONGITUDINAL SECTION

0   5   10   20 FT.

3.68

higher toward the heavens, and their pagan animal motifs were transformed into organic Christian symbols. Finally, in the fourteenth century, such features typically adorned all of Norway's churches.

The existence of the Norwegian stave church gives rise to many questions in the development of wooden architecture. Perhaps the most significant one is what type of building, native or foreign, inspired the Norwegian church patterns from the twelfth century. Lorentz Dietrichson (1890) and Anders Bugge (1955) put forward the theory that these churches were a translation of stone basilicas into wood, even though the stave church's aisles completely surround its nave for structural reasons, whereas a basilica's aisles terminate at the chancel. Today this viewpoint is repudiated on technical grounds: the inherent skeletal properties of wood do not translate easily into load-bearing masonry. In the stave church, lateral stability is provided by the response of the entire cross section of the building, whereas in the Gothic cathedral, it is provided by the massive and monolithic buttresses. In fact, it has been suggested that the medieval wooden bay system was instrumental in the development of Gothic architecture, the latter's skeletal expression being achieved "in spite of stone." [25] The logistics of time also negate the basilican theory. The early wooden churches were contemporaneous with stone basilicas, so there would hardly have been enough time for the transposition of such convincing solutions in wood. Yet, to entirely exclude the influence of stone architecture on Norway's stave churches would be incorrect. The Christian basilica certainly provided a basic model for Norway's churches even though their architectural resolution was completely predicated on wood construction.

Today, a more constructivist trend of thought prevails, which originated with Nicolay Nicolaysen (1890). Håkon Christie, for example, takes an architectural

Fig. 3.71. Interior of Kaupanger Church, ca. 1190, Kaupanger, Sogn. At some point early in the church's history, it was literally cut in half to extend the nave longitudinally. Including those added during the extension, the number of interior posts in Kaupanger is not exceeded by any other church—except Lom, which has been heavily modified.

Fig. 3.72. Interior of Borgund Church, ca. 1150, near Lærdal, Sogn, showing a view of the chancel from the nave.

stance: his studies sequentially trace actual building processes backward over a period of time, illustrating how traditional wooden construction principles inspired stave-church building. The result is a theory that the church could have been a square, central room or building that was adapted or refitted to a religious purpose when the need arose. In many churches, for instance, the aisle around the nave exhibits fine and precise detailing, whereas the joining of chancel to nave reveals a poorer-quality technique, as does the construction of the chancel itself. This indicates that the chancel, in contrast to the nave, was an unfamiliar element in the Norwegian building language. Such a theory then seems quite likely and relates to the idea that an early *hov* might have been an extant room on a farmstead that was later modified for a church's nave.

In some cases, such as in Kaupanger Church, with its long hall of twenty masts, the nave does exhibit Gothic-like qualities (fig. 3.71). But, in fact, excavations at this church have also revealed that the nave was formally separated from the chancel with a wall featuring only a door leading to it. The nave was intended to be an entity unto itself, distinct from the chancel, and this is evident in other churches as well. Borgund Church probably reveals the most about the intentions of the stave-church builders regarding the nave room. While it is neither the oldest, largest, nor most original of the medieval churches, it is the most complete architecturally, having been little altered through the ages. It exhibits all the typical characteristics of the fully developed church and illustrates the usual integration of the square nave and chancel (fig. 3.72). That is, the opening merely continues through the aisle formed of staves without any special configuration or gesture. The exterior ambulatory, which surrounds the entire building, further emphasizes the centralized character of the church rather than that of a basilicalike hall.

Elements of Stave Church Construction

The handling of wood accounts for the unique character of the stave churches. The distinct expression of these churches springs from the consistent use of a material for all such buildings and from construction techniques that were, most likely, continued from earlier traditions rather than imported from abroad. While scant indications of wood-frame systems appear in scattered examples elsewhere in Europe, the stave system exemplified in the Norwegian churches remains unparalleled. More than fifty stave churches in Denmark and Sweden are documented, but none were as advanced as those in Norway.

A stave church is a system of frames. In principle, there is no difference in the structural systems of early nave-and-chancel churches such as Holtålen and later clerestory structures such as Borgund. The stave post is the most obvious component of both types of frames and is essential for joining the horizontal foundation system to the upper horizontal braces. The wall planks (or filling material) fit into this primary frame. In the strictest sense, the corner posts and interior columns—as opposed to the wall planks—are the actual stave elements, as they represent the vertical components of the structural frame.

The word *stav* in Norwegian refers to an upright vertical pole. In describing a church, the word refers specifically to one of the structure's four corner posts. According to ancient law, the posts were a formal qualification for the validity of consecration: as long as the corner posts were standing, the consecration of a church was valid, whereas the dedication was destroyed when the corner posts fell down. According to Peter Anker, a sermon dating from the dedication of a church in Bergen from about 1200 implied that the wooden stave church was considered the normal form of a house of worship in Norway at that time. The elements of the building, which today seem purely functional, were each given a Christian interpretation in the sermon: the four corner columns stood for the four gospels, as their teaching was the strongest support of Christianity; the choir referred to the holy men in Heaven; the nave signified the Christians on Earth; and the altar stood for Christ.[26]

In the early nave-and-chancel churches the foundation beams were laid in a square on top of flat stones, which prevented moisture penetration from the ground. These beams functioned as ground sills, members into which the wall planks were placed. At the corners the stave posts fit over these sill beams, helping to clamp them together. At the top of the wall another beam, the wall plate, consisting of two horizontal members, fit over the wall planks. The roof trusses rested on this beam. The walls of these church types were both structural, resisting gravity and lateral loads, and enclosing, forming the exterior skin.

As the builders moved from one assignment to another, they began to refine the static system of the early churches. The wall planks eventually served a strictly enclosing function while the framing members alone transmitted both vertical and horizontal forces. The clear distinction between load-bearing and enclosing elements was facilitated by the invention of a chassislike foundation frame used in all the later churches with their interior, freestanding posts. The distinguishing feature of the mature stave church was this fully developed foundation system built completely above ground, which forced the central frame to withstand the forces of gravity, along with wind, rain, and snow—all severe elements in Norway.

In these churches, the foundation beams were arranged in two parallel pairs that intersected to form a square, with the beam ends extending beyond the corner intersections. These beams were notched at their outer ends to accommodate the sill plates, which carried only the outer wall planks of the aisles. As in the earlier churches, the aisle sill and wall plates were still joined to the frame system through the exterior posts. The interior intersections of the foundation beams were the original, exterior four corner-post locations of the older system. In the later structural system, the beams functioned as cantilevers, carrying the entire building and significantly helping it to transmit lateral forces.

Along these beams were placed interior, freestanding posts, which carried the central weight of the building and offset lateral forces. At the top of the staves sat the wall plate, consisting of two members. But in this system, the wall plate was the uppermost component of a clerestory because of the addition of aisles. The clerestory was supported and braced by a horizontal member called a *bressummer*, which was also the element on which the aisle roof rested. The *bressummer* was supported by the staves and spanned the distance between them. The wall plate in the nave still clamped the frame system together while it provided a base for the trussed roof of the church. A cube, then, consisting of the foundation beams, the staves, and the wall plate, defined the central nave's frame.

A similar framing system was also used for the chancels. Their foundations were joined directly to the central one. Although a connection of this type could possibly have transmitted complex forces to the main foundation, it did not adversely affect the central section's structural integrity. Furthermore, the construction and joinery in these chancels reveal less care than was applied in the central part of the churches. The spacing of the roof trusses, for example, was uneven compared to similar elements in the nave, and many churches later required additional bracing in the chancels to transmit lateral forces.

Given the exposed locations of these churches and their ambitious height, it is obvious that the bracing of the tall, rectangular central compartment in several directions was the builders' primary concern. The stave system implies a number of advanced technical solutions—bracing, joining, and shoring—that are necessary for the practical application of its basic principles as well as for its final architectural expression.[27]

What distinguishes Norway's stave construction from similar post-and-beam systems, according to Peter Anker, is a framework principle. This principle, found and operative only in stave churches, is dependent on the columns' connection to the foundation beams and to the wall plate and *bressummer*, creating a tall cube. The function of the columns is not only to carry the upper parts of the building, but also to strengthen it so that it can withstand lateral pressures. Because of the rectangular foundation chassis, the east and west columns are as essential as the lateral ones. Similarly, the aisles laterally strengthen and surround the central nave cube and are a structural consequence of the overhanging foundation frame: the aisle walls rest on the ends of the foundation beams. The twelfth-century stave church can be described as two cubes: a tall central nave placed inside a lower, surrounding square formed by the aisles. The cubes are joined together by the columns at the foundation beams and *bressummer*. In this manner, the columns are elements of a three-dimensional framework in which all the members depend on one another. The columns and corner posts are structurally essential, whereas the wall panels serve only to shelter the building like the roof.[28] This construction technique is most obvious in the churches from the second half of the twelfth century when the principle was in common practice, but it is also apparent in the early nave-and-chancel structures. The three-dimensional system of posts linked to frames was distinct from the system of uprights and palisade walls without ground sills that was common in all Scandinavian countries and was an earlier form of stave-church construction.

Many devices within this advanced three-dimensional frame worked together to offset forces and prevent the frame from collapsing. The sheer number of parts, such as brackets, aisle rafters, clamping beams, and Saint Andrew's crosses, testify to the refined level of craftsmanship the church builders had achieved by the twelfth century. A clear example of how these many architectural devices functioned can be found in the cross section of Borgund Church seen in figure 3.76. The various stabilizing components can be easily identified by examining the interior staves from bottom to top.

The first horizontal element above the column's base was an arched quadrant bracket, which spanned the staves. Collectively called *arcading*, this series of brackets offset forces in the plane of the staves. Above these, a horizontal string, or clamping, beam held together the interior posts.

The clamping beams consisted of two flat planks laid edge to edge and pressed together. At this butt joint a semicircular area was cut out of each plank, into which the posts were fitted so that the beams clamped the whole row of posts. Once clamping gained acceptance structurally, builders discovered that the weight of the roof could be supported on fewer interior posts. As they gained experience, the builders stood the posts just from the clamping beams to the roof, omitting them from below the beam to the floor (fig. 3.75). The curved quadrant brackets under the clamping beams allowed the loads from the shortened columns to be transferred to the full-length corner posts.

This development led to a variation of the squarish churches such as those at

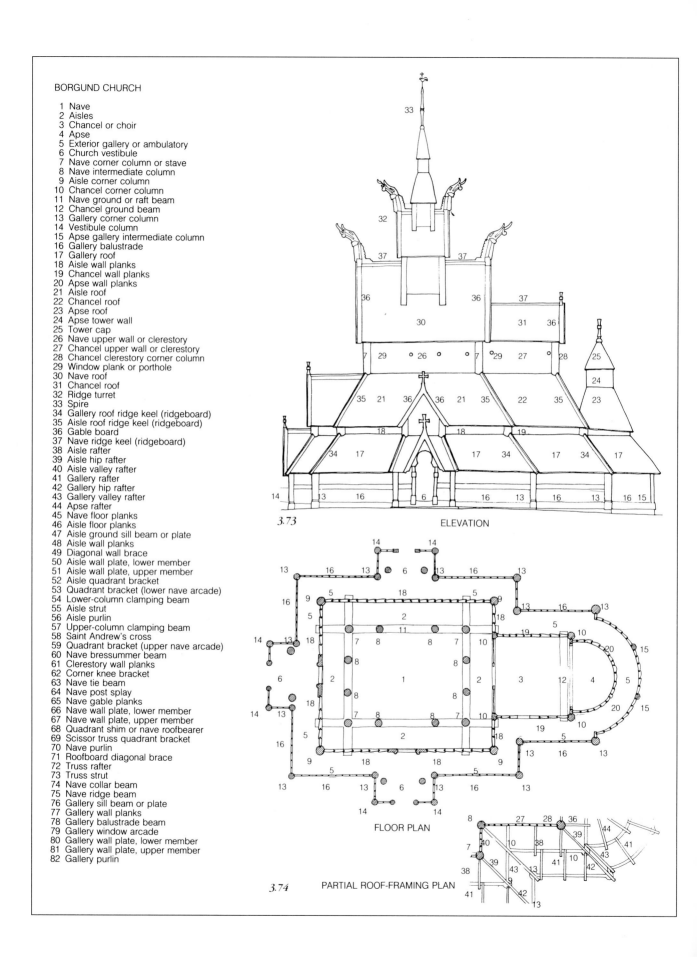

BORGUND CHURCH

1 Nave
2 Aisles
3 Chancel or choir
4 Apse
5 Exterior gallery or ambulatory
6 Church vestibule
7 Nave corner column or stave
8 Nave intermediate column
9 Aisle corner column
10 Chancel corner column
11 Nave ground or raft beam
12 Chancel ground beam
13 Gallery corner column
14 Vestibule column
15 Apse gallery intermediate column
16 Gallery balustrade
17 Gallery roof
18 Aisle wall planks
19 Chancel wall planks
20 Apse wall planks
21 Aisle roof
22 Chancel roof
23 Apse roof
24 Apse tower wall
25 Tower cap
26 Nave upper wall or clerestory
27 Chancel upper wall or clerestory
28 Chancel clerestory corner column
29 Window plank or porthole
30 Nave roof
31 Chancel roof
32 Ridge turret
33 Spire
34 Gallery roof ridge keel (ridgeboard)
35 Aisle roof ridge keel (ridgeboard)
36 Gable board
37 Nave ridge keel (ridgeboard)
38 Aisle rafter
39 Aisle hip rafter
40 Aisle valley rafter
41 Gallery rafter
42 Gallery hip rafter
43 Gallery valley rafter
44 Apse rafter
45 Nave floor planks
46 Aisle floor planks
47 Aisle ground sill beam or plate
48 Aisle wall planks
49 Diagonal wall brace
50 Aisle wall plate, lower member
51 Aisle wall plate, upper member
52 Aisle quadrant bracket
53 Quadrant bracket (lower nave arcade)
54 Lower-column clamping beam
55 Aisle strut
56 Aisle purlin
57 Upper-column clamping beam
58 Saint Andrew's cross
59 Quadrant bracket (upper nave arcade)
60 Nave bressummer beam
61 Clerestory wall planks
62 Corner knee bracket
63 Nave tie beam
64 Nave post splay
65 Nave gable planks
66 Nave wall plate, lower member
67 Nave wall plate, upper member
68 Quadrant shim or nave roofbearer
69 Scissor truss quadrant bracket
70 Nave purlin
71 Roofboard diagonal brace
72 Truss rafter
73 Truss strut
74 Nave collar beam
75 Nave ridge beam
76 Gallery sill beam or plate
77 Gallery wall planks
78 Gallery balustrade beam
79 Gallery window arcade
80 Gallery wall plate, lower member
81 Gallery wall plate, upper member
82 Gallery purlin

3.73   ELEVATION

FLOOR PLAN

3.74   PARTIAL ROOF-FRAMING PLAN

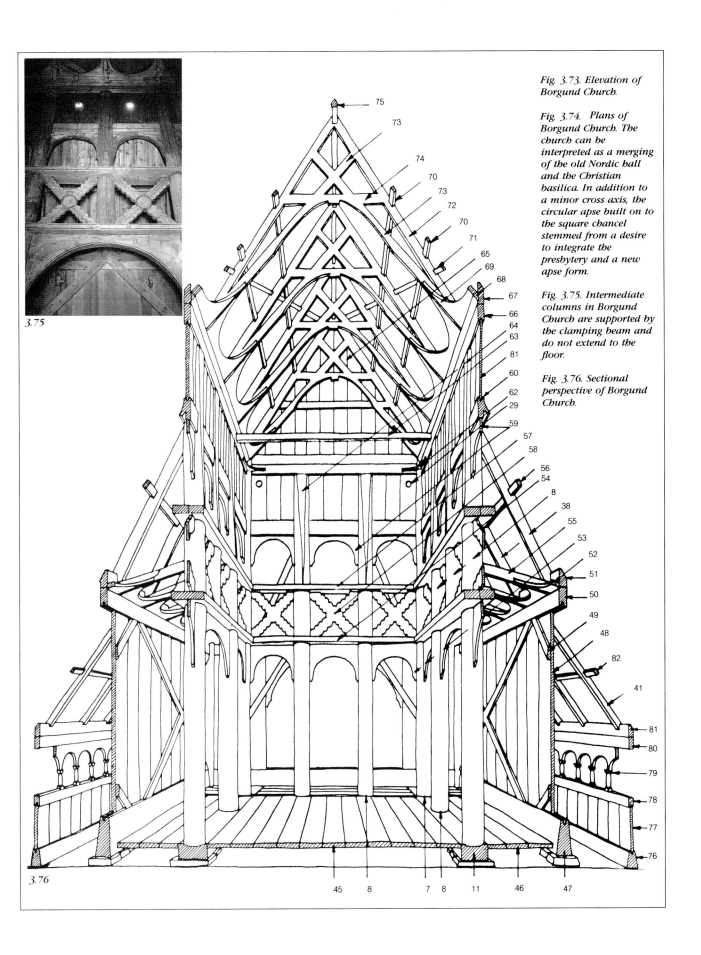

3.75

75
73
74
70
73
72
70
71
65
69
68
67
66
64
63
81
60
62
29
59
57
58
56
54
8
38
55
53
52
51
50
49
48
82
41
81
80
79
78
77
76

45   8   7   8   11   46   47

3.76

Fig. 3.73. Elevation of
Borgund Church.

Fig. 3.74. Plans of
Borgund Church. The
church can be
interpreted as a merging
of the old Nordic hall
and the Christian
basilica. In addition to
a minor cross axis, the
circular apse built on to
the square chancel
stemmed from a desire
to integrate the
presbytery and a new
apse form.

Fig. 3.75. Intermediate
columns in Borgund
Church are supported by
the clamping beam and
do not extend to the
floor.

Fig. 3.76. Sectional
perspective of Borgund
Church.

Borgund and Gol. In Hurum and Lomen churches, only four corner columns in the interior reach the ground at the sills' crossing points (fig. 3.77). This type of plan recalls the older tradition of simple nave-and-chancel structures: it has an almost completely square ground plan and a central disposition.

Above the arcading in many stave churches was a bracing assembly made up of two intersecting diagonal members between each pair of staves. Such assemblies, called Saint Andrew's crosses, first appeared about A.D. 1200 and are probably an influence from medieval churches in France. (The Saint Andrew's crosses, combined with the arcading, were similar to the well-known clerestory triforiums of French naves.) Many of the earlier churches were fitted with such crosses long after the churches themselves had been built. The crosses were probably intended to give greater lateral strength to the assembled staves, but in practice, they did not offer much additional resistance, and in fact, some of the later installations of this component reveal poor joinery that negates the cross's structural capability.

On churches with very tall staves, such as Borgund, a second tier of clamping beams and quadrant brackets was added in the nave to offset the stronger forces created by additional height. Above the brackets and Saint Andrew's crosses in the churches was the important *bressummer*. It was usually placed 1¼ to 2 meters (4 to 6½ feet) below the top of the staves supporting the clerestory walls. It provided further lateral bracing for the nave's central cube compartment and was, simultaneously, the fastening point for the aisle rafters.

Each corner of the nave was fitted with a horizontal knee bracket, sometimes at the level of the *bressummer*, as at Kaupanger, sometimes not, as at Borgund, where it was constructed at the wall plate. This bracket gave the central cube strength to resist the flattening deformations to which a square frame is susceptible when lateral forces are applied. Thus, the frame of the central space of a church was braced longitudinally and laterally.

When the central compartment was finished, the roof was built (fig. 3.78). The roof of a stave church was sharply peaked, generally with a rise of 3:2, vertical to horizontal, or an angle of 56 degrees, to reduce the impact of snow loads. The rafters were braced by a pair of beams, which crossed under the peak of the rafters. This *scissor brace* often had a rise of 1:1, or an angle of 45 degrees. A horizontal collar beam, located in the roof bracing near its mid-height, was generally connected to the rafters and to the scissor braces. Light secondary members, or *purlins*, which ran parallel to the roof ridge, transferred roof loads to the rafters and the roof bracing. In the thirteenth-century stave churches, diagonal bracing was incorporated into the plane of the roof to keep the structural components from collapsing.[29]

Once the rafters and the roof bracing were constructed, light wood planks were added, running down from the ridge to the eaves. Exterior planks were then laid parallel to the roof ridge. The two layers of planking were usually fastened together with wood pins. The oldest roof known, from Urnes Church, had such planking for its covering, and the thin members, exposed to weather, had deteriorated and were in poor condition when the roof was replaced during one of its many restorations. In some of the churches, such as at Borgund, the planking was covered by an additional layer of wood shakes or rough shingles. More resistant to decay than simple planked roofs, shingled roofs also lent a distinct expression to churches. The shakes were cut into unusual shapes, giving the roofs the appearance of fish scales, or in terms of medieval sensibility, dragon skin, and often they were extended over parts of the walls (fig. 3.79).

When the roof was completed, the aisles were added. The roof of the aisles

Fig. 3.77. Interior of Lomen Church, ca. 1175, Vestre Slidre, Valdres. Only four corner columns in the nave support the structure, the other ten are carried by large quadrant brackets in the triforium. There is no indication on the exterior of the church of the nave's aisles because of the later addition of wainscoting, although the structure is clearly intact inside. The spacious feeling of the clerestory is evident despite radical alteration of the chancel and apse after the Reformation.

Fig. 3.78. The nave's roof structure of Gol Church, ca. 1170, from Gol, Hallingdal, now at the Norwegian Folk Museum, Oslo.

Fig. 3.79. Lom Church, ca. 1150–1170, Lom, Gudbrandsdal. The distinctive effect of wooden shingles can be seen on the massive roof of this church. The original clerestoried church, with its squared chancel and apse, was radically altered in the seventeenth and eighteenth centuries. Today, it has a cruciform plan, complete with steeple, although without its original ambulatory. In 1634, the nave was extended in log contruction and somewhat later, transepts were added using stave contruction. Even before renovations, the large church exhibited little stability, and Saint Andrew's crosses and diagonal wall braces were added to the large nave with its twenty freestanding columns.

was lower than that of the raised central compartment and was supported by sloping rafters. The upper end of the sloping rafters was attached to the interior staves with wooden pegs at the *bressummer*. The lower end rested in a notch cut into a horizontal beam, the aisle wall plate, located at the top of the aisle wall. The plate functioned much the same way as the wall plate in the nave. The main weight of the aisle roof was carried by the plate and transferred to the corner posts. Under the aisle rafters was a cross-beam called an *aisle strut*. Between the aisle struts were quadrant brackets, which also resisted horizontal forces parallel to the axes of the nave.

The aisle assemblies surrounding the nave contributed greatly to the lateral strength of these churches. As most of the buildings were placed on exposed sites, wind forces were severe especially on the broad side of the churches. These lateral forces would be first transmitted from the aisle struts to the interior staves. Then they were transmitted across the nave through the roof truss to the leeward staves, aisle struts, and corner posts. Through these framing members, the forces were transmitted to the foundation beams. The stabilizing factor for these cubelike structures was the capacity of the entire cross section of the church to transfer loads efficiently from one side of the building to the ground on the other side.

The final step in constructing a stave church was to fit the vertical wall planks between the sill beams, wall plates, and corner posts. In thirteenth-century churches, an exterior gallery—an ambulatory—or a covered walkway was built or added to existing churches (fig. 3.80). These were informally attached with mortise connections to the wall planks of the main structure, and many did not survive.

Such a covered walkway, called a *svalgang* in Norwegian, usually surrounded the entire building. The purpose of this gallery might have been to provide space for diseased people who could not enter the church proper for services. Or it could have been a convenient place from which to ward off enemies (certainly the church locations themselves were); the shape of Hedal Church's gallery portal is purported to have been advantageous for warriors' weapons. But the gallery also served a mundane purpose. It provided a space for daily transactions of all kinds since the church was a central meeting place for the scattered community. Many documents that have been preserved conclude, "... written in the *svalgang* of the ... church in the year.... "[30] Whatever function the gallery served, it did protect the lower portions of later churches from the ravages of weather.

The ambulatory roof provided the third and lowest tier in the fully developed stave church, as exemplified by Gol Church in its reconstructed form at the Oslo Folk Museum. In the thirteenth century, many churches also were embellished with turrets, lanterns, and bell towers. With their cascading profiles of steep angular gables and roofs topped with carved dragon heads, the later churches convey an

Fig. 3.80. Wall planks and portal from the ambulatory at Hedal Church, ca. 1200, Hedal, Valdres; the ledge at the left would have supported a medieval weapon, probably an arrow.

almost Oriental image; yet, the influences that led to their skeletal expression were derived completely from an early native Nordic wood tradition. When one remembers that the lofty churches of Norway were generally built on visually prominent sites exposed to the full effect of sun, wind, rain, and snow, one realizes how well their particular constructive system suited their climate.

Masterly wood techniques in Norway are directly related to climatic forces. This is evident in the way that individual elements of a church worked together during a storm; the pieces locked into position and the church swayed with each buffet of the wind, almost like the top of a tree. This recalls the membrane planks of tenth-century Viking ships, which were designed to give and take the swelling pressures of the open sea. On the ships, overlapping strakes bound with spruce roots were fastened to a skeletal frame, and under sail the pliable system adapted to forces of the dark Norwegian waters. Both the ships and the churches were built at times when man used wind and wave for counsel, when nature was his inspiration.

Development of Stave Church Techniques

Although the stave church obviously was derived from some particular building pattern, its refined construction methods arose from other factors. Archaeological finds have provided evidence that certain aspects of Norwegian stave construction were not unique to Norway, but that stave construction, defined as a framework system, was a technique not found in other countries. Stave churches belong to the post-and-beam bay structures that were prevalent throughout northwestern Europe in the Middle Ages, yet they reveal technical solutions so carefully worked out that one is forced to suppose a lengthy process of evolution preceded them. However, archaeological evidence seems so primitive that the development of the churches appears to have actually taken place very rapidly.[31] This is especially so in regard to the skillful framework of ground sills, which are not found in earlier excavations. In order to understand the synthesis of stave-church construction, excluding the cantilevered foundation system, one must place the Norwegian developments in the context of framing techniques from other parts of northern Europe.

One of the oldest wooden churches in northern Europe is Saint Andrew's at Greensted, Essex, near London, which dates from about 845. In this structure huge oak logs were spliced in half and embedded, vertically, directly into the ground. The method spread eastward, possibly splitting off into two techniques: the palisade method, similar to the Saint Andrew's system in which the members in the ground form the structural wall; and the half-timbered technique, which consists of a wood-frame structural system infilled with various materials to form the wall. In Norway, both methods were employed in the early Holtålen Church from 1050.

One of the first churches to be erected in Scandinavia employing the palisade method was Saint Maria Minor in Lund, Sweden, dating from about 1050. Interior columns stand a few feet inside its palisade walls and support the roof. This was a common technique of pre-medieval static systems, as evidenced by the many long halls found with interior wood poles surrounded by earthen walls. The primary function of the columns used at Saint Maria's was to support the roof, and Norwegian builders incorporated this principle in their twelfth-century clerestory churches.

In Gotland, Sweden, Hemse Church, from the early eleventh century, displays vertical wall planks embedded on a sill beam above the ground. No corner posts, indicating a framework solution, are found in this highly developed palisade example, although carved door portals are a main feature of this church. With the introduction of the ground sill, planks no longer rotted in the earth, and the frame system that served the stave churches was almost in its final form.

Following the development of half-timbered frame construction in northern Europe, buildings from Stellerburg, Ditmarsken, in northern Germany, from the ninth and tenth centuries were a particularly important development for frame-type systems. In this housing complex building walls consisted of grooved ground sills and wall plates, vertical panels, and four-sided uprights at the corners. These were mortised to house the wall planks and fit snugly over the ground sills. There is not much difference between these buildings and a minor nave-and-chancel frame like the one at Holtålen. According to Peter Anker, in theory, the entire method of construction of the ninth- and tenth-century Stellerburg buildings might have been imported to Norway from northern Germany in the eleventh century, when the Nordic Church was attached to the archdiocese of Bremen-Hamburg.[32]

In contrast, Hermann Phleps, a noted historian of wooden architecture, has suggested that the development of Norwegian stave techniques was influenced by timber or log construction, rather than by the grooved-sills-and-planks technique. Phleps notes that the sill beams, which support the wall planks in stave-church construction, are connected together at their corners in a fashion that resembles log-construction interlocking.

The distinctive central clerestory structure of the majority of stave churches certainly owes its shape to the longhouse, with its rows of interior uprights (from the Iron Age dwellings of the fifth century onward), to the Viking fortresses scattered throughout Scandinavia (from about A.D. 900), and to the church of Saint Maria Minor in Sweden. One can conclude that the separation of columns from walls found in the churches was first and foremost a device to carry the roof (fig. 3.81); it later developed into an important part of the construction system that resisted lateral forces. Christian Norberg-Schulz calls further attention to the relationship between supporting and sheltering elements in these churches. In his studies, he emphasizes the *canopy principle*, which employs continuous uprights passing into the roof to carry its weight. Originally derived from Byzantine architecture and fully developed in Gothic construction, this canopy, or *baldachin* principle, was used to mark special places or events and was a feature of the mature stave churches of the twelfth century.[33] Whether such a purpose for the clerestory was consciously intended in the mature churches is difficult to ascertain. But by the thirteenth century, altar canopies indicate that builders were actively using a similar principle.

Yet, more important, the distinctive central clerestory of the twelfth-century churches is completely dependent on their cantilevered foundation system, and no evidence of the origins of this framework has been discovered anywhere other than in Norway. When and where this significant method of construction was worked out is not known, but the structure of the clerestory, with its returned aisles, is conditioned by such a foundation chassis. The cantilevered construction was a decisive step forward in the history of wooden architecture as it made possible the raising of monumental wood buildings that were durable and solid compared to the smaller wooden structures previously erected, whose walls and supports were placed directly into the ground. What is not surprising is that this invention developed in relation to a religious building: a church's primary expression is always toward the sky.

Beginning with the foundation and the central structure, one arrives at a more qualitative understanding of what the Norwegian stave church resolved. The stave church's advanced structural system reflects the influence of Norway's unique landscape on church construction. As a result of the foundation, the builders could extend the central parts of the churches closer to heaven in their mountainous country. At the same time, the foundation gave the building freedom from Norway's variegated ground, and a church's image could finally be consistent from region to region; it could be set in any part of Norway and convey the same message.

If the stave church is examined in this fashion, the development of its foundation can be seen as an ingenious device that freed churches from specific local sites. At the same time, its very resolution tied it to the multitude of complex land forms found in Norway. It revealed the fact that this landscape had a peculiar structure: it was full of mountains and fjords, with few level expanses of land. More important, perhaps, is that the foundation system allowed the central structure to rise up and consistently dominate the breathtaking terrain in spite of its inherent harsh climatic conditions. The struggle for dominance, the development of refined techniques to allow this lofty, yet frail, wooden structure its height, again reveal something special about the nature of Norway and the nature of a church.

The builder's understanding of their world enabled them to translate its harsh forces into beautiful wooden buildings that expressed religion in a very particular place. A church, by definition, is abstract—a universal structure in which a post not only supported the roof, it also connected the three cosmic levels of heaven, earth, and underworld. Simultaneously, the stave churches were symbols of a specific culture, expressing communal truths abstracted from a shared reality. What kind of perception enabled the master builders to so convincingly combine such strong universal and local influences? An example of the kind of perception manifest in Norway's medieval culture can be found in the following quote from Grette's Icelandic saga, written down sometime in the Middle Ages:

> In the same moment, Torbjørn jumped forward in front of the door with both hands around the spear and drove it into the middle of Atle so that it pierced him through. "There are many of them now, the broad spears," Atle said, in that he got the thrust. Then he fell forward over the threshold.[34]

Atle's last comment—"There are many of them now, the broad spears."—referred to the tool that killed him, nothing else. The reason for his death was never questioned, only its means were abstracted into a truth. If the same type of objective perception molded a stave church, if similar importance was always given to tools, it is no wonder its construction reached such refined heights. The building itself was not questioned, nor what it represented; only *how* it represented was questioned. How could it better serve the purposes of God, how could it resist such wind, such water, how could it be taller, how could it best *be*? With freedom and skill, the Norwegian builders emphasized their churches' peculiar reality and achieved a unique expression in the Christian world.

The act of creating the same type of churches over and over naturally led to exquisite refinements, though the basic structure and methods of joining foundation, sill, stave, and roof remained consistent. But the building pattern only hints at the spirit of a church—it is the way in which the nave and aisles were molded together, the understanding of what would best illuminate the pattern or make it function better, that allowed the master builders to enhance their wooden churches. The beauty of a stave church is ultimately derived from its details. In that realm of building, the perception of the master builders is most apparent; it was inherited from their dark world.

Fig. 3.81. Interior of Gol Church, ca. 1170, from Gol, Hallingdal, now at the Norwegian Folk Museum, Oslo. The reconstructed upper nave parts illustrate the fully developed stave church, with the staves or columns supporting the roof.

4. DETAILS

Every people that has produced architecture
has evolved its own favorite forms, as peculiar
to that people as its language, its dress, or its
folklore. Until the collapse of cultural frontiers
in the last century, there were all over the
world distinctive local shapes and details in
architecture, and the buildings of any locality
were the beautiful children of a happy
marriage between the imagination of the
people and the demands of the countryside.
—Hassan Fathy

Fig. 4.1. Refined log and
stave shapes from the
Finnes loft, ca. 1250,
Voss, Sogn.

D etails are small acts upon which the totality of any building rests. Beyond traditional building types, the refinement of building patterns through these acts reveals an operational idea of beauty. Just as building patterns in Norway enabled a resident of one locale to recognize elements of his own region in another, building details articulated form and generated a character that reflected the culture's disposition.

Fig. 4.2. Stave work from a two-story Telemark stue, ca. 1775–1825, now at the Skien Folk Museum.

Constructive patterns reveal the spirit of a place, they give an underlying structure to the world. Yet, alone, they do not distinguish between the character of a Finnish or a Norwegian *loft* or between a well-built and a beautiful church. It is in a building's details that this distinction is most apparent. In traditional societies, everyone knew the building types and even how to build them; the expertise of craftsmen was only a matter of degree.[1] But the manner in which the typical building skeleton was fleshed out, its details, is the most important aspect of its architectural manifestation: it gives a building its character. This character separates Norwegian buildings from those of other wood cultures.

For example, a Swedish three-room dwelling house is spatially similar to a Norwegian one. But upon close examination, the two are completely different. The distinction can be found primarily in the way the buildings were put together. This is the manifestation of different building skills, and these skills, in turn, were the product of cultural traditions (fig. 4.3).

As in other traditional building cultures, each piece of wood a Norwegian builder shaped revealed an understanding of his world: the growing cycles of a tree; the importance of the grain of wood; the natural way wood joins; the effects of moisture; the physical forces required to erect the structure; the tradition of builders before him; and the natural forces a building must withstand. All of these, along with an idea of the events that would occur within the final building, are manifested in his details. Yet, in Norway, building details seem to reflect an unusual amount of care.

Norway's traditional architecture is characterized by skilled craftsmanship. Historically, the development of the country's arts was tied directly to its building arts through the craft of woodworking. Artists were typically woodworkers and in general, the Norwegians' building craft was their art. In fact, until about 1800, painting and sculpting in Norway were never as popular or expressive as art forms as was wood carving.

During the Viking period specialized woodworkers were common. The two high points of Norway's early art forms are illustrated by the wooden artifacts found on the Oseberg Viking Ship and the carved wooden portal from the first Urnes Church, one of the earliest stave churches (figs. 4.6, 4.7). Wood carving during this period in Norway was a skill unequaled in other Viking cultures—in fact, at this time, other cultures abandoned wood carving in favor of metal or ceramic art forms. Throughout the ages, until the nineteenth century, wood was generally the medium Norwegians used to express their artistic abilities. Few countries have such old and

4.3

4.4

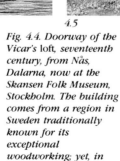

4.5

Fig. 4.3. Eighteenth-century Swedish stue at the Skansen Folk Museum, Stockholm; while the detail work in Swedish and Norwegian dwelling houses vary, the actual building patterns of stuer are similar in the two countries.

Fig. 4.4. Doorway of the Vicar's loft, seventeenth century, from Nås, Dalarna, now at the Skansen Folk Museum, Stockholm. The building comes from a region in Sweden traditionally known for its exceptional woodworking; yet, in contrast to Norwegian loft doors, even the finest Swedish ones are rarely articulated.

Fig. 4.5. Nineteenth-century Finnish loft from South Karelia at the Helsinki Folk Museum. The details of wooden buildings in Finland are precise and carefully executed; they consequently have a somewhat restrained appearance and lack the strong ornamental quality typically found in Norway's buildings.

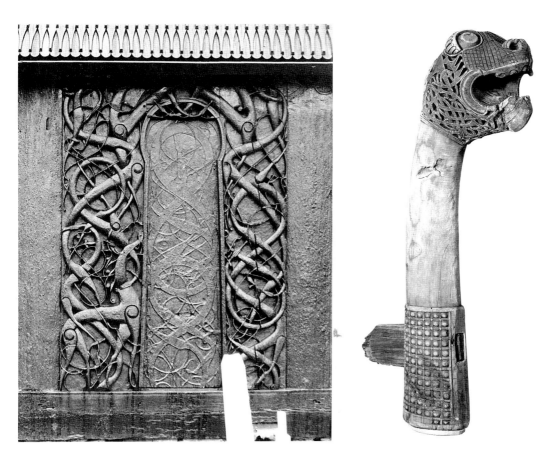

rich traditions in wood carving as Norway, and it is not surprising that timber building endured longer here than in other countries.

The tradition of skilled woodworking is also closely related to the country's pattern of individual farm settlements. Every family was self-sufficient, making or producing all it needed: buildings, tools, clothes, and food. Handwork, especially woodwork, was a daily part of farm life. In this vast rural landscape, until the Industrial Revolution, specialized craftwork was the task of every man and this is most clearly seen in the refined details of each log and stave building. Naturally, stylistic developments resulted from the common practice of such an old, traditional craft.

Traditional settlements are typically characterized by certain motifs that vary according to circumstances.[2] In a culture such as Norway's, various motifs and techniques helped define the aesthetic quality of the building language. This quality was not specially generated for each house; it was handed down through time. As Amos Rapoport explains, "Tradition was the law, the regulator. As long as a shared and accepted image operated, the aesthetic was alive."[3] For instance, the intricately carved door portals on farms and churches were always a special feature of Norway's buildings, in contrast to those in other Scandinavian countries, where they were not so profusely articulated (figs. 4.4, 4.5).

This kind of inherited tradition can also be seen in the prolonged use of the many animal symbols that typified Viking art and that appeared on both farms and churches. On the door portals of farms and churches, the continuous development of the art of wood carving can be traced from the Viking period all the way up to the eighteenth century. On the same portals, stylistic influences from the continent, including Romanesque, Renaissance, and baroque styles, can also be traced. These influences were combined with native motifs in endless variety to reveal the inherent

Fig. 4.6. Original portal from Urnes Church, ca. 1030, Lusterfjord, Sogn, now on the church's north wall. (The existing church itself is from 1130.)

Fig. 4.7. Academician Animal Head, ca. 800–850, discovered in the Oseberg Viking Ship Find of 1904, now at the Viking Ship Museum, Oslo. The function of these well-crafted animal headposts is unknown, but this post is unrivaled in Viking art, reflecting the refined style of wood carving achieved by specialized craftsmen in Norway.

Fig. 4.8. The front elevation of Stærnes loft, ca. 1725, Rollag, Numedal, combines intimately worked out details with fine craftsmanship.

Fig. 4.9. Portal from Torpo Church, ca. 1150–1175, Ål, Hallingdal (Younger Sognefjord type). Woodworkers in the Middle Ages adorned the portals of both their sacred and secular buildings with traditional motifs.

skill of Norwegian craftsmen. Cultural heritage is obviously an important component of the character found in this building tradition. Yet, in a sense, linking building character to cultural motifs is like ascribing it to technical knowledge: both are purely quantitative approaches.

The difference between an aesthetic and beauty revolves around craftsmanship, the mastery of a building language. With good craftsmanship, the expression of form is always elevated because the craftsman applies his understanding of how a thing is used and how it should be made. His process is executed with a definite intent—the intent to make something better. In making something better, the traditional Norwegian builder fashioned his details in accordance with their functions: beauty was not a goal in itself—it was the result of resolving and expressing the natural forces acting upon a building. The craftsmen's knowledge was the most important tradition that was handed down through time in Norway. The skill in handling wood for hundreds of years, the knowledge of what it could and could not do, enabled Norwegian builders to express their language in an artistic way.

In this culture, as in other traditional building languages, the subtle irregularities, the seemingly unconscious changes in forms or carving, are significant. Starting with a simple outline—the main features or skeleton of a building—a builder began to elaborate typical details. He held a piece of wood in his hand, knowing what function it must perform, and began to shape it accordingly. Certain pieces or joints inevitably received more attention than others, and it is in this extra attention that we begin to see the craftsman's artistic sense and to pinpoint the quality found in Norwegian architecture. If a builder distinguished an important part of a building, it was tied

to a particular situation, whether it was a difficult connection (such as a *loft*'s log joints) or a place that was significant for nonstructural reasons (such as a church's doorway). Naturally, the most difficult construction problems received the most care, engaged Norwegian builders most.

In this manner, details manifest reality. To the extent that details were authentic reflections of a building situation, they formed the foundation for beauty. Each piece of an exceptional Norwegian building articulated both a well-known construction method and its own place within the system. But in order for details to be accurate, the builders had to be rooted in the everyday experience of making things and be rooted, too, in the *love* of making things. In view of the historical relationship of wood and woodworkers in Norway, it is no wonder the buildings allowed the craftsmen's solutions to dominate the forms.

Because most of the "how" was already specified for the Norwegian builders, they were not concerned with *whether* there would be a window or a door, but rather with its form, placement, and orientation. In a building culture where everyone was familiar with the basic techniques, the distinguishing characteristic of a Norwegian building was its execution, or its making. Just as traditional building types were used over and over yet varied to fit each situation, so were their components. These served the same function from building to building, and it is only in the handling of typical shapes that differences are found.

Each building, each piece of building, has its own geometric structure, its own presence. In Norway, the woodworker's task was to make building forms better express this presence, their "being" in the world. The repetitive act of making the

Fig. 4.10. Detail of the Finnes loft, ca. 1250, Voss, Sogn. The corner post was one of the most significant junctions in loft building.

Fig. 4.11. Suigard Berdal loft, 1749, from Vinje, Telemark, now at the Norwegian Folk Museum, Oslo. Such important constructive elements as the lower corner posts and cantilevered gallery supports were always highly articulated.

same kinds of buildings over a long period of time helped this occur. The buildings had their own lives, independent of the craftsmen, which were embedded in the building pattern itself. Any farmer, for example, knew how to make a good, solid door in a log wall. Furthermore, the similarity of buildings also lessened the difference between master builders and skilled workers so that the components of Norway's building language always reflected their own peculiar cultural quality.

A column was hewn in a certain way because it worked best in that form for a particular building type. Its shape was used repeatedly because of this common knowledge. Yet, as in any traditional culture, a master craftsman would further shape a column so that it emphasized a specific situation, so that the column was anchored in its place. The expertise of craftsmen was rooted in their sense of form and seeing; it told them if a certain detail or procedure was appropriate or not. If a column's base was important functionally, it was cut and carved differently; if its cross section needed to vary, it was narrowed or broadened accordingly. What appears to be a decorative shape or motif on a Norwegian post is only the emphasis of a particular function; or, conversely, the particular function of such a column led to its unique detailing. The Norwegian craftsmen knew that if a detail was executed well, it enhanced reality: its function became the ornament and this was its beauty.

This is the underlying ornamental quality one senses in Norwegian farms and churches. Beautiful shapes are completely ornamental, and at the same time, they are based upon use, upon a repeatedly experienced reality. Ornament is the poetic process of construction that binds it to human experience. Such a process includes beauty and goes beyond function—it enters the realm of feeling: the values inherent in a society, the choice behind a pattern, the thought behind construction. In the words of Christian Norberg-Schulz, "Ornament clarifies a structure, it gives character to buildings, it gives architecture a substance which goes beyond mere geometrical relations."[4]

The refinement of a building pattern or element, its detailing, is the essence of its beauty. This process demands a craftsman's understanding because the refinement must match the reality of a situation in order to reveal it. The Greeks have a word that describes the process best—*techne*—a word that originally meant to make something appear, as something present, among the things that were already present. It was a creative "revealing" of truth and belonged to *poiesis*, which is the "making."[5]

If examined in this fashion, details highlight the experience of buildings and tell us something about the world from which they came. Thus, the buildings illuminate our own experience. A person within such a traditional space is more centered in the world, more alive, and the whole idea of beauty seems to be deeply rooted in the question of what it means to *be* in a certain place. Consequently, the distinction between farms and churches is not so important at this level of examination: craftsmanship is the only criterion needed. The various details of a structure should illuminate our experience of the building and, if well executed, should illuminate the world from which they came. To make this determination, one must look at the shapes of the logs and staves themselves and remember that it was these the builders held in their hands (fig. 4.12).

Fig. 4.12. Voss, Sogn. A traditional Norwegian builder shaped his building components according to the nature of wood.

Log Detailing

An important ground rule of timber architecture is that the shaping or contouring does not efface the basic shape of individual members. In fact, it is delicately proportioned decorative features which give timberwork its singular air of refinement. One perceives the lines of the original piece of material. The observer finds himself attracted not only by the pleasing interplay of shape itself, but also by the sense that he is looking at wood.
—Hermann Phleps

By applying appropriate tools and techniques to a good piece of timber, a woodworker's imagination is limited only by the nature of his material—a material that often seems to have a life of its own. Nevertheless, under a craftsman's skilled hands, the pliancy of wood becomes an easy accomplice to artistic expression. In architecture, the quality of "aliveness" that we find in log buildings—its comfortable proportions and its sensuous texture—is one we respond to warmly. In Norway, with its abundant forests, it is not surprising that wood was sometimes thought of in human terms. As the writer Knut Hamsen describes it:

> All these trees bordering the path were good friends of his. In the spring, he had drained their sap; in the winter, he had been almost like a father to them, releasing them from the snow which weighed their branches down.[6]

Log building in Scandinavia is known for its sensitive matching of tools to the nature of wood. The exacting interplay between the cornering technique, the tools used, and the building material produced the artistic and ornamental qualities one perceives in Norway's log buildings. Log construction is an art that is demanding of builders because the logs must be accurately hewn, fitted on top of one another, and then joined at the corners.

The tools used for timber building included a variety of axes, adzes, wedges, planes, chisels, and gouges. The Scandinavians also made expert use of an old Germanic tool known as a *klingeisen*, a curved drawknife. The use of the drawknife, in fact, had an important influence on the appearance of log buildings in Scandinavia. The shaping of the logs themselves was probably a result of the drawknife. Tools affected the styles of log building in that certain construction methods emphasized the nature of wood. For example, a saw cuts across the grain of wood, so with this tool, a builder is relatively free to ignore the character of wood. In contrast, an ax cut is actually dependent on the direction of the wood grain, and a builder is aware of it with every stroke he makes. Consequently, in areas where the saw did not come into general use until relatively late, as was the case in Norway, the natural and distinctive log styles survived longer than in regions such as Germany and Poland where the saw emerged earlier.[7]

Over the years in Norway the sensitive expression of log building produced a language that echoed the lessons of pine forests. Wood was seasoned and then shaped according to the forces it needed to withstand. Norwegian craftsmen carefully molded their trees into logs and joined them to make dwellings. In the expression of *loft* and *stuer*, in their details, the sensitivity typically associated with wooden architecture is most apparent.

Shaping and Joining

Fig. 4.14. Uv stue, *ca. 1300, Uv, Rennebo. The* megaron stue, *comprised of a large room and an enclosed porch, reveals refined, oval log shapes with ornamental log heads and door construction from the Middle Ages.*

The cross section of a tree was the starting point for log building. Typically, once a tree was felled, it was limbed to the crown (the branches were cut off, leaving only a few remaining at the top, to draw out the sap), which was removed when its needles died and most of the sap had drained from the wood. Portions of the bark were peeled off to aid the curing process. In general, it was considered necessary to air-dry the trees for two years before they could be hewn.

On the oldest preserved Norwegian log houses, the logs are usually small and round in cross section, as the Rolstad *loft* illustrates (fig. 4.36). The gaps between the logs were often filled with moss or oakum, or sometimes even with a woolen material stained red or blue. The undersides of the logs had V grooves cut out along their entire lengths, into which the logs below fit. The point of contact between logs was near the sapwood, or within it, not in the heartwood. (Heartwood is the hard, unyielding wood at the core of a tree, whereas sapwood is the softer wood between the heartwood and the outer bark.) Once the bark was removed, the sapwood was the portion of a log most often molded to a builder's needs. This grooving technique was widely used throughout Norway and was also occasionally borrowed by other wood cultures who saw the advantages of its tight joints and resistance to severe weather.

Because of sapwood's pliancy, the stacked logs were gradually pressed together snugly in the V groove, thus preventing them from twisting in opposing directions. To guard against shrinkage in the wrong direction, logs were laid on top of one another in alternating sequences so that the root end of one log lay upon the top, or head, part of the log below it. Logs were also finished as smoothly as possible, permitting them to shed rain and thereby preventing them from absorbing water.

As builders in Norway became familiar with log construction in the Middle Ages, the rounded forms gave way to logs oval in cross section, reflecting the craftsmen's understanding of their building material. This shape moderated *checking* in the wood, an unnatural grain separation caused by improper seasoning. The oval shape was also quite efficient, as it gave the largest amount of wood to the central section of the log, where the vertical, load-bearing axis was under the most stress. The functional form reveals the actual structural forces occurring in the log.

The oval log shape was usually employed on the more important buildings, such as the *loft* and *stuer*. With this shape, the profile is deflected toward the next stalk so that the contour of a stack of log heads appears as a fine wavy line. The ends of such logs were sometimes grooved, reemphasizing their geometric form. Log heads could easily be decorated and were thus marked by taste and fashion to a larger degree than the log joint itself, in which the cut of the wood was more determined by function and skill.[8] For similar emphasis, the lengths of the logs were sometimes etched in a horizontal direction. This embellishment was applied on the exterior, where two logs came together, as the eye would naturally be drawn to this joint and would thus perceive the logs as individual members.

In Norway the old styles of grooving and molding timberwork persisted longer than in other countries. While it would seem unlikely that contouring of such delicate

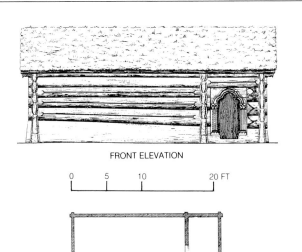

FRONT ELEVATION

0   5   10   20 FT

Stue room

Gallery porch

FLOOR PLAN

0   5   10   20 FT.

EXTERIOR DOOR ELEVATION

INTERIOR ELEVATION OF MAIN DOOR

0   1   2   3   4   5 FT.

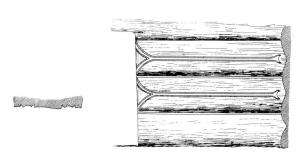

WOOD-CARVING PROFILES

PLAN SECTION OF DOOR PORTAL
AND LOG CONNECTION

FRONT ELEVATION

SIDE ELEVATION

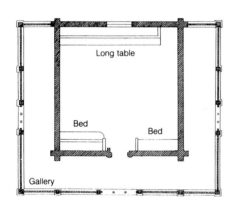

Long table

Bed

Bed

Gallery

SECOND FLOOR PLAN

PROFILE OF WOOD CARVING
OVER FIRST FLOOR DOOR

0   5   10   20 FT.

FIRST FLOOR DOOR ELEVATION

SECOND FLOOR DOOR ELEVATION

WINDOW PORTAL
ELEVATIONS

0   1   2   4 FT.

proportions could affect the appearance of heavy log work, in fact, it gives an air of refinement and can almost be considered a natural feature, since only a few slivers of wood were removed with a chisel or gouge from the wood's surface to create the contours. The use of decorative grooving illustrates that knowledge of tools was accompanied by a deep sense of intimacy with the natural character of wood. The groove itself developed as the work progressed, growing organically out of the basic design contour. Beveling and fluting were seldom used in Norwegian work until the Renaissance period, and where they do exist, they appear to have been imported from abroad.[9]

Logs hewn into an oval cross section were invariably used for the best buildings in Norway, even in the High Middle Ages, when they were used on buildings belonging to the aristocracy. Norway's oldest *stuer*, such as the Raulandstua and the Uv *stue* from 1300, employ the form, as do the Stave and Finnes *loft*, both from 1250 (figs. 4.1, 4.15). Archaeological evidence from secular structures is lacking in Norway, so little remains to trace the form from the Middle Ages to the sixteenth century in *stuer*. The oldest *loft* from the rich period of the sixteenth and seventeenth centuries that bears such logs is the Rygnestad *loft* from 1600 (figs. 4.16, 4.17; pl. 7). Its highly developed oval shapes lead one to believe the form was quite common and of much older origin. The oval log is an example of outstanding craftsmanship; however, despite its efficiency, it was rarely used outside of Norway.

Throughout the 1600s and 1700s, oval logs were used on Norwegian farm buildings, especially in Setesdal and Telemark. The precision of their shapes illustrates that the builders were paying attention to more than just functional considerations, especially if the exposed ends were formed for aesthetic purposes. Yet, if oval logs were formed for ornamental reasons, they were certainly functional as well, and each intention enhanced the other.

Fig. 4.15. Stave loft, ca. 1250, from Ål, Hallingdal, now at the Hallingdal Folk Museum, Nesbyen. The medieval construction features oval logs, Romanesque door portals, and slim, Gothic stave members.

Fig. 4.16. Second Rygnestad loft, ca. 1600, Rygnestad, Setesdal. The large logs of the loft clearly reveal their enclosing function.

Fig. 4.17. The oval shape of the logs on the second Rygnestad loft is emphasized by a chiseled groove.

Fig. 4.18. Small log heads from the Sevle long loft, ca. 1600, Nore, Numedal. Although precisely shaped, the faces of the oval logs were formed with six straight edges rather than oval profiles.

Fig. 4.19. Log-notching techniques.

During the sixteenth and seventeenth centuries, emphasis was placed on large dimensions in log work, as evidenced by the increasing size of log cross sections. The refinements that developed are best seen in the late Setesdal *loft* from 1500–1700, an excellent example being the second Rygnestad *loft* discussed above. In this building the first floor is defined by a height of only three logs, the size of which are hardly exceeded in any other wooden structure in Norway. The logs lose their circular cross section almost entirely and express their enclosing function clearly.

During the seventeenth and eighteenth centuries, smaller log members were unusual, and when they were used, their details did not receive much attention. Heads of logs were shaped into six-sided forms or irregular ovals, and the grooves on the log faces were less carefully executed than in past centuries or were left off altogether (fig. 4.18). At this time, large dimensions and proportions became more important than individual components. It was the contrast between log and stave work in the galleries and entrances, for example, that shaped the character of Norway's later log buildings.[10]

Once a log was shaped, its joint could be fashioned. Together with shaping, the process of joining determines the very character of Norwegian log buildings. Because it was the primary challenge in this type of building, joint work forced Norwegian builders to devise exquisite solutions. Whereas Swedish buildings reveal a picturesque tendency in the shaping of their log heads, Norwegian developments in timber architecture refined the joint itself. According to Hermann Phleps, "The end treatment so cherished by the Swedes would have appeared fussy on the oval-hewn Norwegian log work."[11]

The main structural support for log buildings was provided by their interlocking corners, and much care was taken with them in order to ensure the rigidity of the walls. The earliest form of corner joints, or head-log joints, consisted of simple round

SWEDISH LOCK NOTCHING   NORWEGIAN LOCK NOTCHING

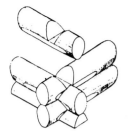

LOCK NOTCHING

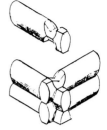

LOCK NOTCHING

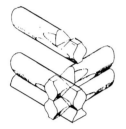

LOCK NOTCHING

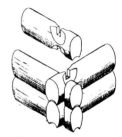

LOCK-AND-STEP NOTCHING

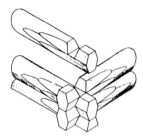

LOCK NOTCHING

EARLY LOCK NOTCHING WITH
LOGS FITTED ONLY ON TOP

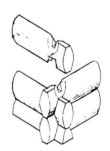

LOCK-AND-STEP NOTCHING

LOCK NOTCHING

EARLY LOCK NOTCHING WITH
LOGS FITTED ON TOP AND BOTTOM

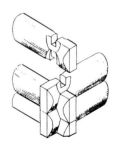

LOCK-AND-STEP NOTCHING

LOCK-AND-STEP NOTCHING

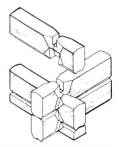

LOCK-AND-STEP NOTCHING

Fig. 4.20. Head-log joint on a loft *from Ose, Setesdal, ca. 1700, now at the Norwegian Folk Museum, Oslo. The precise interlocking of large, oval members is highlighted by a sensitive carving which marks the transition from head logs to an overhanging gallery support.*

notching, with only the upper half of a log carved out for the log above. Later, lock notching was developed, with logs notched on both their top and bottom surfaces (fig. 4.19).

In the past, the head-log joint has been used to date old wooden structures and, in general, this method can be accurate. However, the type of head-log joint used does not always reveal the age of a building. It seems that, at least in Norway, the best houses were always distinguished by the best notching.

In an effort to achieve a tight-fitting joint at the corners, builders devised a variety of joining methods, and the demanding work this required inspired craftsmen to make the joint a distinct decorative motif. The methods involved skilled ax work for the notching, and the builders scribed or scored the wood first to show where it would be cut. Various joints reveal innovations such as lock-and-step systems, with locks on the shoulders of the joint: some even included additional corner dowels embedded in the protruding log heads to prevent twisting.

The length of the neck, or head, to the shoulder in the grooved joint determined its rigidity, and this was varied for different structural members. Generally, the shoulders were cut across the log's grain at an angle slightly less than ninety degrees to the log's surface. The neck ran parallel to the log's surface and was what remained after the shoulders had been cut. The depth of the shoulders and width of the neck determined how logs would lock together, and they are the basis for distinction between different types of notching.

An example of fine joinery is found on the *loft* from Ose, Setesdal (fig. 4.20). The logs were cut with exacting precision, ensuring snugness and rigidity. If one were to dismantle the wall, the notches would illustrate differing neck and shoulder lengths. The overhanging logs (which form the base of the second floor) have a shallower cut than their counterparts below.

A head-log joint must also allow for shrinkage, a major consideration in any type of wood building. The Norwegians treated this "enemy" as an "ally" in their joint work. When logs were laid on top of one another with a scooped-out surface between them—that is, with the logs touching only in a long ridge or spine—compression caused greater settling in the walls than in the interlocked head-log joints. Because of this, extra space was cut into these keyed joints to allow for subsequent settling. As a result, the gradual shrinking of log members due to moisture loss actually reinforced the tightness of the joint and, consequently, the structure.

Yet, by itself, the keying and fitting at the corners of log walls were inadequate to hold them in alignment. Wood continually moves because of shrinkage and drying, and this causes logs to twist in and out of a wall, depending on how their grain runs. To prevent this, oak dowels or pegs were driven through the logs at regular intervals and staggered for each course of logs.

It was natural that great emphasis should be placed on the forming of the logs and head-log joints, especially in Norway's wet climate; otherwise, these buildings might not have withstood the ravages of time. In order for a house to be solid and tight, all the details, especially the log joints, had to be as precise as possible. The time, effort, and care taken in joining the logs reveal the nature of this building method: it was a system of well-crafted joints.

Portals and Motifs

The feeling of solidity one perceives in Norway's log buildings is characteristic of construction that uses large wooden members. While such walls often appear impregnable—necessarily so in such a landscape—they did need openings.

Making the door is one of the most important structural concerns in a log building, and this is evident in the way Norwegians constructed their thresholds. Historically, doorways existed before windows and were also used to permit light to enter a structure. Windows did not appear in log buildings until well after door framing had reached an advanced stage of evolution, and in Norway they were not common until the seventeenth and eighteenth centuries. A number of factors prompted their adoption, among them the addition of ceilings and the installation of chimneys, which closed off roof openings for the exit of smoke and entry of light. But in the Middle Ages, when windows were sometimes needed, narrow slits were simply chopped or cut out of the walls starting from the joint between two logs. Gradually, these grew in size to become small apertures fitted with splines connecting the log wall and window frame.[12]

Door openings in the Middle Ages were usually small to avoid weakening the log wall, as the Raulandstua illustrates (fig. 4.22). The builders would cut away a minimum number of log courses, leaving a rather low opening, and the logs that had their central portions removed for the door were discontinuous. This could eventually lead to problems of uneven wall settlement because of the differing log heights in portions of the wall. The central portion of a wall over the door consisted of perhaps two or three logs, while the portions to either side of the opening consisted of six or seven logs. Wood shrinks greatly in its width but minimally in its length, and this is always a major concern in log building, especially at the door opening. As a result, when fashioning doors in log structures, builders were always concerned with reinforcing the discontinuous logs and with a wall's eventual settlement.

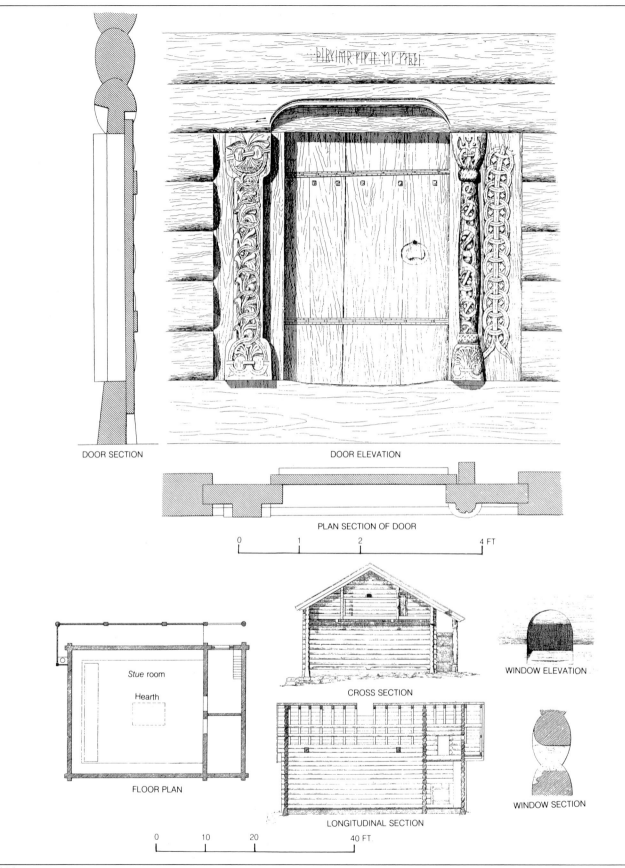

DOOR SECTION

DOOR ELEVATION

PLAN SECTION OF DOOR

0   1   2   4 FT

Stue room

Hearth

FLOOR PLAN

CROSS SECTION

LONGITUDINAL SECTION

WINDOW ELEVATION

WINDOW SECTION

0   10   20   40 FT.

4.21

Traditional door constructions in European timber buildings can be categorized according to three different methods, all of which were known prior to the Middle Ages: Celtic, or Celtic-German; Scandinavian; and Bavarian. In contrast to the Scandinavian and Celtic constructions, the Bavarian method involved delaying installation of the doorposts until the log walls were fully settled. Consequently, the doorposts were more restrained in the use of artistic embellishment.

The salient features of the Celtic and Scandinavian methods were that the ends of the discontinuous logs were joined to trimmer posts, which later evolved into doorposts, in a mortise or groove or with a tenon, and that these vertical trimmer posts were erected at the same time as the walls. Perhaps even more important, the mortise in the posts' header log, or lintel, was made deep enough so that ample space was left above the trimmer posts for the downward settling of the log members, as illustrated in figure 4.21. (The header log was the first continuous log over the door opening.)

This type of construction which dated from the Bronze Age, allowed the horizontal logs and vertical doorposts freedom to contract in the direction of their shrinkage and also provided for a very tight door. Wood can shrink up to thirty centimeters, or one foot, in its width, while the shrinkage in its length is negligible. Therefore, while the horizontal logs shrank, the vertical doorposts retained their original height. In discussing a *stue* from Hardanger, Hermann Phleps notes that the extent to which the building would settle had been calculated so precisely that when the log work did come to rest, the gap between the lintel and trimmer post was tightly sealed.[13] In a harsh climate such as Norway's, the great amount of care exhibited in door constructions was absolutely necessary.

According to Phleps, early Scandinavian doorposts were simple vertical splines, or trimmer posts, set into the sill and header logs of an opening. To provide a stop

Fig. 4.21. Raulandstua, ca. 1250–1300, from Uvdal, Numedal, now at the Norwegian Folk Museum, Oslo. A traditional three-room plan illustrating Scandinavian door construction and a medieval window.

Fig. 4.22. One of the oldest stue in Norway, the Raulandstua features a typically small medieval entrance.

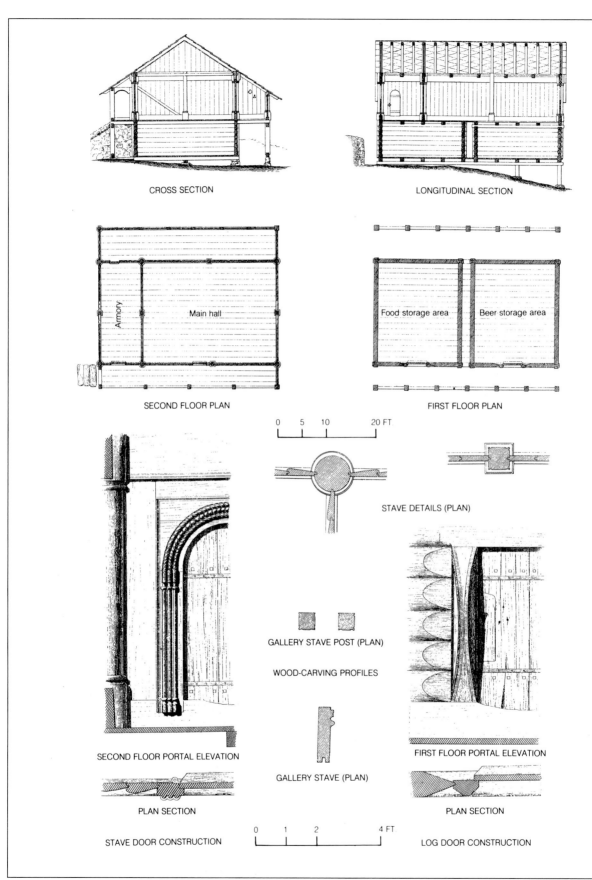

CROSS SECTION

LONGITUDINAL SECTION

SECOND FLOOR PLAN

Armory

Main hall

FIRST FLOOR PLAN

Food storage area

Beer storage area

0 5 10 20 FT

STAVE DETAILS (PLAN)

GALLERY STAVE POST (PLAN)

WOOD-CARVING PROFILES

SECOND FLOOR PORTAL ELEVATION

FIRST FLOOR PORTAL ELEVATION

PLAN SECTION

GALLERY STAVE (PLAN)

PLAN SECTION

STAVE DOOR CONSTRUCTION

0 1 2 4 FT

LOG DOOR CONSTRUCTION

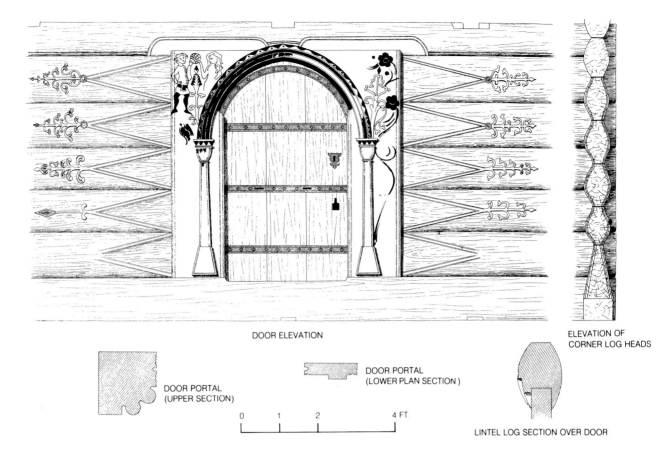

DOOR ELEVATION

DOOR PORTAL
(UPPER SECTION)

DOOR PORTAL
(LOWER PLAN SECTION)

0   1   2   4 FT.

ELEVATION OF
CORNER LOG HEADS

LINTEL LOG SECTION OVER DOOR

for the door plank itself, the spline was increased in size until it became a sturdy plank. When this in turn became a doorpost of a thickness almost equaling that of the log walls, its top was tenoned or tapered into the lintel log, with space for settling.[14]

A few techniques prevailed for the joining of logs to portal planks, and the Scandinavians evolved brilliant expressions for this important connection. In its most basic form, the full thickness of the doorposts was housed into a mortise in the logs. (A "housing" joint is a solid connection made by placing the full thickness of one member into another.) As the planks became thicker, a tongue-and-groove approach was used. A joining technique peculiar to Scandinavian door framing, known from at least the seventeenth century, was the use of V and W grooves, which provided the tightest joint: the sides of the door planks were V-grooved and they fit snugly into a W groove in the logs' mortise slot.

Such early methods of joining portal plank and log were well known in the Middle Ages. According to Håkon Christie, the oldest Scandinavian joining method was a technique whereby the logs were planed thinner at their ends so that the whole section of a log fit into the thick mortised portal panel (figs. 4.23, 4.24). It is one of the most popular Scandinavian methods, and in Norway many doors illustrate this medieval, architectonic solution with the planed logs emphasizing the silhouette of the door.

The thickness and width of Norway's portals reveal the great rigidity they gave to the log wall's interruption. Norwegian doorposts can usually be distinguished by their size and the way in which they were formed. In the southern, western, and border regions of the country, the door planks are even more notable. In these areas, the planks were not rectangular in cross section but were often given a

Fig. 4.23. Plans and elevations of stave- and log-door constructions from the Finnes loft, ca. 1250, Voss, Sogn.

Fig. 4.24. Medieval inner door of the Lydva loft, ca. 1250, Voss, Sogn. The double-line grooving on planed logs at entries highlights the door and was a traditional Scandinavian detail.

Fig. 4.25. Door from the Ose loft, ca. 1700, from Ose, Setesdal, now at the Norwegian Folk Museum, Oslo. The carved door planks were influenced by Renaissance wood carving while the flanking portals reflect medieval styles.

Fig. 4.26. Second Rygnestad loft, ca. 1600, Rygnestad, Setesdal. The rounded portal, with its medieval braided rope carving and lightly grooved oval log, illustrates how the geometry of building elements were precisely articulated.

Fig. 4.27. Wide door portals from the loft at Helle Uppigard Farm, 1582, Helle, Setesdal. The deeply grooved portals contrast with the shallow carving of the door plank.

rounded shape on their exterior faces. This strong, unique design mirrored basic structural forces much as the oval-hewn logs did. The doorposts have the same breath of vitality in their bowed forms as do the oval logs, suggesting the exertion imposed upon them by the logs above. Both posts and logs reveal the eloquence native to Norwegian craftsmen. Hermann Phleps notes of these rounded forms: "The dynamics created by this exceptional feel for the work ranks with the crowning achievements in the language of wooden architecture. In the age of Classical architecture, this distinctive form was used on stonework as well, although stone itself could never have inspired the stone masterpieces of entasis."[15]

Because doors in Norway were the focus of so much attention—both in structural terms and as the threshold to man's dwellings—it is natural that craftsmen further refined their doorposts with fine wood carving. The carvers were intimately guided by the longitudinal fibers of the wood, while the carvings reinforced the vertical, often bulging, shape of the posts.

In Setesdal, doors exhibit a strength unrivaled by those of other regions—a function of both fine joinery and rich decorative work (figs. 4.25, 4.26, 4.27). The huge dimensions of the wood used in this part of the country made the tenon type of joint the most efficient way to join portal and log. The portals stiffened the opening at the large discontinuous logs and were thick and extremely wide, sometimes half the width of the door. The door itself tended to be broader than in other areas. In this region, also, the actual door planks were sometimes carved—an unusual practice.

The carving on both the door itself and its portals reemphasized proportional relationships through the use of shallow relief on their broad surfaces. If the doorposts were hewn into oval shapes, their vertical forms were further enhanced by the taut profile of the carvings. The intensity of the carvings, as well as the generous dimensions of the door, were necessary if these doorways were to stand out against the large logs of the buildings and appear as individual entities.

In Norway, thick wooden doors were elaborately carved in imitation of stone portals and arches, or even coils of braided ropes and chains (figs. 4.28, 4.29). Rhythmic geometric plant or animal forms decorated doorways, and doorposts were topped with guardian lions, masklike faces, or mythological creatures—reinforcing the quality of fantasy that had always distinguished the Norwegians' world.

In the Middle Ages, doorways on *loft* and *stuer* were decorated with Romanesque and Gothic motifs from stone architecture, such as arches, half-

Fig. 4.28. Door from the Stave loft, ca. 1250, from Ål, Hallingdal, now at the Hallingdal Folk Museum, Nesbyen. The medieval detailing of this portal resembles that found on stone architecture.

Fig. 4.29. Interior door of the Finnes loft, ca. 1250, Voss, Sogn. The traditional rope coils imitate the sculpting found on stone portals.

4.26

4.27

4.29

4.30

4.31

4.32

columns, and lions. These were blended with influences from the stave-church portals, which depicted Viking monsters, dragons, and worms, intertwined with vine tendrils—a Christian motif—and Byzantine flowers. Wood-carving styles between 1250 and 1350, especially on furniture, illustrate the blending of such motifs from unlike origins. Circular and intertwined patterns of Gothic vine leaves, rings of braided chains, wild beasts, and human masks were all combined, and these strongly inspired wood carving in the sixteenth and seventeenth centuries. In some areas, older medieval traditions persisted because of geographical isolation. In Numedal, Setesdal, and Telemark in the south, for instance, local schools of craftsmen were hardly affected by the Renaissance and baroque movements until the late 1700s. As the Rygnestad *loft* portal illustrates (fig. 4.26), unmistakable medieval patterns persisted in wood carving long after the era had passed.

In addition to native patterns, the wood carving that appeared on Norway's farms in the sixteenth and seventeenth centuries was influenced by other factors. The rising number of cities in the 1500s resulted in a closer relationship between urban centers and rural communities. Craftsmen from the *bygder* discovered more opportunities in the cities, and by the early 1600s the formation of craft guilds, with specialized training and formal education, began. Since the Middle Ages there had been a tendency to concentrate commerce and handicrafts in cities, and by 1680, this resulted in guild laws that forbade members to practice in *bygder* while it strengthened their ranks and gave them official status. Even more significant, a new, specialized class of cabinetmakers developed in the cities, responding to the more precise demands of fine Renaissance and baroque furniture, which had formerly been imported from England and France. With increased communication between urban and rural areas in Norway, the work of this guild class was to eventually affect local craftsmen throughout the country.

The influence of the Renaissance style on farm portal carving was ushered in relatively slowly in Norway, sometime in the sixteenth or seventeenth century. The influence was not the same everywhere, and it varied in degree from primitive expressions to masterpieces in the art of wood carving.

The European Renaissance styles were introduced primarily through religious architecture at the time of the Reformation in Norway, but they were also introduced by way of the imported furniture that was occupying the larger *stuer* built in the sixteenth and seventeenth centuries. In the seventeenth century, the guild cabinetmakers with specialized tools hastened the development of international styles. During the Renaissance, planes, curved gouges, skew chisels, and spindles were used by many woodworkers. In the *bygder*, local woodworkers copied professional cabinetmakers and styles, without, perhaps, comprehending the actual technical aspects of the craft. Nevertheless, international styles in certain regions of Norway can be detected but they developed independently in different parts of the country.

Renaissance wood-carving patterns popularized architectural motifs such as triglyphs, gables, and arches, and evolved into an art of "flat" carving with geometric patterns of circles and lines, fashioned by compasses and rulers (fig. 4.30). On farm portals, the carving was either cut deeply or just inscribed on the wood's surfaces. It had a sharp, edgelike character, and the technique was soon transferred to different motifs. These included organic and geometric shapes such as flowers, stars, and diamonds, all combined in endless variety and regular repetition (figs. 4.31, 4.32). This anonymous style of wood carving was quite simple and did not demand much skill, nor did it allow as much room for individual expression as the ancient figurative styles had.[16]

Fig. 4.30. Early example of geometric flat carving on the door of the Sevle long loft, ca. 1600, Nore, Numedal.

Fig. 4.31. Organic and geometric flat carving on the doorway of the Parsonage loft, 1719, Rollag, Numedal.

Fig. 4.32. Organic flat carving on the door of the Stærnes loft, 1725, Rollag, Numedal.

Early in the 1700s in the isolated southern regions of Norway such as Setesdal, Numedal, and Telemark, flat carving took firm root in local crafts. In these regions, medieval wood-carving traditions were most preserved in organic motifs and circular bands that were braided under and over each other—motifs that had been popular throughout the 1600s. It was the last expression of medieval traditions. During the Renaissance, flat carving was transferred to the medieval vine and double vine motifs and was combined with the new geometric forms. The technique was quite popular in these regions, and it can be seen most frequently on the door portals and columns of *stuer* and *loft*. In parts of Telemark, it was even combined with gouging in deep relief and gave the building portals a monumental character. In Setesdal and Telemark, the archaic custom of decorating *loft* portals with old leaf and vine forms persisted longest.

Along the old Royal Road from Oslo to Trondheim, stylistic influences from the cities easily penetrated into wood-carving traditions from the Renaissance onward. The strongest influence that affected local woodworkers was related to church art. In 1700 guild cabinetmakers in Oslo were carving sacred furniture in deep relief, depicting the acanthus flower with thick, wavy leaves. The plant was an old Christian motif, well known from Greek and Roman art, and its leaves resembled a dandelion with pointed stems.

From Oslo all the way to Trondheim, the use of this motif heralded a whole new wood-carving movement. In Gudbrandsdal especially, the three-dimensional baroque acanthus motif was incorporated and transformed into a local trademark, appearing everywhere on buildings, furniture, and small household objects (figs. 4.33, 4.34). By 1749 the style was well established, and it began to travel eastward and northward to areas where large numbers of self-taught woodworkers existed. The artist Jakob Klukstad represented the best of such self-trained men. His many students and followers formed a school that is considered one of the high points in Norwegian art. While these carvers lacked the perfection of the guild workers, they had an abundant supply of spontaneity which they applied to their work in these regions, especially to the *stuer*; the *loft* were never as finely detailed.

In 1780, guild members in cities complained of strong competition from the rural woodworkers, and a law was passed that allowed these cabinetmakers to practice in the *bygder*. The professionals moved to large farming communities such as Gudbrandsdal and Trøndelag, which could support their services and where they could find employment alongside local craftsmen. From then on, styles from abroad developed quickly. By 1800 the acanthus, blended with rococo forms, was the main motif found in Trøndelag.

In Telemark, Numedal, and Setesdal, wood carving remained a more secular art, and flat carving was always too popular for the baroque acanthus to invade local traditions. Instead, by the middle of the 1700s, the rococo style and a particular form of acanthus were easily integrated in the flatly carved doorways (fig. 4.35). In Telemark, open vines appeared with fewer details than in the usual, finely detailed flat carving. By the end of the eighteenth century, self-taught craftsmen such as Jarand Aasmundson Rønjom had transformed the rococo C form into a basic three-dimensional motif out of which vines and flowers grew. The development can be seen clearly in *loft* from Telemark; their architectonic portals became the main feature of *loft* building.

Toward the end of the eighteenth century, wood carving became a less significant craft. By this time, *loft* building had begun to decline, with *loft* increasingly displaying features from Swiss chalet styles rather than native woodworking forms.

4.33

4.34

4.35

Instead of using traditional carving motifs to highlight their buildings, builders frequently adorned them with red and white colors. Simultaneously, the art of *rosemaling*, or rose painting, superseded woodcarving as the way to decorate *stuer*. *Rosemaling* spread widely throughout southern regions, less so in northern areas. In Telemark, the art form generated exceptionally fine styles of expression. There, self-taught painters such as Ola Hansson decorated *stuer* and furniture with robust flowers of bright colors and the craft became quite popular. Not surprisingly, the art is still practiced today in many parts of Norway (pl. 13).

Fig. 4.36. Rolstad loft, ca. 1300, from Sør-Fron, Gudbrandsdal, now at the Norwegian Folk Museum, Oslo. This finely crafted medieval building illustrates how early Norwegian builders mastered the art of reisverk, a combination of stave and log construction techniques.

Reisverk

If the character of a building is realized in its joining and binding—in the way the structure is put together—then the *loft* expresses Norway's building language most completely, more so than the *stue*. Both buildings, the most important on a farm, obviously received the most detail work in all areas of the country. And, in turn, the detail work was directed to the most important components of these log buildings: the log heads, doors, and galleries.

It is in the *loft*, however, that the woodworkers' skills are most evident. The use of both logs and staves, which were combined in *reisverk*, were distinctly articulated and expressed the elegance achieved in the Norwegian *loft*. The interaction of stave and log techniques, their contrasting forces, is the essence of *loft* building in Norway. In the constructive details of the *loft*, one sees most clearly the refined synthesis of the two building methods that served the Norwegians through the ages.

The exquisite manner in which these storage buildings were made reflect the importance of the structure, its place on a farm, and a masterly building method. The Norwegian *loft*, purely a system of joints, could be taken down and set up in different places, as was the case when a bride took this building with her as a customary wedding gift. Traditionally, a *loft* was full of symbolic value, and it was natural that the farmers lavished their best skills upon it. The *loft* was always built with especially fine materials and marked by refined carpentry work. Logs, door parts, corner posts, staves, and important joints in the exterior were typically highlighted with wood carving. If a farmer had the means, he employed a specialist to build his *loft*. If he built it himself with the help of kinsmen, he used his culture's high-quality building standard as a familiar guide. In either case, the buildings were meticulously constructed, and their details exemplified the special pride farmers always had in their *loft*.

The details of the Havsten *loft*, a classic Telemark building, reveal a precise integration of stave and log techniques (fig. 4.37). The log structure is the core on which the staved gallery is supported, and the *loft*'s construction is the direct resolution of this structural force. It is possible that this system, with its overhanging gallery, was related to the cantilevered foundation structure of the stave churches. The top logs of the first story flare out to support the gallery, and these important members are carefully shaped, not just put in place. The manner in which builders sought to make the transition from the vertical line of the log ends to the horizontal gallery beams was a distinguishing feature of *loft* building. It was a natural response, as the logs' supporting function was the essence of their building method.

A number of logs were combined to create this transition, which was further emphasized by the use of oval-hewn logs. The configurations of interlocked log

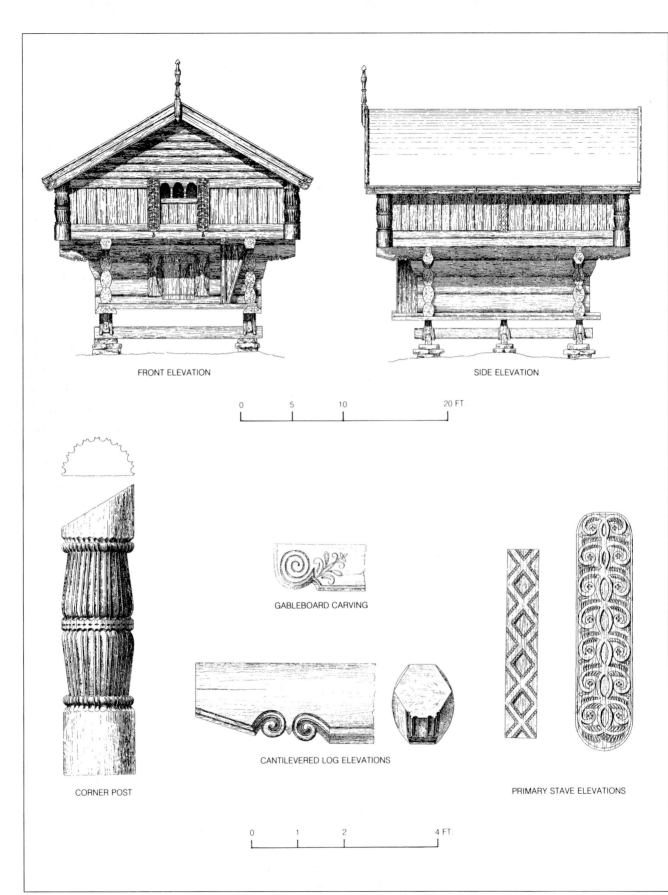

FRONT ELEVATION

SIDE ELEVATION

0   5   10   20 FT

GABLEBOARD CARVING

CANTILEVERED LOG ELEVATIONS

CORNER POST

PRIMARY STAVE ELEVATIONS

0   1   2   4 FT

4.37

heads led the eye up to the supporting logs' outermost ends, which topped off the exuberant system. A notch was usually featured on the lowermost, overhanging log, which arrested the upward line of the corner work. Beginning at the flare, this detail originated with the craftsmen's practice of notching to indicate the ending of the log beneath it. The gesture resulted in wonderful designs that emphasized an important process and a significant aspect of the building system (fig. 4.38).

On top of these overhanging beams stood the corner posts of the gallery. These posts supported and stiffened the frame of the staved gallery and its balustrades. Called *stolper* in Norwegian, they were sometimes inclined outward to shed water and to offset the settling of the core's log walls. The posts were joined to the beams above and below with a large double-forked mortise, a feature also known in stave-church construction. The shapes of these posts could be round or square and always contrasted with the repetitive, flat infilling planks. In keeping with the nature of squared or rounded timber, the posts were first hewn using a broadax, finer detail being added with a drawknife and chisel. Builders usually started shaping their *stolper* from each end of a log, and this practice naturally led to a decorative band at the middle of a post. If a builder also wished to distinguish the connection of an upright to its horizontal members, he had to taper these ends back into the shaft of an upright. At these points, the procedure was also emphasized with decorative bands on a column. Such tapering gave posts a bulging expression that reflected the dynamics of applied vertical forces (fig. 4.39).

When the bottom porch was enclosed with infilling members, as in the southern parts of Norway, similar posts performed a similar function. The builders then chose between distinguishing the lower posts from the upper posts—as they did in Telemark, where the top posts had rounded forms and the bottom ones were square—or blending them, as the builders did in Numedal, where both the upper and lower

Fig. 4.37. Building details of Havsten loft, ca. 1600, Gransherad, Telemark, illustrating carving on important log and stave members.

Fig. 4.38. Supporting log work under the gallery of Havsten loft.

Fig. 4.39. Upper corner post with carved bands and gouging from the Havsten loft.

4.40

4.41

4.42

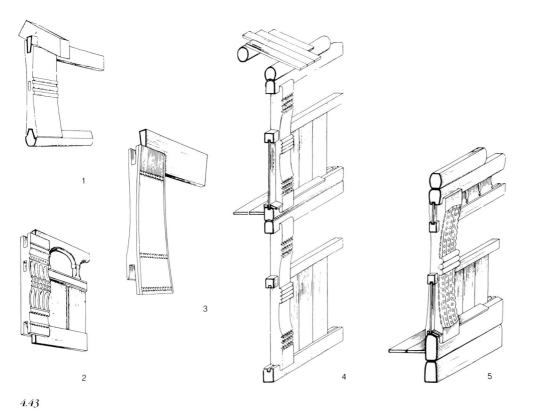

4.43

Fig. 4.40. Upper corner
post from the Rauland
loft, ca. 1730, from
Rauland, Telemark, now
at the Skien Folk
Museum.

Fig. 4.41. Lower corner
post from the Rauland
loft. A variety of
ornamentation, inspired
by nature, characterizes
Norwegian loft, giving
them an animistic
quality.

Fig. 4.42. Upper and
lower corner posts of the
Suigard Berdal loft,
1749, from Vinje,
Telemark now at the
Norwegian Folk
Museum, Oslo. The loft
of Telemark
traditionally had
different shapes on their
upper and lower posts,
whereas the posts of loft
in Numedal all had the
same form.

Fig. 4.43. Gallery details
of primary stave
members: numbers 1–3
are from Telemark, 4
and 5 are from
Gudbrandsdal. The
decorative bands at the
center of the staves
derived from the practice
of rough hewing a
member from each end,
to its center. This left a
small band of wood in
the middle of the
component which the
builder usually chiseled
or carved for a finished
effect.

stolper were usually round (figs. 4.40, 4.41, 4.42). Different geometric shapes could also be created within their individual cross sections—square or round—or different kinds of carvings could be placed on the same shapes, or similar kinds of carvings on different shapes.

The staved members of the galleries were also distinguished in their joining and shaping. The primary vertical staves, that is, the secondary structural members, fit over the beam on which they rested and helped to stiffen the wall of infilling planks (fig. 4.43). Widened at top and bottom and decorated slightly, this shape demonstrated superbly the members' grasping function and, at the same time, prevented water from entering the mortised groove. In contrast, regular wall planks were inserted into the beam, offsetting the primary staves' forces, and the beam's exterior face was sloped to deflect water penetration. The important stave members were always specially carved to reflect their significance, whereas the regular staves, which took the brunt of climatic conditions and were periodically replaced, were not carved in any distinctive manner.

The window portals in these enclosed galleries were also natural areas for emphasis. Where the openings occurred, the framing staves were usually carved. If the balustrades had posts, they were carved in various shapes, often based on organic or geometric forms or characters from fairy tales.

When the *loft* were raised off the ground and became *stabbur*, the higher elevation aided the overhanging roof in keeping rain and snow out of the building's lower portions. The exposed supports held the building off the ground and were supported by sill beams. The small posts resembled corner posts in their double-mortise connections, and these stumps were also carved, although more primitively. The sill log, raised above the ground and resting on stones, reflected its simple but important function in a triangular cross section. Upon the stumps rested a long half-

Fig. 4.44. Corner posts of the Kleivi loft, ca. 1783, Åmotsdal, Telemark.

Fig. 4.45. Even the foundation members of the Kleivi loft were articulated.

round log distinct from the oval logs stacked upon it. The building depended greatly on the stability of this member, and builders used a thicker log for this course and often took special care to select certain species for the durability of their "bottom-rounds."

It is interesting to see the different expressions from building to building—to see which members received the wood-carvers' knives (usually the verticals) and which did not (usually the horizontals), to see why one builder did one thing and another did not because of regional traditions or structural considerations. Of course, stylistic influences from the Continent affected certain elements within the system of *loft* building. The medieval tendency was to repeat similar shapes such as staves in the galleries, and posts were slender, with a Gothic character. With the advent of Renaissance and baroque styles, a differentiation of parts began that expressed structural functions. The corner and middle columns of the gallery took on different shapes and were thicker and more robust than previously. In the seventeenth and eighteenth centuries, the secondary structural members were either distinguished from the primary structural members or both were made with similar constructive shapes in order to achieve a particular effect.

One can see how *loft* variations became endless, were adopted to fit the situation in each instance. One can also see order in the possibility of chaos: the basic patterns of joining stave and log members remained consistent from the Middle Ages until the beginning of the nineteenth century.

The high point of *loft* building occurred in Telemark in the eighteenth century. In this region builders strove for a distinguishing effect between buildings and between building elements. Because of Telemark's irregular *tun*, the buildings stood separately and became individual pieces of sculpture, each striving for attention in the courtyard. As a result, building details were individually and precisely articulated,

similar in manner to those of classical buildings, where each building member expressed an individual function. The Kleivi *loft* is probably the best example of a *loft* by a well-known building master that clearly expressed its different structural functions (figs. 4.44, 4.45; pl. 9). The oval log structure supported staved galleries on both upper and lower floors, and three different types of vertical structural elements were used in them: the first-story corner columns were flattened to emphasize the lower staved façade, while the upper-story *stolper* were rounded to turn the corner of the dominant gallery. The secondary stave members were richly carved with baroque and rococo plants, whereas the main structural components received geometric flat carving. Each part of the building stands out as an individual entity, with a different geometry for each shape and contrasting plantlike and geometric carving.

If wood-carving patterns seem decorative, the emphasis of building details was dictated by the whole setting of a farm complex and its buildings. As was seen in Telemark, each detail of the *loft* and *stuer* was individually carved to stand out in a haphazard *tun*, in order to pull the *tun* form together. If a building was set apart from its neighbors, as in the southern and border regions, its individual members, the corner posts or log heads, for example, were distinguished (figs. 4.46, 4.47). If a building was part of a whole complex, as in the western and eastern regions, its details were probably not so marked (figs. 4.48, 4.49, 4.50). Similarly, in the north, the precise geometry of an ordered *tun* overrode any need for emphasizing the individual buildings or any of their details.

In each region building details naturally followed the established character of their *tun* and building forms. Seen in this way, the expression of *loft* and *stue* details is not decorative. The way these details were made, their execution, reiterated a farm's original disposition, while at the same time, they reinforced it.

Fig. 4.46. Decorated upper and lower corner posts of the Parsonage loft, *1719, Rollag, Numedal. The square courtyards in this region resulted in regular building placements and, consequently, detailing was more repetitive. The main building components are emphasized to achieve a precise, rule-like effect.*

Fig. 4.47. Large door from the second Rygnestad loft, *ca. 1600, Rygnestad, Setesdal. In the southern row* tun, *buildings were emphasized by their size, as well as the size of their components (unlike the western regions that only emphasized the size of the buildings). Building details in Setesdal were precisely articulated to emphasize the large structures.*

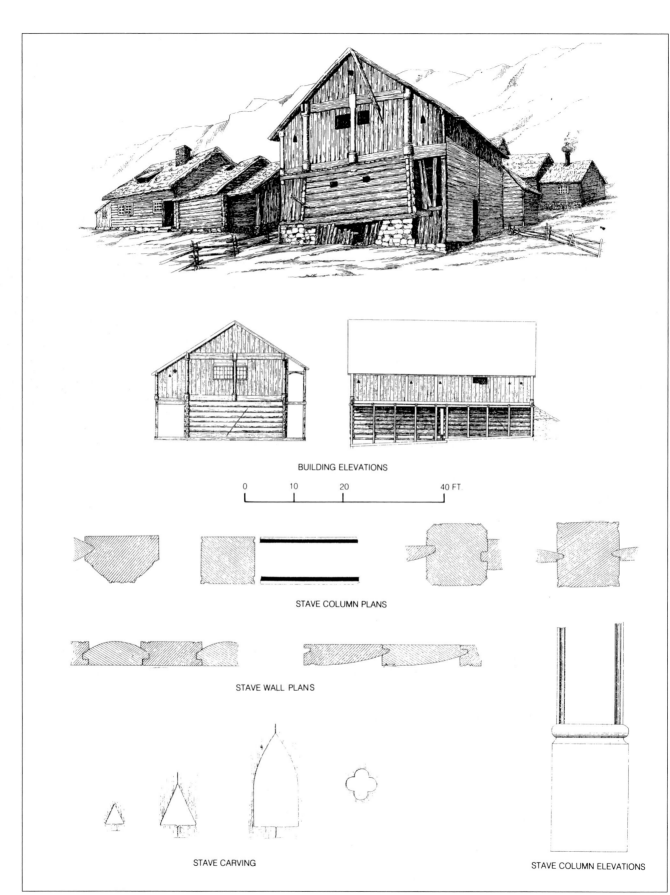

BUILDING ELEVATIONS

0   10   20   40 FT.

STAVE COLUMN PLANS

STAVE WALL PLANS

STAVE CARVING

STAVE COLUMN ELEVATIONS

4.49

Fig. 4.48. Stave work details from the Finnes loft, ca. 1250, Voss, Sogn, as it appeared in the nineteenth century. In western regions, buildings were emphasized by size rather than distinct details in order for them to stand out amidst the jumble of a cluster tun. Compared to Telemark, details are not so noticeable, nor as important as the homogeneous stave work which served as a covering over the farm, concealing differences in individual buildings. As a result, staves were the most important building elements on these farms and their detailing gave the farm its overall character.

Fig. 4.49. Two loft from the Bjørnstad Farm, ca. eighteenth century, from Heidal, Gudbrandsdal, now at Maihaugen Folk Museum, Lillehammer. In eastern regions, only the staved galleries were carved. The blending of all the buildings with such façades strengthened and enhanced the symmetry of the square tun.

Fig. 4.50. Stave members of a stue from the Bjørnstad Farm have the same shape as those on its companion loft.

4.50

Stave Detailing

In the church the fisherman enters his pew. From his seat, he recognizes that the column has the same dimension as his mast. Through this recognition he feels secure. He sits by his column, a form also acknowledged by the gentle touch of his fingers. On the open sea, the tree was a symbol he trusted, it brought him safely home.
—Sverre Fehn

In the making of a stave church an extraordinary amount of craftsmanship is evident. The pieces that comprise a church were not only cut and put in place, they were carefully molded to their tasks and it is not surprising that the beautiful simplicity of each form in a stave church seems to derive from a structural function. Yet, a deeper understanding was also reflected in their final forms, and the building components seem put together to achieve a vertical and wholistic expression. All the various parts visually support and help each other in order to reveal their truth. This notion of cooperation is a basic Christian premise and an underlying principle in the churches' details.

The pieces of a stave church fit together as precisely as a well-made piece of furniture; wood is used the way it should be, and all the pieces lock together, working in harmony. This is seen not only in obvious parts, like the posts and beams, but in every part. The apparent simplicity is actually a refined expertise.

Because the churches attracted the best skills available in a community, it is possible that certain shipbuilding methods were incorporated into these buildings. Indeed, the medieval period's expert understanding of wood is obvious in the Viking ships and sagas of shipbuilders, such as that of the man who built King Tryggvason's great ship in the years 995–1000. The builders of the Viking ships were the first to adopt sails in Europe's far northern regions, and the boats were a perfect marriage between form and function: their wide hulls provided purchase against a rough sea and the deep, masterly keels on these vessels allowed them to be rigged for tacking while their foes still sailed with the wind (fig. 4.52). Their functional shapes render them outstanding examples of technology, and the boats' details reflect extensive knowledge: the changing size of T-shaped keels from front to back accommodated the varying degrees of water pressure at each point along the keels' lengths; a thicker strake was placed precisely at the waterline where pressure was greatest.

Such precision is also apparent in the details of stave churches and thus Norway's medieval churches can be categorized with Viking ships. Both the churches and ships break the horizon, symbolize an important historical period, are distinguished by excellent construction techniques, and represent an artistic climax in Norway's use of wood. In discussing the churches, the architect Sverre Fehn compares their details to nautical handicrafts: the window circles of church buildings are cut out of the middle of a plank (like the oar holes on the Viking ships) rather than being half circles cut from two parallel edges of planks, which would have been a car-

Fig. 4.51. Post, ca. 1030, from Urnes Church, ca. 1130, Lusterfjord, Sogn. The rounded bottom of the gallery corner post resembles the mast of a ship and consists of casing around the column's base.

penter's solution (fig. 4.58). He even relates the column posts to a ship's mast, the beams to a boom.

These and other church details reflect a similar way of thinking, a similar way of putting things together in this medieval society. For example, the rounded bases at the bottom of early church columns resemble a Viking ship's mast, which was rounded at its base (fig. 4.51). The rounded form facilitated the erecting of the masts on the ships as the large posts could be rolled, rather than carried, into place. The wood carving and spherical form of column bases on churches were also reminiscent of rope coils or withes, which were entwined crosswise around the intersecting ends of the horizontal sills and the corner staves on buildings. After being tarred, this kind of knot would bind a corner together firmly. Descriptions from literature suggest that interlacing was common in Scandinavian architecture during the Viking age, although the binding was perishable and no remains exist.[17]

The famed quality of Viking ships also obviously influenced church builders' standards to a large degree. To what extent this occurred is impossible to determine, but it is evident that the dexterity of Norsemen with wood and their ability to manipulate strong natural forces affected the churches: they were erected with the same finesse that marked the ships. What certainly influenced the churches' unique expression was the highly refined wood carving that was an integral part of Viking culture and art forms.

The artistic and prolific wood carving on the churches is powerfully expressed, and it is easy to understand why early researchers used the exuberant carving for dating churches. But it was really the manipulation of the basic frame system, not the carving, that allowed master builders to merge artistic sensibilities with refined techniques. More than questions of plan and elevation, the details of the stave churches, the way in which their members were shaped and joined, were responsible for the total architectural expression of these buildings.

Shaping and Joining

Obviously, many initial considerations determined the shapes that made up a stave church and these helped preserve the long life of the wooden building. Great care was taken in selecting the trees to be used in church construction. The finest woods were always chosen for important structural members, specifically, the stave and corner columns, and were well seasoned. Long tree trunks were chosen for the staves, and before being felled, their tops were removed. The outer sapwood was scraped off, and the trunks were left standing for five to eight years. The trees died gradually, and the remaining heartwood became impregnated with its own resin— hence the relatively few cracks found today in the churches' main members. In general, the staves, wall planks, and other structural components were hewn from Scotch pine, an abundant species in Norway. The wood for many of the curved brackets was from a species of birch, and that used for many of the pins and other connectors was a common juniper, a dense softwood.[18] Norwegian folktales sometimes even mention master builders who planted groves of pine trees specifically for use in constructing their churches.

Although the builder's art is not well documented, the church builders were clearly extraordinary craftsmen. Evidence suggests that traveling craftsmen and church-building specialists existed in the Middle Ages. Certainly the churches' grand door portals were created by master craftsmen. The church builders might have been specialized craftsmen who worked on commission. Yet, it is impossible to say definitely whether a master builder traveled around with a team—a kind of itinerant builder's lodge—or was presented with his craftsmen at the building site.[19]

Specialized or not, the significant amount of preparation given to wood is evident in the final forms of these ancient buildings. In addition to the prolonged seasoning of wood, the size of the churches' main structural members has contributed to their longevity. Staves as tall as eleven meters (thirty-six feet) can be found with diameters of thirty to forty centimeters (twelve to sixteen inches). Foundation beams are approximately thirty by forty centimeters (twelve by sixteen inches). Structural members were sized intuitively in those times, and it is not surprising to learn that these components were stressed at very low levels, which enabled them to function for so long. The stave poles themselves only use approximately one-tenth of their potential capacities to resist stress. Larger wooden members also took time to burn through; thus, a stave church might survive a fire without structural collapse and require only secondary-member replacement.[20]

The life of a church began with such timbers which were cut in the forest and transported, a few years later, to the building site in almost finished form. Planks and beams were hewn directly from the tree trunks. The planks were normally formed by splitting the trunk into two halves, which were then trimmed or planed. The arches and other curved supports were formed from the intersection of the roots and stem of a tree, which had grown naturally into curved shapes, a further explanation for the structures' durability. The longer pieces of bent wood, such as the nave's quadrant arches, were made out of several pieces, so precisely joined that even today it is difficult to detect the connection points. All the pieces of a wall were skillfully put together in a systematic order and, sometimes, whole sections of walls were joined prior to being carefully hoisted into place (fig. 4.53).

In contrast to this superior craftsmanship and the large size of church elements, the builders' tools were simple: the common ax, the chisel, the plane, the auger, and the knife. It is unlikely that builders used saws (although they were known)

Fig. 4.53. A hypothetical version of the construction of a stave church.

either because of the dearth of metal and/or because of the tool's insensitive nature. Such simple tools, combined with their skillful handling, preserved the quality of wood, which is inherent in the structure of a stave church. Today, this quality can still be sensed and it is most apparent in a church's primary members.

Naturally, the shaping of important structural components received the most attention in a church's final building form. If the structure of a church is a system of frames consisting primarily of stave members, then this should be discernible in its details. One can examine the basic constructive frame, both its vertical and horizontal components, and see how the significant elements developed, how they were made, to articulate the experience of a building.

The most important members of a stave church are its vertical posts. If the exterior corner posts in early eleventh-century churches are examined, the tops of the exterior columns usually reveal little or no evidence of a capital—the diameter of its wood shaft was large enough to hold the upper two framing beams. In contrast, the bases are usually thick, heavy, and semirounded (sometimes with diameters as large as one meter) since they had to clamp over and join the large sill beams that held the structure off the ground, as in Urnes and Holtålen churches. These bases stabilized any eccentric, or unsymmetrical, forces and their shapes expressed their constructive function. Because the function of exterior corner posts became less significant in twelfth-century churches, as interior posts were added, the bases of some later columns were not as large, though they were still larger than their shafts so that the sill plates could be clamped together.

It was probably difficult to find pine trees with such generous diameters, even in Norway. The largest bases actually consisted of a protective casing that enveloped the column bases, and it appears the casings were later removed when exterior galleries were constructed. This casing protected the vertical fibers of wood that would have been exposed to rain when the tree's larger base was carved in toward the post's slimmer shaft. This would have caused fissures, or wood splitting along the grain, on an important structural member. At Kaupanger Church, evidence reveals that such casing even extended around the entire church, over its sills and wall planks, where climatic exposure was also critical.[21] The preserved casing at Urnes Church provides the best example of the covering's durability (fig. 4.51).

If one were to look at the cross sections of the various columns in a later, twelfth-century church, the exterior posts in the galleries and the four corner posts of the central nave generally remained circular (they were joined to the frame in two directions). In contrast, the interior freestanding posts were sometimes oval in cross section (they were joined to the frame in only one direction). In fact, in these later churches, above the *bressummer*, the freestanding posts are almost rectangular in cross section. The oval shape is best seen in Kaupanger Church, in which the tall staves extended to the top of the raised clerestory, carrying the roof (figs. 4.56, 4.57, 4.58). These separated the aisles from the nave and were the most significant framing elements, connecting the ground beams to the central roof structure. Such significant members would logically engage the builders' attention, and as a result, different shapes and details for stave posts evolved.

In comparing naves and the form of their posts, it is best to study churches of a similar type, such as Urnes and Kaupanger, both of which have long-naved halls (fig. 4.59). Each church has its own definite characteristics, but they both represent the salient features of the building type associated with the Sognefjord region.

In Urnes the posts have bases and Norman capitals on their lower section,

Fig. 4.54. Holtålen Church, ca. 1050, from Gauldalen, Trøndelag, now at the Trøndelag Folk Museum, Trondheim. The ground sill's shape can be discerned in its exposed section in the column bases. The upper and lower members of the upper wall plate (a double beam) can be seen housed above in the nave's corner column.

Fig. 4.55. The corner post of Torpo Church has a smaller base than older churches, ca. 1150–1175, Ål, Hallingdal.

4.56

Fig. 4.56. Interior nave of Kaupanger Church, ca. 1190, Kaupanger, Sogn. The tall staves lack the fully developed triforium found in other churches, but the pure vertical expression of the columns is not matched by any other church, as they continue uninterrupted from the floor to the ceiling of the church.

4.57

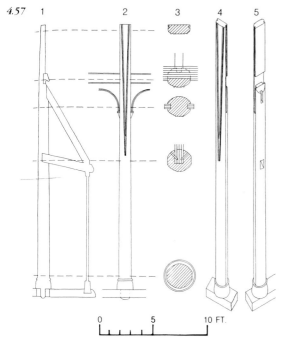

0   5   10 FT.

Fig. 4.57. Detail of an intermediate post from the nave of Kaupanger Church: 1—vertical section through the post and the aisle; 2—nave elevation; 3—cross sections through the post; 4 and 5—isometric perspectives of the post.

Fig. 4.58. Flattened upper part of the columns in Kaupanger Church. The ceiling was added in the seventeenth century, but the wall planks still illustrate how window ports were usually cut from the middle of a plank, like the oar holes of Viking ships. The simple clerestory shows the quadrant brackets, bressummer, and carved splay.

4.58

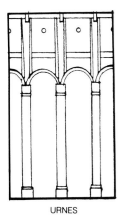

URNES

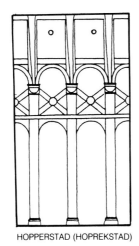

HOPPERSTAD (HOPREKSTAD)

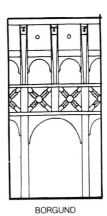

BORGUND

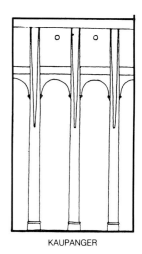

KAUPANGER

Fig. 4.59. A comparison of nave elevations from churches in the Sognefjord region.

Fig. 4.60. Interior columns of Urnes Church, ca. 1130, Lusterfjord, Sogn. With sixteen interior freestanding posts, the church's nave has a longitudinal configuration; its elements recall Romanesque stone architecture.

probably a stylistic influence from stone ornamentation or perhaps an influence from early round-bottomed posts (fig. 4.60). But although capitals are unusual features for a stave post, Urnes' capitals properly carry arched quadrant brackets, lending the configuration an almost Romanesque feeling. The posts continue to the ceiling, becoming oval, then flatten into rectangular shapes as they frame the upper stave members in the clerestory. It should be noted that the cube form of the capital was ill suited to round timber. The cube often had its projecting corners nailed onto the round post behind it. As a result, the Norwegian cylinder capital developed and was used in later churches, as in Lomen Church (fig. 3.64).

In contrast to capitals, the cylindrical bases of staves are a natural form for wood, as the broadening of the post at this point was the logical result of a tree being larger at its bottom. The carved band between the base and shaft also reveals an innate feel for the essential character of wood as it highlights the important transition a wood-carver made when he curved his base inward to meet the column's slender shaft.

The pure expression of Kaupanger's posts is different than that found at Urnes. The unbroken line of its posts from floor to roof is Kaupanger's most distinguishing characteristic and it reveals accurately the masts' function in the building system. The church is one of the best preserved constructionally, and although it is the only remaining building with such columns, it can be assumed these posts were a typical feature of the region, given their similarity to the posts of Urnes and Borgund churches.

Kaupanger's interior posts had only bases, and each post continued to the clerestory in an oval shape. The longer axis of the oval offset the operative moment forces as the ellipse's long dimension was in the longitudinal direction of the posts. Above the *bressummer*, if one were to look at its cross section, the post continued to the ceiling in a rectangular shape. In contrast to Urnes, the arched brackets in Kaupanger were grooved into the posts to offset racking movement; consequently, they had no capitals, giving them a Gothic appearance. The tops of the posts were flattened to join the upper wall plate, and a small bracket approximately fifteen centimeters (six inches) long, now gone, formed the transition to the roof.

The slender staves convey a truly vertical expression, which is further enhanced by the carved splays on their faces—the dominant feature of Kaupanger's columns. The splays have a simple, triangular geometry, with their bases at the wall plates, and point downward, extending halfway down the post. They are emphasized with delicate molding, and according to Kristian Bjerknes, a stave-church historian, "The splay has the specific intention of performing a beautiful transition between the post and horizontal wall plate: it leads the eye upward to the roof and the vertical impression is uninterrupted by horizontal elements. Seen in a general context, the post, its splay, and the roof rafters all accentuate the vertical effect of the nave."[22]

The splays illustrate how the builders used wood carving to emphasize a structural function, how this particular function provided a basis for a shape's ornamental quality. An ornamental shape reveals a true and unique situation, and in contrast to a purely decorative element, an ornament emphasizes this reality. In its deepest sense, if made well, an ornamental shape enhances truth and is the function itself. In this sense, the splays on Kaupanger's columns were functional elements that accentuated the workings of a specific structural system.

Such splays were a common feature of stave churches. But in churches where the staves are more elaborately connected to the horizontal elements, such as at Urnes, the splays are not as noticeable, and attention is drawn to the capitals, brackets,

Fig. 4.61. Carved wooden masks in Borgund Church, ca. 1150, near Lærdal, Sogn.

and crossbeams instead. In these churches, the splays were usually crowned with carved wooden faces to draw the eye upward. Excellent preserved examples of such carvings can be found at Gol and Borgund churches (figs. 4.61, 4.68). Some churches have these demonlike faces topping their masts; others do not, such as at Kaupanger where the original sculptures have since disappeared. Finishing the interior masts in such a manner certainly had symbolic value: it assured worshippers safety from evil spirits. The act was also a typical craftsman's gesture: it highlighted a very special junction in the building's structure. Where the important vertical staves ended and where they carried the horizontal wall plate on which the roof rested, the masks were carved and they marked this structural connection in the frame-type system. From this point, too, the tall, steep roof sprang and began its ascent to heaven.

In examining the horizontal shapes of a church's frame, one notes that they, too, were shaped for functional reasons, as can be seen at Holtålen Church (fig. 4.54). The sill beam's trapezoidal shape underscored its role—that of holding the planks—and its wide bottom allowed for ample contact with the rectangular raft beams. The wall plate clamped the planks at their tops; its otherwise simple shape might be specially carved in the portions that extended beyond the corner posts. However, inside, where a rectangular shape would have sufficed, the builders sloped the plate's face from its base upward and outward to the roof members to emphasize the nave's vertical effect. On the interior of twelfth-century, clerestory stave churches, the additional wall plates in the nave were given an angled cut and shim to provide better support for the roof rafters and quadrant brackets. Also on these later churches, as in Borgund Church, the important *bressummer* was clearly shaped for its function. The slanting exterior surface shed water, and in addition to weep holes, it contained a regletlike drip to support the roof planks and deflect moisture.

The shape of the bracketing devices, more than that of any other members,

Figs. 4.62–4.64.
Quadrant brackets from
Kaupanger Church, ca.
1190, Kaupanger, Sogn.
The brackets are placed:
fig. 4.62—vertically
between posts; fig. 4.63—
horizontally between
aisle rafters; fig. 4.64—at
a corner column.

gave the stave church its animistic sense of living nature, illuminating its frame system as a skeletal network of tendons and connective tissue. These arched elements were structurally joined to the frame, bracing it in all planes: vertically, between posts; horizontally, between aisle struts and at aisle corners; and between the central roof trusses.

The arched shape was purely functional, as the longer section of wood was needed where racking was heaviest, where the bracket met the column, strut, or truss. Given the frame-type structure of the churches, the arched form of these elements was natural. But in order to emphasize their important role, the builders accented the brackets' character even further, outlining their geometrical shapes with ornamental grooves, which sometimes ended in small organic or animistic carvings, as can be found at Gol Church, for example (figs. 4.67, 4.68, 4.69). These grooves are found on most of the secondary, and sometimes primary, framing members and even in the upper, dark reaches of the roof trusses. Hidden from view, the delicate relief is carried from the quadrant bracket onto the trusses' interior struts and from there to the collar beam. Thus, there was a definite purpose behind the carver's knife; there existed an operative idea of beauty. As in the carved splays on the columns, a shape's functional geometry was emphasized and its function became the ornament.

In Norway this chiseling was done with a tool called a *geitsfuss*, meaning "goat's foot" (a reference to the shape of the tool, which resembled the animal's cloven hooves). Applied parallel to the grain of the wood, the *geitsfuss* produced a double-line relief that visually accented individual building members as distinct entities while at the same time giving them a refined, integrated appearance. The same tool was used on Norway's log buildings and on the strakes of the Viking ships where the edgework served similar ornamental purposes.

The Saint Andrew's crosses found in many of the twelfth- and thirteenth-century churches were also a focal point for the woodworker's knife (fig. 4.70). Organic carvings on some of the crosses and geometric patterns on others reveal that they were always given special attention. Since they were, in most churches, the only diagonal other than the arches in the system, their articulation emphasized their different role. Although the cross's structural contribution has been disputed, its distinctiveness illuminated the forces operative in a frame system.

The configuration of the roof truss and the shaping and carving of its individual

Fig. 4.65, 4.66. Geitsfuss carving on an aisle strut and quadrant bracket in Kaupanger Church. The quadrant bracket strengthens the connection between aisle strut and wall plate and it is difficult to see where one starts and the other ends. At the nave post, the bracket ends in a slight curve, achieving an ornamental effect.

4.67

4.69

Fig. 4.67. Interior of Gol
Church, ca. 1170, from
Gol, Hallingdal, now at
the Norwegian Folk
Museum, Oslo. The
church's constructive
elements have been
articulated with
geitsfuss.

Fig. 4.68. The dark
ceiling of Gol Church
was emphasized with
carving on all its
important members; the
collar beam was also
given a distinct shape to
mark its significant
function.

Fig. 4.69. Ends of two
quadrant brackets in
Gol Church, one of
them featuring a
carved animal head.

Fig. 4.70. Saint Andrew's crosses in Lomen Church, ca. 1175, Vestre Slidres, Valdres.

members also reveals an ornamental expression. An assembly found in many old European wood buildings was the German truss, or scissor truss, consisting of two diagonal rafters, two diagonal interior struts (the "scissors"), and a vertical member, which connected the two diagonal systems. Truss design was not formalized until the beginning of the sixteenth century, and before that time local solutions to engineering problems were worked out by trial and error. The steep roof assembly of rafters, scissor braces, and collar beams in a stave church resembled an orthodox truss structure but did not function like one.

In the scissor braces of a stave-church roof, the vertical member was conspicuously absent. In its place was a horizontal collar beam, the function of which was to connect the rafters and scissor braces. As a result, the brace did not operate as an ideal truss; an analysis of the structure shows that many of the truss's beams were subject to bending forces in addition to tension and compression. The twelfth-century Norwegian builders did not construct an ideal truss because the collar beam served the important function of redistributing vertical forces in the assembly, thereby minimizing the horizontal forces delivered to the walls. If the collar beam had been absent, the tops of the walls could have been pushed apart under a heavy snow load.[23]

An integral part of the stave church's refined framing system, the important collar beam was naturally highlighted by the builders. In the few churches where the truss system can still be seen, this member is always distinguished by special shaping and carving. The lower edge is formed with an upward curve, accenting verticality, which merges into the scissor braces and follows the contour of the quadrant brackets so that all the elements become one final expressive form.

On top of the trusses, church builders added planking and wood shakes. The shingles' rough appearance was further enhanced by placing finely carved dragon heads on the gabled roofs. Much like those that adorned the prows of Viking ships, these dragon heads, rather than crosses, reveal the silhouette of a church. The heads are often larger and more dramatic than the crosses, which were placed on the lower roof tiers, and in the perception of medieval citizens, the ancient dragons wielded more power than traditional Christian icons in keeping away evil, even after Christianity itself was accepted.

The shaping of the wall planks between the main framing members reveals

many different forms from church to church, and by the twelfth century, these planks were no longer structural elements. As a result, much variety is apparent in their shapes—some have a tongue and groove for each plank, some only tongues or grooves, some are splined, some are rectangular, and early planks are half-round. The choice of a particular shape might be based on considerations of water drainage, stiffening, or perhaps a completed visual effect. Certain joints between planks were particularly susceptible to water penetration and were therefore not used. Conversely, some joints were stiffer and stronger than others for joining the wall planks together. Like other building elements in the churches, the planking was embellished on the exterior with exceptionally fine grooved chiseling along its edges (fig. 4.71). The result of such careful detailing is noted by Kristian Bjerknes: "The chiseling is most evident when the sun shines on the wall planks. Each plank casts a shadow on the next, revealing the shape of the planks and giving life to the chisel grooves."[24] Often the sills and wall plates had similar grooves that achieved the same effect. In contrast, the wall planks were smooth on their dark interiors to provide a neutral background for the altar and nave posts and perhaps to emphasize the elaborate roof construction.

The individual components of a stave church were just as carefully joined as they were shaped. As in the log buildings, the shapes of the basic members differ from church to church, while the types of joints remain relatively consistent. In fact, it was such exacting joinery that enabled the buildings to work so well. In view of the simple tools at the builders' disposal, such joinery is particularly impressive.

The foundation beams were joined at their intersecting corners by mortises or meshing notches. In order to connect the foundation beams to the stave posts, builders projected tenons from the bases of the posts, which fit into accompanying mortises in the beams; these strong tenons extended completely through the beams and the joint was well wedged from pressure above. At the joint between intersecting foundation beams, these tenons also strengthened the beams' meshing notch.

The overhanging outer ends of the foundation beams were notched to accommodate the sill beams. The joinery between sill and foundation rafter was quite precise and reflected careful planning of the junctions between important constructive parts. The "slot" mortise and tenon was used for this connection. A portion of the sill's base was removed at the point at which it sank into the notch of the raft beam. This provided solid surface contact between the two members and prevented the sill from moving lengthwise and crosswise in addition to preventing it from twisting.[25] Where the sill plates came together at right angles, they were solidly connected by a joint resembling the head-log joint in log construction. Each sill had a neck and shoulder that fit into the neck and shoulder of the intersecting sill, and their wide bases reinforced a strong connection.

At the top of the masts, the wall plate was placed. Both the wall plate and the sill beam were mortised to accept the tenons that projected from the top and bottom of each wall plank. The exterior corner posts clamped the beams together above and below in a huge double-forked mortise joint, which held the basic framework together.

Inside the churches, the vertical quadrant brackets between staves each consisted of an arched horizontal lintel and two vertical brackets. The brackets and lintels were tongued into stave posts—the long tongues prevented racking—and were reinforced with wooden pegs. In certain instances, however, the arched lintel penetrated completely through a stave post rather than tonguing into it. In Kaupanger's western nave wall, for example, a lower arched bracket defined the nave's entrance between the staves and supported a truncated stave post that extended to the roof. Where the half post met the higher row of main quadrant brackets, the arched lintel extended completely through the column, thereby reducing the pressure on the lower quadrant bracket.[26]

In most churches, the lintels and Saint Andrew's crosses were fastened to horizontal beams by round wood pegs about twenty-five millimeters (one inch) in diameter. Some of the pegs were held by enlarged heads, but in many instances, they were fixed in place by a wooden wedge driven into their outer ends.[27]

The generous depth of the joint between *bressummer* and stave post indicated its importance and the connection was indeed one of the most intricate details of stave-church construction (fig. 4.72). The *bressummer* was the point at which the aisle rafters met the columns; it supported the clerestory walls; and it braced the nave longitudinally. Naturally, this member was placed deeply into the post. The *bressummer* also had a notch cut out of its width for gripping the post, which prevented the element from moving longitudinally. In addition, mortises for the wall planks on both stave post and *bressummer* were precisely aligned. At intersecting corners, the *bressummers* were solidly inserted into the corner columns and met inside the columns at right angles. This connection in particular demonstrates how the junctions of all a stave church's constructive elements were carefully worked out, and their dependency on each other mandated that there was a prescribed order in which all the intricate pieces were put together.

While the types of joinery used to connect wood members in the stave churches were common for frame buildings in medieval times, their precision was extraordinary. In some parts of the churches, it is only because of accurate joinery that the frame system works. A significant example is the capacity of a church's cross section

Fig. 4.71. Øye Church, ca. 1175–1200, Øye, Valdres. The triangular notches on the ground sill are drain holes; fine geitsfuss *grooving marks the wall planks and sill beam.*

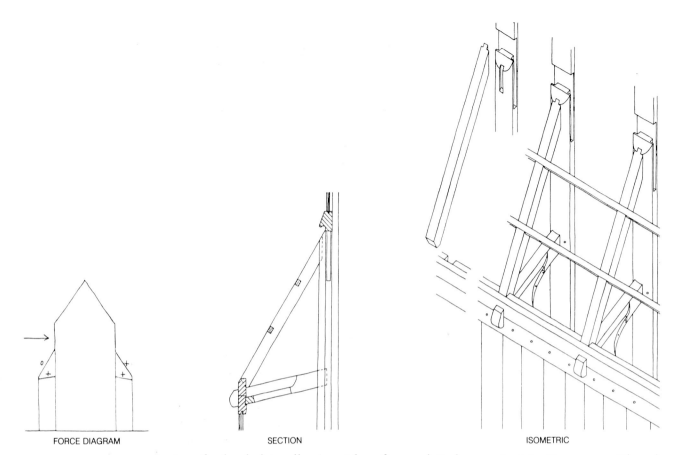

FORCE DIAGRAM   SECTION   ISOMETRIC

Fig. 4.72. Diagrams of aisle rafters and struts inserted into the wall plate and nave posts in Kaupanger Church, ca. 1190, Kaupanger, Sogn. The bressummer *was inserted into the nave posts above the aisle rafters and the quadrant brackets were mortised into the posts below it.*

to transfer loads laterally. An aisle rafter and its lower strut in Kaupanger Church illustrate the typical configuration of this detail (fig. 4.72). The aisle rafter was merely set between the wall plate (or the aisle wall's upper sill plate) and the post, not fastened. One end of the aisle strut, however, was firmly secured to the wall plate in a locking joint that had neck and shoulders similar to those used in log construction, while its other end was driven deeply into the post; both ends were secured with pegs.

If one pictures the church in its short cross section with a gust of wind blowing against its north nave wall, one sees how the joints work in resisting lateral forces: the rafter on the left side will have no significance—it has no tensile strength; the rafter to the right will withstand the pressure; but both aisle struts will come into play, tension on the left side, compression on the right.[28] It is evident, then, that the aisle strut has the most significance for the stability of the church, and its joinery is critical for a church's overall structural integrity.

Only if the grooving, notching, and shaping of all the connecting members in a church were accurate would the vertical and horizontal forces be transferred efficiently with no distress to the building. But the master builders had other forces to contend with. The natural drying and shrinking of wood in Norway's moist climate could have distorted the fibers of the wood and destroyed any kind of precision achieved through joinery. For example, along the *bressummer* and the outside of the sill beam the potential for rotting is great. Water runs down the wall planks until it is stopped by these horizontal beams, where it collects and penetrates the joint in which the planks rest. To counteract this problem, builders made small drainage holes at intervals of a few meters along the *bressummers* and sill beams to permit the water to escape (fig. 4.71). This is one of the weak points of a church's construction as the beams were constantly exposed to varying degrees of moisture, and sill beams in some churches show signs of continuous repair. Although this detail was not original to Norwegian sill techniques, the church builders used it wisely. Today, one is astonished to find the majority of original sill beams free from decay.

Other factors naturally contributed to the buildings' survival in this harsh landscape. Wood to be used in church building was always cut so that the grain ran in its most logical direction; thus all structural members were used in their most efficient capacities. Most significant, the wood was always properly seasoned and tarred. Perhaps it is because climatic forces in Norway are so severe that the churches were built so well. Paying attention to small, but important, details, builders assured their churches a longevity that even today one can hardly expect with wood.

Portals and Motifs

A common reaction to confronting a stave church's entrance portal for the first time is to step backward, unsure of whether the wriggling dragons carved everywhere beckon welcome or scream warning. As Dan Lindholm and Walther Roggenkamp describe the experience, "Anyone who enters a stave church has to face, for a moment, the turmoil of animal qualities hidden deep in man's being."[29]

In any church, the doorway represents a junction between two worlds. Norway's medieval structures were no exception. The door illustrates the apex of the Norwegian wood-carver's skill and one of the most important elements of the church, artistically as well as symbolically. Through the door, man enters a holy house to commune with God, leaving the everyday world behind. Although these masterpieces were built only of perishable wood, they are comparable to the finest medieval stone entrances.

The Norwegian stave-church door is probably the high point of this period's artistic sensibility. The specialists who executed these doors between 1050 and 1350 were obviously gifted in portraying their world—all its icons with a range of symbolic meanings can be found on the portals. The best wood-carvers were contracted by master builders to create portals for each church, and these men probably came from cultural centers or from the few cities such as Oslo, Bergen, or Trondheim that existed at the time.

Structurally, the portals consisted of vertical planks, slightly thicker than the typical wallboards, with the sill plate housed into them at the bottom and the wall staves tenoned to their sides. Often, wooden dowels reinforced the connection between the sill and heavy portal staves. A horizontal arched plank rested on their tops. The portals were not a difficult structural or technical problem in stave construction. Rather, their task was to convey a message. On the back of a few preserved portals, preliminary carvings can be seen where the master worked out the general outline of his animistic symbols; it was their story that was most important. The use of animal motifs to convey a Christian warning had, in fact, pre-Christian roots.

Complex pagan motifs originating in Nordic art were the starting point for the development of portal carving in Norway. According to Peter Anker, the aesthetic principle of this art was ornamental and abstract, using animal imagery to convey magical intentions. Characterized by an asymmetrical linear rhythm, such ornamentation was a subjective expression that suggested spiritual powers were present

in the animals. In contrast, classical Christian art was representational—it usually depicted divine or saintly individuals—and rational: divine truth appeared in human, objective forms.[30]

From the first animal motifs in the fifth century, Nordic art displays an unbroken continuity until the early thirteenth century. The art can be divided into two periods: an early heathen period and another that arose with the influx of styles that occurred when Christianity was introduced. Consequently, the tradition from pagan times was uninterrupted until the arrival of Gothic art toward the end of the twelfth century.[31] The sources of pagan art are found in busts of coins from the Roman empire, which were translated into Germanic animal heads and geometric patterns. The art is marked by a distinct absence of plant ornamentation and developed throughout Scandinavia prior to the advent of the Viking period.

The climax of the first rich artistic period was revealed with the discovery of the Oseberg Viking Ship in 1904 (fig. 4.73). On the keel of Queen Oseberg's ship (ca. 850–900) is a gripping beast with a large head that was the inspiration for the animal motifs found on the later church portals. On the boat, the beast is depicted in a frieze, rhythmically alternating with the tail of one beast in the mouth of the next.

The second period in Nordic art corresponded to the rise of the Romanesque style in western Europe and was a confrontation between Viking and Christian traditions. In the Middle Ages, the ancient Norse poetry of the skalds, with its powerful worm-and-dragon imagery, was a living tradition. Merging with the Romanesque lion idiom and with motifs from stone architecture, this imagery developed into a folk art that thrived for another 400 years.[32] The final synthesis was expressed in the craft of stave-church portal carving.

The earliest door decorated solely with animal motifs is from the first church at Urnes and dates from approximately 1030–1060 (fig. 4.74). (There were two, possibly three churches built on the same site at Urnes: the first known one dates from about 1030; the second and extant one, is from approximately 1130; there

may also have been a third, earlier church on the site, but this has yet to be determined.) Known as the Urnes, or Stave Church, style, the wood carving on this door represents the last vestiges of true Viking art. In this style, the gripping beast from the Viking ship had been transformed into three different animals with heads and limbs: a quadruped or great lion; a serpentine animal with one foreleg; and a ribbonlike serpent with no legs. The animals were usually portrayed with long intertwined tendrils representing either limbs or snakes, typically in deep relief, and configured in scroll or figure-eight patterns. As an art form, the style spread westward, and in Ireland, by 1123, for example, instances of this type of ornamentation were found everywhere. Yet, because of its overt heathen symbolism, clerical authorities in Norway relegated the portal, and its animal carving style, to the church's north wall in the second half of the eleventh century and may even have tried to stifle the craft of portal carving completely. At about the same time, the custom of decorating the outside walls also vanished. Soon after, it was only in the patterns of the main western portals that the development of the dragon motif, with vinelike tendrils—a feature of all later Norwegian stave churches—could be traced.

Although it is difficult to establish an artistic style chronologically, the idiom of the scrolled beast or dragon here provides a tool for dating Viking art's Christian transformation in the portal carvings. The great beast, with its scrolls, on the first main portal at Urnes marks the last pure animal carving found on the stave churches before it gave way to writhing animals and vines of Christian content and finally disintegrated into geometric and organic forms. On church portals that were crafted after the first Urnes Church portal, the pagan animal images were reinterpreted and transformed into dragon-and-tendril styles. The exact dating of the styles that were generated in portal carving in the twelfth and thirteenth centuries is difficult to ascertain, however, the imprecise concept of "older" and "younger" carvings enables one to follow a craftsman's motif through stages of its development. Typically, for example, a lower-quality motif implies either an early and formative or late and degenerative stage within a particular style.

Fig. 4.74. The original portal, ca. 1030, of Urnes Church, Lusterfjord, Sogn, which is now on the north wall, marks the end of Viking art and the beginning of the Stave Church style in Norwegian art.

Portal carving was reestablished as an acceptable craft by the church probably sometime in the late eleventh or early twelfth century. Initially, this wood carving was mixed with influences from Romanesque stone architecture. Portals were adorned with capitals, archivolts, and half-columns. One of these earlier styles, known as the Archaic type, is distinguished by a minimal amount of animal carving. The door found on Holtålen Church is a good illustration of the type (fig. 4.75).

Perhaps because church authorities recognized that pagan motifs were still powerful, and perhaps because the mythological characters were popular among craftsmen, later portal carving in the twelfth century reinstated animal imagery once again. In an era when ancient Norse poetry was still alive and based on pagan myths, Viking symbols—imbued with magic—were familiar to most Scandinavians and exerted a strong hold, even after the supremacy of the Christian church had been established. Privately, Norwegians still adhered to the legends and imagery of the fading mythology.[33] The clergy understood this and gave the Nordic images a place on the churches. The popular craft of animistic carving continued because the church redefined the power and tenacity of pre-Christian forms. The pagan legends were reinterpreted in Christian terms: for example, the fight between a Romanesque lion and dragon serpents became Christ's battle with evil; or the great beast represented the Lion of Judah, a symbol of Christ.

The twelfth-century church portals skillfully blended Romanesque features with such native idioms and it was the traditional craft of wood carving that provided the continuity for carrying on ancient themes although beliefs had, by then, changed. This return to animal imagery first manifests itself in the Sognefjord type portals.

In the Older Sognefjord type represented by the Ål and Hedal church portals, two beasts at the bottom of each portal, above a palmette, spew vines that terminate in Byzantine blossoms (figs. 4.76, 4.77, 4.79). As one follows the deep relief-carving upward in this type of portal, one sees that it covers the flanking columns and becomes the tendrils of two dragons with wings. On the upper half of the door and from each side, these winged snakelike creatures attack a smaller, central dragon whose head protrudes into the door space. The small dragon almost completely covers the door's archivolt. On the Ål portal two Romanesque lions grace the column capitals, defying evil to enter such a structure. The vines, the wings, and the lions were all Romanesque motifs integrated into the native style of scrolled and intertwined animal carving.

The Younger Sognefjord type is typified by the portal of Borgund Church (figs. 4.78, 4.80). The style has all the elements of the Older type except that the carving is in lower relief and is confined to the columns; the archivolt is separated totally from the struggle of the three dragons. The central dragon no longer penetrates the doorway with its head, and the winged animals seem less graceful—they are more constricted in the overall composition of the portal and are not as well-formed as the Older Sognefjord dragons. The plant motifs appear to have overpowered the animal icons, as exemplified in the portal at Torpo Church (fig. 4.9).

A few later, twelfth- and thirteenth-century portals include carved narratives of popular myths. The first known example is from Hyllestad Church in Setesdal from about the middle of the thirteenth century. Events from moral tales such as "Sigurd Slaying the Dragon" are carved in medallionlike frames and portrayed in sequence. These Figure-type portals are more Christian in character, employing human representations rather than the ancient creatures.

The last stage of portal development is illustrated by the Degenerate type, which is represented at Lom Church (fig. 4.81). This style does not follow the pattern of

Fig. 4.75. The portal of Holtålen Church, ca. 1050, from Gauldalen, Trøndelag, now at the Trøndelag Folk Museum, Trondheim, is an example of the Archaic type.

Fig. 4.76. Drawing of the existing portal at Hedal Church, ca. 1175, Hedalen, Valdres, an Older Sognefjord type showing a small central dragon above the portal being attacked by beasts on both sides.

4.77

Fig. 4.77. Portal from Ål
Church, ca. 1150, from
Ål, Hallingdal,
illustrating the Older
Sognefjord type. The
lions atop the columns
are motifs adapted
directly from
Romanesque influences;
the columns resemble
similar stone structures.
The church no longer
exists but this portal is
now at the History
Museum, Oslo.

Fig. 4.78. Portal from
Borgund Church, ca.
1150, near Lærdal, Sogn,
illustrating the Younger
Sognefjord type.

4.78

4.79

Fig. 4.79. Detail from the
portal of Ål Church. The
snake-like head of a
pagan creature is
framed between two
Romanesque lions.

Fig. 4.80. Detail from the
portal of Borgund
Church, showing the
ancient, intertwined
wood-carving style.

4.80

the typical dragon doorways: some of these portals are narrative, some are symmetrical, most use primarily plant motifs, and none are carved on their flanking staves. The portals usually consist only of half-columns with capitals and an archivolt. Not many portals of the type are preserved, probably because they were not built as well in this last period of stave-church construction.

In looking at the elaborate doors of the stave churches, one should bear in mind that the few portals existing today undoubtedly represent the best of their time, as the minor portals were probably destroyed. Therefore, they cannot be regarded as typical. In spite of uncertain dates, the mature, fully developed Norwegian stave-church portals, such as that of Ål Church, provide an instructive lesson on the strength of the ancient Nordic motifs: their ability to survive, adapting themselves completely to the peaceful conditions—in contrast to their turbulent Viking origins—of Christian society.[34]

In their symbolism, their well-composed and rhythmic motifs, and their skillful execution, the portals achieved a rare elegance. Their artistic expression represents a certain time in a specific place. The portals reveal a medieval perception just as other church details reveal other aspects of a specifically Norwegian world. It is evident that for the master builders, technical problems were the easiest to resolve—were, in fact, only a means to an end. The exemplary building method represented by the churches was based on continuous experience, a result of repetitive techniques and a conscious striving for improvement. Without such traditional procedures, the builders of the stave churches could not have created structures that functioned so well in this harsh climate. But without precise craftsmanship, the builders could not have created beautiful churches. And it is the craftsman's approach to building that truly distinguished these churches.

If viewed in this context, the Norwegians' building technology can be seen to express a deeper desire. The builders pursued criteria beyond structural soundness or functional efficiency. The details of a church, in fact, could have taken different and equally valid forms if these were the only goals. For instance, in the interior of the stave church, each part adapted its form from a constructive function. Nevertheless, it is important to note that function does not dominate a shape. Different shapes could have satisfied these functional demands, and this enabled a choice to be made when the question of form arose. This forces one to look not only at the constructive problems, but also at the choices of form: they reveal how individual forms were adapted to one another in order to obtain a greater effect of unity. The procedure was *techne*, achieved through *poiesis*.

This is most apparent in the use of minor constructive elements such as the Saint Andrew's crosses: sometimes they were carefully chiseled; other times they were poorly crafted or not used at all. It can also be seen in the use of capitals in some churches and their absence in others and it is particularly evident in the *geitsfuss* carvings, which emphasized the geometrical quality of important members. The choice of details, or the way they were made, express a craftsman's way of thinking.

For the master builders, ornament and function were similar means toward a common end. Using building skills as artists would, the builders emphasized a truth: by distinguishing significant parts of a church, as in a stave's oval shape, the craftsmen revealed a structure, a particular reality; by enhancing this reality, as in the stave's carved splay, they gave the churches life, a beautiful ornamental quality all their own.

Fig. 4.81. Original portal of Lom Church, now on the north transept, ca. 1150–1170, Lom, Gudbrandsdal, illustrating the Degenerate type.

Notes

1. INTRODUCTION

Headnote. John Brinckerhoff Jackson, *Discovering the Vernacular Landscape* (New Haven, Connecticut: Yale University Press, 1984), xii.

1. Christian Norberg-Schulz, *Architecture: Meaning and Place* (New York: Rizzoli, 1988), 108.
2. Peter Anker, *The Art of Scandinavia*, vol. 1 (London: Paul Hamlyn, 1970), 5.
3. Christian Norberg-Schulz, *Mellom Jord og Himmel* (Oslo: Universitetsforlaget, 1978), 82–84.
4. Christian Norberg-Schulz, *Genius Loci* (New York: Rizzoli, 1980), 23.
5. Peter Anker, *Folkekunst i Norge* (Oslo: J. W. Cappelens Forlag A/S, 1975), 15.
6. Peter Anker, *The Art of Scandinavia*, vol. 1 (London: Paul Hamlyn, 1970), 207.
7. Christian Norberg-Schulz, *Genius Loci* (New York: Rizzoli, 1980), 23.
8. Christopher Alexander, *A Timeless Way of Building* (New York: Oxford University Press, 1979), 65–74.
9. Ibid. 71–101.
10. Sōetsu Yanagi, *The Unknown Craftsmen: A Japanese Insight into Beauty* (Tokyo: Kodansha International Ltd., 1982), 111.
11. John Lobell, *Between Silence and Light: Spirit in the Architecture of Louis I. Kahn* (Boulder, Colorado: Shambhala Publications, 1979), 26.
12. Knut Hamsun, *Mysteries* (London: Picador Edition, Pan Books, 1976), 91, 92.

2. SITE

Headnote. Henrik Ibsen, "St. John's Night," in *The Oxford Ibsen*, vol. 1 (London: Oxford University Press, 1970), 3.

1. Christian Norberg-Schulz, *Genius Loci* (New York: Rizzoli, 1980), 18.
2. Spiro Kostof, *A History of Architecture, Settings and Rituals* (New York: Oxford University Press, 1985), 17.
3. Norberg-Schulz, op. cit., 42.
4. Amos Rapoport, *House, Form, and Culture* (Englewood Cliffs, New Jersey: Prentice-Hall, Inc., 1969), 83.
5. Henrik Ibsen, 'The Grouse in Justedal," in *The Oxford Ibsen*, vol. 1 (London: Oxford University Press, 1970), 431.
6. Christian Norberg-Schulz, *Mellom Jord og Himmel* (Oslo: Universitetsforlaget, 1978), 30, 31.

Farms

Headnote. Peter Anker and István Rácz, *Norsk Folkekunst* (Oslo: J. W. Cappelens Forlag A/S, 1975), 10.

7. Gunnar Bugge and Christian Norberg-Schulz, *Stav og Laft* (Oslo: Norske Arkitekters Landsforbund, 1969), 13.
8. P. Foote and D. Wilson, *The Viking Achievement* (London: University of London Press, 1980), 82.
9. Christian Norberg-Schulz, *Mellom Jord og Himmel* (Oslo: Universitetsforlaget, 1978), 42.
10. Rapoport, op. cit., 48.
11. Christian Norberg-Schulz, *Genius Loci* (New York: Rizzoli, 1980), 61.
12. Foote and Wilson, op. cit., 36.
13. Martin Heidegger, *Poetry, Language, Thought* (New York: Harper and Row, 1971), 150.

Churches

Headnote. Christian Norberg-Schulz, "Våre Stavkirker," *Byggekunst* 3 (1961): 11, 12.

14. Jon Børre Jahnsen, *Bygget av Levende Stene, Middelalderens Kirkelige Forhold i Valdres* (Aurdal, Norway: P. T. Dreyer, 1983).
15. Ibid., 61.
16. Peter Anker, *The Art of Scandinavia*, vol. 1 (London: Paul Hamlyn, 1970), 201.

3. BUILDINGS

Headnote. Christopher Alexander quoted in Stephen Grabow, *Christopher Alexander* (London: Oriel Press, 1983), 226.

1. Spiro Kostof, *A History of Architecture, Settings and Rituals* (New York: Oxford University Press, 1985), 35.
2. Christopher Alexander, *A Timeless Way of Building* (New York: Oxford University Press, 1979), 347.
3. Amos Rapoport, *House, Form, and Culture* (Englewood Cliffs, New Jersey: Prentice-Hall, Inc., 1969), 85.
4. Christian Norberg-Schulz, *Genius Loci* (New York: Rizzoli, 1980), 42.
5. Ibid., 69, 70.
6. Alexander, op. cit., 88, 89.

Farms

Headnote. Sōetsu Yanagi, *The Unknown Craftsmen: A Japanese Insight into Beauty* (Tokyo: Kodansha International Ltd., 1982), 198.

7. Gunnar Bugge and Christian Norberg-Schulz, *Stav og Laft* (Oslo: Norske Arkitekters Landsforbund, 1969), 9.
8. Ibid., 13.
9. Christian Norberg-Schulz, *Architecture: Meaning and Place* (New York: Rizzoli, 1988), 119.
10. Bugge and Norberg-Schulz, op. cit., 17.
11. Peter Anker and István Rácz, *Norsk Folkekunst* (Oslo: J. W. Cappelens Forlag A/S, 1975), 30.

12. Ibid., 82.

13. Christian Norberg-Schulz, *Mellom Jord og Himmel* (Oslo: Universitetsforlaget, 1978), 92.

14. Gaston Bachelard, *The Poetics of Space* (Boston: Beacon Press, 1969), 41.

15. Bjørn Myhre and Arne-Emil Christensen, "Laftehusets Opprinnelse og Eldste Historie," *Foreningen til Norske Fortidsminnesmerkers Bevaring* (1983): 165–172.

Churches

Headnote. Sverre Fehn quoted in Per Olaf Fjeld, *Sverre Fehn: The Thought of Construction* (New York: Rizzoli, 1983), 27.

16. Dan Lindholm and Walther Roggenkamp, *Stave Churches in Norway* (London: Rudolf Steiner Press, 1969), 47.

17. Peter Anker, *The Art of Scandinavia*, vol. 1 (London: Paul Hamlyn, 1970), 418.

18. Lindholm and Roggenkamp, op. cit., 47.

19. Anker, op. cit., 391.

20. Ibid., 394.

21. Bugge and Norberg-Schulz, op. cit., 23.

22. Anker, op. cit., 388.

23. Ibid., 390.

24. Ibid., 418.

25. Walter Horn, "On the Origins of the Medieval Bay System," *Journal of the Society of Architectural Historians* 17, no. 2: 2–23.

26. Anker, op. cit., 379.

27. Ibid., 378.

28. Ibid., 377, 378.

29. Petter Aune, Ronald L. Sack, and Arne Selberg, "The Stave Churches of Norway," *Scientific American* 249, no. 2: 102.

30. Lindholm and Roggenkamp, op. cit., 16.

31. Anker, op. cit., 380.

32. Ibid., 384.

33. Christian Norberg-Schulz, "Våre Stavkirker," *Byggekunst* 3 (1961): 12.

34. Jorge Luis Borges, *Den Nørrone Litteratur* (Oslo: J. W. Cappelens Forlag A/S, 1969), 25.

4. DETAILS

Headnote. Hassan Fathy, *Architecture for the Poor* (Chicago: University of Chicago Press, 1973), 19.

1. Amos Rapoport, *House, Form, and Culture* (Englewood Cliffs, New Jersey: Prentice-Hall, Inc., 1969), 4.

2. Christian Norberg-Schulz, *Genius Loci* (New York: Rizzoli, 1980), 180.

3. Rapoport, op. cit., 6.

4. Christian Norberg-Schulz, "Arkitekturornament," *Byggekunst* 5 (1965): 116.

5. Martin Heidegger, *Poetry, Language, Thought* (New York: Harper and Row, 1971), 159, 215.

Log Detailing

Headnote. Hermann Phleps, *The Craft of Log Building* (Ontario: Lee Valley Tools, Ltd., 1982), 23–27.

6. Knut Hamsun, *Victoria* (London: Souvenir Press Ltd., 1974), 4.

7. Hermann Phleps, *The Craft of Log Building* (Ontario: Lee Valley Tools, Ltd., 1982), 46.

8. Håkon Christie, *Middelalderen Bygger i Tre* (Oslo: Universitetsforlaget, 1974), 40.

9. Phleps, op. cit., 291.

10. Peter Anker and István Rácz, *Norsk Folkekunst* (Oslo: J. W. Cappelens Forlag A/S, 1975), 60.

11. Phleps, op. cit., 61.

12. Ibid., 227.

13. Ibid., 220.

14. Ibid., 166.

15. Ibid., 281.

16. Peter Anker, *Folkekunst i Norge* (Oslo: J. W. Cappelens Forlag A/S, 1975), 132.

Stave Detailing

Headnote. Sverre Fehn quoted in Per Olaf Fjeld, *Sverre Fehn: The Thought of Construction* (New York: Rizzoli, 1983), 46.

17. Anders Bugge, *Norske Stavkirker* (Oslo: Dreyers Forlag A/S, 1953), 16.

18. Petter Aune, Ronald L. Sack, and Arne Selberg, "The Stave Churches of Norway," *Scientific American* 249, no. 2: 103.

19. Hans Jürgen Hansen, et al., *Architecture in Wood* (New York: Viking Press, 1971), 42.

20. Aune, Sack, and Selberg, op. cit., 104.

21. Kristian Bjerknes and Hans-Emil Lidén, "The Stave Churches of Kaupanger," *Riksantikvaren Skrifter*, bulletin no. 1 (1975): 71.

22. Ibid., 61.

23. Aune, Sack, and Selberg, op. cit., 102.

24. Bjerknes and Lidén, op. cit., 84.

25. Ibid., 66.

26. Ibid., 101.

27. Aune, Sack, and Selberg, op. cit., 101.

28. Bjerknes and Lidén, op. cit., 96.

29. Dan Lindholm and Walther Roggenkamp, *Stave Churches in Norway* (London: Rudolf Steiner Press, 1969), 54.

30. Peter Anker, *The Art of Scandinavia*, vol. 1 (London: Paul Hamlyn, 1970), 5.

31. Ibid., 6.

32. Ibid., 418.

33. Lindholm and Roggenkamp, op. cit., 47.

34. Anker, op. cit., 394.

Bibliography

Alexander, Christopher. *A Timeless Way of Building*. New York: Oxford University Press, 1979.

————. "The Nature of Order." Unpublished manuscript, University of California, Berkeley, 1982.

Anker, Peter. *The Art of Scandinavia*, vol. 1. London: Paul Hamlyn, 1970.

————, and István Rácz. *Norsk Folkekunst*. Oslo: J. W. Cappelens Forlag A/S, 1975.

————. *Folkekunst i Norge*. Oslo: J. W. Cappelens Forlag A/S, 1975.

————. "Folkekunsten." In *Norges Kunsthistorie*, vol. 3, 317–428. Oslo: Gyldendal Norsk Forlag A/S, 1982.

Aune, Petter, Ronald L. Sack, and Arne Selberg. "The Stave Churches of Norway." *Scientific American* 249, no. 2: 96–105.

Bachelard, Gaston. *The Poetics of Space*. Boston: Beacon Press, 1969.

Berg, Arne. *Norske Gardstun*. Oslo: Universitetsforlaget, 1968.

Bjerknes, Kristian, and Hans-Emil Lidén. "The Stave Churches of Kaupanger." *Riksantikvarens Skrifter*, bulletin no. 1 (1975): entire issue, 155 pages.

Blindheim, Martin. *Norwegian Romanesque Decorative Sculpture, 1090–1210*. London: A. Tiranti, 1965.

Borges, Jorge Luis. *Den Norrøne Litteratur*. Oslo: J. W. Cappelens Forlag A/S, 1969.

Brochmann, Odd. *Bygget i Norge*, vol. 1. Oslo: Gyldendal Norsk Forlag, 1979.

Bugge, Anders. *Norske Stavkirker*. Oslo: Dreyers Forlag A/S, 1953.

Bugge, Gunnar. *Stave Churches in Norway*. Oslo: Dreyers Forlag A/S, 1983.

————, and Christian Norberg-Schulz. *Stav og Laft*. Oslo: Norske Arkitekters Landsforbund, 1969.

Christie, Håkon. "Urnes Stavkirke Forløper Belyst ved Utgravninger under Kirken." *Foreningen til Norske Fortidsminnesmerkers Bevaring* (1958): 49–74.

————. *Stavkirkene i Bygningshistorisk Sammenheng*. Reykjavik: National Museum of Iceland, 1970.

————. *Middelalderen Bygger i Tre*. Oslo: Universitetsforlaget, 1974.

————. "Nes Stavkirke." *Riksantikvarens Skrifter*, bulletin no. 3 (1979): entire issue, 111 pages.

————. "Stavkirkene-Arkitektur." In *Norges Kunsthistorie*, vol. 1, 139–251. Oslo: Gyldendal Norsk Forlag A/S, 1981.

Dietrichson, Lorentz. *De Norske Stavkirker*. Kristiania (Oslo) and Copenhagen: Alb. Cammermeyers Forlag, 1892.

————, and H. Munthe. *Die Holzbaukunst Norwegens*. 1893. Reprint. Hannover, West Germany: Th. Schäfer Gmbh, Edition Libri Rari.

Eliade, Mircea. *The Sacred and Profane*. New York: Harcourt, Brace, and World, Inc., 1959.

Erixon, Sigurd. *Svensk Byggnadskultur*. 1947. Reprint. Lund, Sweden: Ekstrand, 1982.

Fathy, Hassan. *Architecture for the Poor*. Chicago: University of Chicago Press, 1973.

Fjeld, Per Olaf. *Sverre Fehn, The Thought of Construction*. New York: Rizzoli, 1983.

Foote, P., and D. Wilson. *The Viking Achievement*. London: University of London Press, 1980.

Fuglesang, Signe Horn. "Vikingtidens Kunst." In *Norges Kunsthistorie*, vol. 1, 36–138. Oslo: Gyldendal Norsk Forlag A/S, 1981.

Futagawa, Yukio, Christian Norberg-Schulz, and Makoto Suzuki. *Wooden Houses in Europe*. New York: Harry N. Abrams, Inc., 1979.

Grabow, Stephen. *Christopher Alexander*. London: Oriel Press, 1983.

Hamsun, Knut. *Victoria*. London: Souvenir Press, Ltd., 1974.

————. *Mysteries*. London: Picador Edition, Pan Books, 1976.

Hansen, Hans Jürgen, et al. *European Folk Art in Europe and the Americas*. London: Thames and Hudson, 1968.

————, et al. *Architecture in Wood*. New York: Viking Press, 1971.

Hauglid, Roar, et al. *Native Art of Norway*. Oslo: Dreyers Forlag, 1965.

————. *Norske Stavkirker*. Oslo: Dreyers Forlag A/S, 1976.

————. "Features of the Origin and Development of the Stave Churches in Norway." *Acta Archaeologica* 49 (1978): 37–60.

————. *Laftekunst, Laftehusets Opprinnelse og Eldste Historie*. Oslo: Dreyers Forlag, 1980.

Heidegger, Martin. *Poetry, Language, Thought*. New York: Harper and Row, 1971.

Herteig, A., H. E. Lidén, and C. Blindheim. *Archaeological Contributions to the Early History of Urban Communities in Norway*. Oslo: Universitetsforlaget, 1975.

Hohler, Erla Bergendahl. "Stavkirkene: Den Dekorative Skurd." In *Norges Kunsthistorie*, vol. 1, 253–255. Oslo: Gyldendal Norsk Forlag A/S, 1981.

Holan, Jerri. "A Norwegian Pattern of Vernacular Architecture." Master's Thesis, University of California, Berkeley, 1983.

Horn, Walter. "On the Origins of the Medieval Bay System." *Journal of the Society of Architectural Historians* 17 (2): 2–23.

Ibsen, Henrik. "St. John's Night." In *The Oxford Ibsen*, vol. 1. London: Oxford University Press, 1970.

————. "The Grouse in Justedal." In *The Oxford Ibsen*, vol. 1. London: Oxford University Press, 1970.

Jahnsen, Jon Børre. *Bygget av Levende Stene, Midde-*

lalderens Kirkelige Forhold i Valdres. Aurdal, Norway: P. T. Dreyer, 1983.

Jackson, John Brinckerhoff. *Discovering the Vernacular Landscape*. New Haven, Connecticut: Yale University Press, 1984.

Kostof, Spiro. *A History of Architecture, Settings and Rituals*. New York: Oxford University Press, 1985.

Lerup, Lars. "Movable Houses." *Architectural Digest* 41 (1): 134–140.

Lexow, Jan Hendrich. "Arkitektur, 1536–1815." In *Norges Kunsthistorie*, vol. 3, 7–119. Oslo: Gyldendal Norsk Forlag A/S, 1982.

Lidén, Hans-Emil. "From Pagan Sanctuary to Christian Church: The Excavation of Mære Church in Trøndelag." *Norwegian Archaeological Review* 2 (1969): 3–32.

Lindholm, Dan, and Walther Roggenkamp. *Stave Churches in Norway*. London: Rudolf Steiner Press, 1969.

Lobell, John. *Between Silence and Light, Spirit in the Architecture of Louis I. Kahn*. Boulder, Colorado: Shambhala Publications, 1979.

Lundberg, Erik. *Svensk Bostad*. Stockholm: Nordisk Rotogravyr, 1942.

Mikkola, Kirmo. *Architecture in Finland*. Huhmari, Finland: Finnish-American Cultural Institute, 1981.

Myhre, Bjørn, and Arne-Emil Christensen. "Laftehusets Opprinnelse og Eldste Historie." *Foreningen til Norske Fortidsminnesmerkers Bevaring* (1983): 165–172.

Nicolaysen, Nicolay. *Kunst og Haandverk fra Norges Fortid*. Kristiania (Oslo): Foreningen til Norske Fortidsminnesmerkers Bevaring, 1894.

Norberg-Schulz, Christian. "Våre Stavkirker." *Byggekunst* 3 (1961): 11, 12.

———. "Arkitekturornament." *Byggekunst* 5 (1965): 114–117.

———. *Mellom Jord og Himmel*. Oslo: Universitetsforlaget, 1978.

———. *Genius Loci*. New York: Rizzoli, 1980.

———. *Architecture: Meaning and Place*. New York: Rizzoli, 1988.

Olsen, Olaf. "Hørg, Hov og Kirke." *Aarbøger for Nordisk Oldkyndighed og Historie* (1965): 277–288.

Phleps, Hermann. *Holzbaukunst: Der Blockbau*. Karlsruhe, West Germany: Fachblattverlag, 1942.

———. *Die Norwegischen Stabkirchen*. Karlsruhe, West Germany: Bruderverlag, 1958.

———. *The Craft of Log Building*. Ontario: Lee Valley Tools, Ltd., 1982.

Polak, Ada. "Kunsthåndverk og Kunstindustri." In *Norges Kunsthistorie*, vol. 3, 247–316. Oslo: Gyldendal Norsk Forlag A/S, 1982.

Rapoport, Amos. *House, Form and Culture*. Englewood Cliffs, New Jersey: Prentice-Hall, Inc., 1969.

Reimers, Egill, and Peter Anker. "Trearkitektur i Bygd og By." In *Norges Kunsthistorie*, vol. 1, 356–427. Oslo: Gyldendal Norsk Forlag A/S, 1981.

Sjøvold, Thorleif. *The Viking Ships in Oslo*. Oslo: Universitetets Oldsaksamling, 1979.

Undset, Sigrid. *Kristian Lavransdatter*. New York: Alfred A. Knopf, Inc., 1927.

Visted, Kristofer, and Hilmar Stigum. *Vår Gamle Bondekultur*, vols. 1 and 2. Oslo: J. W. Cappelens, 1951–52.

Vreim, Halvor. *Norsk Trearkitektur*. Oslo: Gyldendal, 1947.

———. *Laftehus, Tomring og Torvtekning*. Oslo: Norske Arkitekters Landsforbund, 1943.

Wilson, Forrest. *The Joy of Building*. New York: Van Nostrand Reinhold, 1979.

Yanagi, Sōetsu. *The Unknown Craftsmen: A Japanese Insight into Beauty*. Tokyo: Kodansha International Ltd., 1982.

Index

PHOTOGRAPHY CREDITS